# American Law Enforcement:
# A History

# American Law Enforcement: A History

**David R. Johnson**

*University of Texas*

Forum Press, Inc.
Arlington Heights, Illinois

Library of Congress Catalog Card Number: 80-68810
ISBN 0-88273-270-6 (pbk.)
ISBN 0-88273-271-4

Text and cover design by Jerry Moore and Janet Moody

Manufactured in the United States of America
91 90 89 88 87
7 6 5 4 3
MG

# Contents

# Preface

Although law enforcement has been a pervasive concern for more than a century, Americans know relatively little about its actual history. Scholars have only recently begun to explore the development of policing in an effort to place current debates about its strengths and weaknesses in perspective. This book is an attempt to draw together in a single volume their discoveries about the history of law enforcement. It deals not only with urban police departments, but also with state and federal policing.

In an effort to impose some order on such a diffuse topic, I have chosen to focus on three themes. First, I attempt to stress the importance of the political framework within which policing developed. America's particular brand of local self-government gives ordinary citizens and professional politicians considerable influence in law enforcement. The need to respond to the diverse, often conflicting demands of various constituencies has given American policing a unique character which affects its efficiency as well as its reputation. However one views the police today, it is essential to understand how the theory and practice of politics influenced the nature, successes, and problems of law enforcement.

Reform is the second major theme. The effort to improve the police (however "improvement" is defined) has been a constant concern of many citizens since the mid-nineteenth century. Since Americans were not very original in their particular reform proposals, however, I have tried to deal with European ideas and activities wherever possible.

Europeans were, at least for much of the nineteenth and early twentieth centuries, more innovative than Americans in their efforts to improve policing. Regardless of its sources, reform has not only affected local law enforcement. Urban police departments in this century have increasingly operated in the shadow of reputedly more effective federal agencies. Federal law enforcement did not originally develop as a reform movement, but advocates of increased federal participation in the twentieth century often played upon public concern over crime to promote their own causes. Their activities can be viewed as part of the general reform effort to improve law enforcement. But their success has seriously challenged prevailing political traditions which emphasize local policing. By the early 1970s, then, reform in its various guises had produced some fundamental changes in the assumptions and practices of policing. The intentions and consequences of the major reform movements are therefore vital to our understanding of the achievements and limitations of contemporary law enforcement.

Historical trends in the nature and extent of crime form the third theme of this book. This is a subject which is even less understood than the history of policing. Crime trends and criminal behavior respond to broad social and economic developments which are not related to law enforcement. But controlling crime is obviously an integral part of the police mission, and therefore requires more attention than it has previously received. Public fears about crime, misconceptions about "organized" crime, and the activities of criminals themselves had important consequences for the development of policing. Oftentimes it was the public's perceptions, rather than the actual behavior of criminals, which had the greatest impact on the police. Misunderstandings about the nature and extent of criminal activity frequently influenced public attitudes toward law enforcement and fueled the demands for reform. In the absence of accurate information, fear often became the basis for changes in policing which did not necessarily solve the problems of controlling crime. We therefore need to examine criminal behavior as a separate phenomenon in order to understand the limited effectiveness of the police when they deal with assorted criminals.

Each of these themes is treated within a broad chronological context which surveys law enforcement from colonial times to the present. Separate chapters deal with each theme, or, in some cases, with various combinations of them. At the end of each chapter I have listed suggestions for further reading. These suggestions will introduce students to the most important studies which are the basis for each chapter.

As with any enterprise of this sort, I have accumulated a number of debts to others who, in various ways, have made this book possible. Peter Stearns offered me the opportunity to write it and has served as a superb editor, incisive critic, and helpful coach throughout this endeavor. Humbert Nelli provided timely encouragement and advice. Mark Haller, in numerous conversations through the years, supplied the insights which made sense of modern illegal enterprise. Numerous historians of crime besides myself are indebted to his pioneering work, and the brief summary of his contributions to that field (in chapter 9) is only a small tribute to his influence. James Richardson read the entire manuscript with great care and offered many helpful suggestions. My debt to all the historians working on law enforcement and crime is only partially indicated in the bibliographical aids. This book is, I hope, a reflection of what we know, and what we need to know, about these important subjects.

# 1

# Colonial
# Law Enforcement

**L**aw enforcement in colonial America seems rather uncomplicated in comparison with modern policing. A startlingly small number of peace officers protected their communities from a handful of criminals and miscellaneous miscreants. But the colonial period is important to an understanding of the history of law enforcement because many of the basic ideas which influence modern policing were developed during that era. Specifically, the colonial period transmitted three legacies to contemporary policing. First, borrowing from English precedents and traditions, the colonists committed themselves to local, as opposed to centralized, law enforcement. The American colonists then reinforced that commitment by creating a theory of government called republicanism. While this theory had no direct impact on policing at the time, it did establish the political framework within which law enforcement developed after the colonial era. Finally, English reformers struggling with an apparently overwhelming crime problem invented the theory of crime prevention. This new idea would later become the basis for the emergence of modern law enforcement agencies. These legacies, then, make an examination of the colonial period essential to any study of contemporary policing.

## Local Law Enforcement in England

Local law enforcement had become an important custom in England long before the first American colonies were established. This custom probably developed from necessity. Saxon England's population was

1

distributed in small rural hamlets and villages because agricultural methods and the level of economic activity did not allow or require large concentrations of people in cities. A scattered population posed practical problems in maintaining law and order. Prior to 1066, Saxon kings had neither a large standing army to enforce their wishes nor a centralized court system whose officers had the ability or authority to interfere in community affairs. In the absence of effective royal authority, local communities had to assume the burden of keeping the peace. Upholding the law became the obligation of each subject. With this as a basis for law enforcement, each community divided its members into small groups of about ten families called tythings. Each person was responsible for the behavior of everyone in his tything. If any member committed a crime, the other members were expected to hold him for trial in the local court, or, if they failed in that, they were required to make compensation. In essence then, Saxon law enforcement rested upon the idea of collective responsibility for criminal behavior.

The Norman conquest in 1066 caused some changes in these simple arrangements, but the obligation to enforce the law remained with local government. As a conquering people, the Normans were anxious to subjugate the Saxon population as rapidly as possible. To accomplish that goal, Norman kings promulgated a few new laws which tightened Saxon procedures regarding the duties of tythings and appointed many Normans as manorial lords (a manor was a district embracing many local communities in which a feudal lord had control). Repression eased by the end of the twelfth century, but the changes which the Normans had imposed remained. Among the most important of these were a shift in responsibility for supervising communities and the emergence of a specific official charged with maintaining order. Manorial courts superseded the tythings as the main agencies for overseeing local affairs. These courts combined executive and judicial functions in their many duties. They conducted their work through officers elected from (but not by) the local population. One of these officers had charge of all matters relating to law and order. In 1252 a royal statute conferred upon this official the prestigious title of constable. Initially, constables had been officers of the royal court. During the two centuries following the Norman conquest, this officer gradually emerged as one of the manorial courts' elected officials.

In 1285, Saxon customs and Norman innovations in law enforcement were codified in the Statute of Winchester. This law was the basis for English policing until 1829, when the Metropolitan Police Act undermined it. The Statute of Winchester reaffirmed local responsibility for law enforcement, attempted to establish a standardized organization which would make policing effective, and distinguished urban from rural law enforcement for the first time. First, the Statute created the watch and ward system to aid city constables in their duties. Constables now had the authority to enroll every male inhabitant on a roster from which they chose several individuals as watchmen every night. These watchmen guarded the town gates and turned over anyone they arrested to the constables each morning. The second provision of the Statute resurrected the Saxon practice of the hue and cry. Watchmen who encountered resistance could raise the hue and cry, in effect calling upon all residents to assist them. Anyone who refused this summons was regarded as aiding and abetting the criminal, and was therefore subject to arrest also. Finally, the Statute ordered that all the king's subjects must maintain arms in their homes for use during a hue and cry. Officials known as high constables were to conduct semi-annual inspections to make sure this part of the Statute was being obeyed. In sum, the English system of policing which evolved by the end of the thirteenth century relied upon unpaid amateurs who had no special knowledge, skills, or commitment to dealing with crime.

This police system became extremely ineffective during the next five hundred years. There were many reasons for this, but foremost among them prior to the eighteenth century was the transformation of the constable from an eminent local official to a public joke. Initially, the more prominent people in a community served in this office. With the passage of time, however, the abilities of the men who served declined because of the nature of the work. Pursuing criminals was only part, and indeed a small part, of a constable's job. While the average constable might occasionally arrest a thief, he more often brought ordinary people into court for some petty offense affecting the community's welfare. Typical offenders included a neighbor who failed to fence his hogs; another who refused to help repair a local road or bridge; a baker who sold bread which weighed less than the legally prescribed minimum; and a man who emptied his chamber pot in a public thoroughfare. Constables also had to watch for strangers who might become a public burden; he had to supervise the watch; and he had to appear in court to make regular reports regarding local conditions. Failure to do any of these things could result in fines. And all these responsibilities were to be undertaken as part of his obligations to his community. He was not paid a salary for his work. In these circumstances, Englishmen who could afford to began to pay substitutes to serve their terms as constables. By the seventeenth century only those who could not hire a substitute actually assumed these onerous duties. Once started, this practice introduced to police work those who were less and less qualified to do the work. Eventually illiterate constables who could not read a summons or write out a complaint struggled to maintain order. Many constables were too old or infirm to fulfill their responsibilities. This reliance upon incompetent men to serve as constables threatened to undermine the whole system of policing.

### Colonial American Law Enforcement: Seventeenth Century

The first colonists transplanted this police system, with all its virtues and faults, to America during the seventeenth century. Local circumstances, though, prevented the problems which had developed in England from becoming particularly serious during the initial years of settlement. The settlers, scattered in several colonies and living in extremely primitive conditions, occupied themselves with erecting homes and planting crops. Their social backgrounds helped prevent any widespread ordinary crime. The first settlers were not impoverished Englishmen but rather individuals and families from the solid, respectable ranks of English society. Some servants accompanied these first settlers, and there was a very small slave population, but most of these people were not a source of concern because they lived under close supervision.

New Amsterdam, the Dutch colony of New York founded in 1625, was to some extent an exception to this picture of generally crime-free society. Dutch officials discovered to their considerable annoyance that their small trading post settlement on the Hudson River was rapidly becoming a haven for runaway servants and slaves during the 1640s. This unattached population quickly created the first crime wave in America by indulging in petty thefts and disorderly behavior. Irritated by this development, the Dutch imposed severe penalties on these offenders and brought them under control early in the 1650s.

Elsewhere in the colonies, however, violations of the law most often involved some individual who ran afoul of community obligations or morals. With the definition of crime so firmly rooted in community standards, policing typically concentrated on the behavior of ordinary people. Colonists found themselves in court for such conduct as working on the sabbath, failing to pen animals properly, begetting a bastard child, and cursing in public places. Outside of New York, two serious crime waves occurred in Massachusetts in the seventeenth century. In both cases, the offenses appear alien to modern ideas about the nature of crime. In the first case, between 1656 and 1665, Quakers who dared challenge the religious conformity of the Puritan colony were whipped, banished, and, in three instances, hanged in the community's effort to rid itself of these people. The second crime wave centered on an even more bizarre crime, witchcraft. Though shorter in duration, the Salem witchcraft episode of 1692 shook the very foundations of the Puritan colony. Several alleged witches were hanged, and dozens of people accused of this crime by their hysterical neighbors languished many months in prison before calm returned to the colony. Both episodes were important for what they revealed about Puritan society, but obviously neither indicated that a serious problem with more ordinary crime existed.

Primitive living conditions, small populations whose members generally conformed to a recognized set of community ideals, and a familiarity with established institutions for enforcing laws meant that the first colonists did not have to give much thought to what kind of formal policing arrangements they should establish. As soon as the colonists had settled into villages like Boston (1630), Charleston (1680), and Philadelphia (1682), local ordinances provided for the appointment of constables whose duties and terms of service differed insignificantly from their English predecessors. (Virginia was an exception to this development. There, a widely dispersed population living on plantations required a different approach to law enforcement. County governments, again drawing upon English precedents, appointed sheriffs as their principal peace officers.) Shortly thereafter, village governments, led by Boston in 1631, created watches to safeguard the lives and property of their inhabitants at night.

Service as a constable or watchman was obligatory, as it had been in England, and for a few years it seems that citizens did not resent this duty. But as soon as the towns grew to sufficient size to make law enforcement more onerous and time consuming, the colonists, like their English counterparts, began to evade this responsibility whenever possible. By the 1650s Bostonians had become so adept at avoiding service that the colony's government had to threaten citizens with huge fines to make them assume their obligations. The settlers' reluctance at taking their turn on the night watches also began to cause problems by mid-century. New York's Dutch officials attempted to overcome this resistance by introducing a paid watch in 1658. Boston tried this solution in 1663. The expense of this idea quickly caused both towns to abandon these first experiments with a paid police. Local residents might dislike serving on the watch, but they liked paying someone else to do so even less. New York revived paid watches occasionally during the remainder of the century, but this practice was not adopted elsewhere. In the 1690s most colonists still relied upon volunteers to staff their policing agencies.

### Colonial Law Enforcement: Eighteenth Century

Unfortunately for the reputations of their towns and the safety of their streets, as citizen willingness to serve as constables and watchmen declined the problems of crime and social order increased. All the initial settlements had grown to fairly sizable colonies by the beginning of the eighteenth century. They were much more prosperous, and they were attracting a more mixed population than had been true earlier.

Many of these changes were most obvious in the small but bustling seaports. An enterprising merchant class had created a thriving economy based on an exchange of colonial raw materials for European finished goods. As their economies expanded, the seaports began to experience some social problems associated with success. The overseas trade, for example, required large numbers of ships and crews to sail them. But sailors in port cities demanded diversions, and some local residents found profits in fulfilling these seafarers' needs. Taverns sprouted up close to the dock areas, and public drunkenness and brawls increased. Women who had to find some means of support due to the death of their husbands or some other misfortune turned to prostitution, thereby providing a service to sailors and a public nuisance to the authorities. Economic development and the emergence of wealthier residents also increased the demand for servants. Large numbers of Englishmen, Germans, and blacks were imported into the colonies to meet this demand during the first half of the new century. Indulgent or careless masters, however, failed to supervise these people closely, and some servants turned to theft to finance their diversions in local taverns. White servants who had served out their contracts and who had failed to find employment as free persons began forming into America's first poverty-stricken class. A few of these people also became thieves as a way to earn a living.

Economic growth and the appearance of a small criminal class in the colonies probably made service as constables and watchmen even less popular than before. Ordinary citizens scrambling to climb the ladder of economic success and social prestige now had less time to devote to civic duties. The increasing chances of having to deal with drunken sailors and an occasional thief further underscored the unpleasantness of jobs which were too time-consuming and troublesome in the best of circumstances. Moreover, the prosperity of these years gave more people than ever before the ability to avoid their obligations. Fines which forced compliance with civic responsibilities in the seventeenth century were no longer sufficient inducements to serve. Too many men now had more than enough cash to pay these fines. As the eighteenth century progressed, more and more citizens escaped their turns as peace officers by paying their fines. This practice threw the burden for law enforcement upon those who could not afford the fines—as had been the case in England much earlier.

By the middle of the eighteenth century the colonists faced a dilemma which some residents felt they could no longer ignore. The towns had become large enough to need a reliable police, but their best citizens habitually refused this duty and the men who did serve were not as effective as they needed to be. Circumstances, not incompetence, dictated this ineffectiveness. Watchmen who worked all day at other jobs could hardly stay awake, let alone maintain order at night. Some cities did pay their watchmen, but not enough to allow someone to earn his living by law enforcement. The idea of citizen participation in policing was breaking down, and something was needed to replace it.

Philadelphia's inhabitants provided a solution to this problem in 1749. They prodded their colonial legislature into passing a law which restructured the watch in ways which would presumably solve the problems of law enforcement. Under the provisions of this legislation, officials called wardens had the authority to hire as many watchmen as they needed. The powers of the watch were increased, and the legislature provided for a tax to pay for the watch. All male citizens were no longer subject to be called upon to act as watchmen; only those interested in earning money applied to the wardens. These provisions did not prevent someone who worked all day from serving as a watchman, but the wardens had the power to dismiss men who were inefficient. Although Philadelphia's reform fell far short of creating an effective police, it improved law enforcement sufficiently to inspire other cities to make similar alterations in their police.

The reform of the watch did not cause a complete rejection of the principle of collective responsibility in policing. Nothing in the new structure of the watch affected the methods for selecting constables. These lawmen continued to be appointed from the ranks of ordinary citizens, and many of those chosen preferred to pay fines rather than suffer the duties of the office. The character and abilities of those who did serve seems to have continued to decline, so much so that complaints began to be heard in the last half of the century regarding the behavior of constables. Some were even whispered to be accepting bribes not to do their duty. Considering the problems of finding capable men, it is surprising that the quality of constables remained relatively high as long as it did. The complaints, it should be noted, did not cause any change in the methods of choosing constables, nor did they prompt any movement to pay these officers adequately for their work. Constables did receive certain fees for serving court papers, and for making arrests, but these sums were never equal to the effort involved.

Massive social and political unrest from mid-century until the 1780s caused law enforcement problems to increase still further. First, the French and Indian War, fought between England and France from 1756 to 1763, disrupted colonial society. Some colonists profited from the military's demands for goods and services while others, caught up in the fighting, lost everything and drifted into the cities looking for safety and a fresh start. Peace was a disaster for the Americans when the war ended in 1763. A major depression struck and impoverished many citizens. Then a dramatic shift in British imperial policy led to American independence. During the war which followed, from 1775 to 1783, both urban and rural society suffered from troop movements, battles, and population shifts. Finally, the end of the fighting brought yet another depression which lasted until the late 1780s. Once again, large numbers of people who had already suffered considerably found themselves struggling to survive.

In these circumstances crime became commonplace, and law enforcement agencies simply failed to cope with it. The dimensions of the problem swamped both the watch and the constabulary. Burglary, robbery, assault, and numerous other offenses flourished. Most of these crimes were probably committed by the victims of the tremendous convulsions afflicting American society, but some career criminals had wide latitude to exercise their talents as well. Counterfeiters, for instance, copied the paper currencies of many state governments and the money issued by the Continental Congress. Wherever possible, peace officers sought to control these criminals, but only a return to stable social conditions in the 1790s solved the basic causes of the long crime wave.

### Republicanism and Policing

The conflict with England not only produced widespread social upheavals, it also prodded Americans to rethink their ideas about the nature of political power. Republicanism, a new theory of politics, was the result. Most of the basic concepts which combined to form this theory had evolved slowly during the colonial period through practical experience and political bickering between the colonists and Parliament. Local policing problems had not figured in these discussions. Weightier issues, such as the authority of crown-appointed governors and the powers of colonial legislatures, had been the central points of controversy. As the colonists struggled to justify their behavior, and then to explain their opposition to English policies after 1763, they invented a set of ideas with genuinely revolutionary implications. These principles, incorporated into the United States Constitution, and eventually into every state constitution, provide the framework for understanding the nation's social, economic, and political development.

Republicanism asserts that political power can be divided. This is its essential point. Several other ideas and practices derive from that central point, two of the most important being a commitment to written constitutions and an insistence on an idea known as actual representation. Americans developed the conviction that a written constitution was necessary in order to protect essential rights and to prevent arbitrary acts by governors, judges, and legislators. The concept of actual representation was based upon long experience with colonial assemblies prior to the Revolution. These legislatures had frequently opposed Parliament's intervention into their colonies' internal affairs on the grounds that members of Parliament did not, and could not, understand the colonists' problems. From this followed the idea that only those persons who actually lived in a locality had any right to represent that area and to legislate for it.

When it was first created, the theory of republicanism had no immediate effect on the structure and conduct of policing. There was no debate among the founding fathers as to whether the new nation should have a national police force, because such an idea did not occur to them. Indeed, there is nothing in the Constitution which assigns any role in maintaining public order or pursuing criminals to the federal government (except under the President's power in national emergencies). The task of safeguarding the internal peace and security of local communities was left to the states by the Tenth Amendment. And yet republicanism is of utmost importance to the history of American law enforcement because it established the political framework within which the police would develop over the next two hundred years. Republicanism, furthermore, helped determine the special strengths and weaknesses of policing in this country due to the ways in which this theory shaped the structure and practices of local government.

Although republicanism is an original and brilliant political theory, it contains a critical dilemma. The theory relies upon local interests to promote the general welfare. Here lies the origins of an enormous amount of controversy over law enforcement in America. Most people can agree that the police ought to protect lives and property from assorted criminals. But how many policemen are needed to achieve that goal, and how should they be distributed? In any particular city, the chief of police might be expected to have the knowledge to answer those questions. But within the framework of republicanism, neighborhood groups and economic interest blocs have the power to challenge his decisions, and often have, historically. Thus the police frequently have had to divert scarce resources to areas where they are less useful in solving a general problem with crime in order to relieve localized problems or fears. Hiring more policemen seems an obvious solution to this situation, but, again, local interests intervene. Historically, police forces have been relatively small because urban residents have been reluctant to pay the taxes required to maintain larger departments. As long as the people in a particular neighborhood feel safe, and as long as they can exert pressure to obtain the amount of protection they want, they feel little need to pay higher taxes to help protect the whole city. Opposition to higher taxes even extends to a willingness among some residents to pay for private police protection rather than vote for increased rates which could be used to employ more officers on the city police.

The tensions between the general welfare and local interests became even more intense when there was no consensus regarding particular law enforcement policies. Everyone could agree that burglars ought to be arrested and prosecuted, but what about gamblers and prostitutes? Significant segments of local communities denounced these people as criminals and demanded their suppression. But other local groups either tolerated gambling and prostitution or actively supported both. And just to make matters even more complex, the structure of republican politics would eventually permit these people to have an active role in the enforcement decisions which affected their businesses. By the middle of the nineteenth century many gamblers had become important local politicians whose views on police activities had to be considered. The reputation and morale of the police suffered in these circumstances; no matter what they did, they offended someone who had the ability to make life unpleasant for them.

Finally, the emphasis on actual representation would make politics a vital concern to every police department and officer on the beat. The wide adoption of the ward system as the basis for urban politics created neighborhood spokesmen whose views on law enforcement usually represented local interests quite accurately. These politicians naturally shaped arrest policies regarding particular crimes, but they also became embroiled in other issues as well. Not every city resident looked at policing solely from the perspective of law enforcement; many regarded the police as a source of economic opportunity and social prestige. A job as a cop meant security, decent wages, good fringe benefits, and the respect of one's neighbors. But what kinds of people should be appointed to these very desirable positions? Should candidates have to demonstrate their sobriety, reliability, and industriousness? Or should they merely be willing to serve and have the right political connections? Since no one group had the power to decide these questions, due to the structure of politics under the republican system, the qualifications of applicants to the police would become a major issue. The controversy over what kinds of men should be policemen was related to other problems which also became involved in politics. Unfit or brutal officers undermined public respect and confidence and raised the issue of police effectiveness. How could the police be made to behave and to do their work efficiently? Various proposals would be fought out in the political arena before any solutions emerged.

Thus republicanism guaranteed that most of the critical issues in law enforcement would become matters for public debate and political maneuvering. From one perspective, this was a considerable benefit to the people whom the police served. But there was also a price to pay in that the police would never satisfy everyone. By definition, then, the reputation and effectiveness of the police constantly suffered. This became one of the unintended legacies of eighteenth century America's ideas about political theory.

## Crime Prevention and Policing

Simultaneously with the emergence of republicanism, events in England led to the development of yet another theory which would significantly shape law enforcement after 1800. During the eighteenth century, policing under the ancient system of constables and watchmen finally collapsed. Widespread incompetence among peace officers contributed to this breakdown, but the more fundamental reasons for its downfall arose from a massive social and economic transformation of English society. The ineffectiveness of constables and watchmen which became painfully apparent by mid-century did not, however, prompt any immediate reforms. Instead, most Englishmen preferred to retain the existing police arrangements in spite of mounting evidence that something else was needed. Although indifference and outright hostility blocked any reform in the basis of law enforcement, a few men began work on the ideas which would eventually create an entirely new police system organized around the theory of crime prevention.

The number of Englishmen doubled between 1700 and 1800. This extraordinary increase was the basis for the changes which troubled Britain during the eighteenth century. Urbanization and the stirrings of industrialization further complicated matters because both of these developments concentrated huge numbers of people in the nation's cities and towns. London, for example, grew to nearly a million people by 1800, and many other cities dramatically increased their size as well. None of these cities were equipped to deal with this mass influx of newcomers. Urban squalor, crime, and general disorder combined with wretched, even oppressive, working conditions in the new factories and mines to create an enormous challenge to established traditions in local government and society.

Parliament took no interest in solving the difficulties arising from social change. It thus fell to each municipality or county to solve a general problem in a piecemeal fashion. After 1750, practically every English city adopted measures which dealt with a wide range of issues without attempting any fundamental reorganization of existing arrangements. In spite of the enormous increase in crime and disorder, town officials simply increased the number of watchmen and constables without considering whether this approach to law enforcement worked any longer. The only innovation adopted, and then not in every case, was a switch to a paid rather than a volunteer watch. Since this change did not affect the quality or behavior of watchmen, who continued to be ineffective, many citizens turned to private associations which offered rewards for the arrest and conviction of criminals as their principal defense against crime.

Little was done even in London, the capital city, to alter basic institutions. The city had become an "infernal wen"; whole districts had developed into criminal haunts where no law penetrated and no honest citizen ventured. Thieves became extremely bold, even knocking down their victims on the streets in broad daylight. In the early 1700s, under the direction of Jonathan Wild, London's most famous fence, many criminals joined an organization which systematically plundered the city's homes. The victims of these crimes arranged the return of their property by paying Wild to negotiate for them with the thieves. Although Wild was eventually hanged, his blatant behavior and tremendous success demonstrated how corrupt and unreliable law enforcement had become in London. In spite of this state of affairs, Englishmen preferred the existing police arrangements to any new ideas. They viewed proposals to reorganize the police as a threat to their liberties. Rather than suffer any loss of their personal freedoms, they resorted to arming themselves and offering rewards as their principal new defenses against crime.

In spite of the obstacles to success, a small number of concerned Englishmen, officials as well as private citizens, began to experiment with new solutions to London's crime problem. Their efforts had little immediate effect, but they did lay the foundations upon which subsequent reformers would build. Henry and John Fielding, and Patrick Colquhoun were the most important men in these early attempts to invent a new basis for law enforcement.

Henry Fielding was a famous novelist who developed an interest in policing through his writing. Several of his works are vivid, accurate portrayals of London crime and the extraordinary corruption in law enforcement during the first half of the eighteenth century. His reputation and extensive knowledge led to his appointment as chief magistrate of Bow Street in 1748. The Bow Street magistrate occupied a rather unusual position in London's legal system. It was, unlike other minor judicial offices, a salaried position with close connections to Parliament. This magistrate, presumably, could afford to ignore the opportunities for corrupt money which daily came the way of other city justices because of his salary. He could also depend upon the central government for some aid in dealing with the crime problem.

As Bow Street magistrate, Henry Fielding made two contributions to the eventual reform of the police. First, and most importantly, he used his writing talents to establish himself as one of England's most advanced theorists regarding the nature of crime and its punishment.

Essentially, he argued that the incredible severity of the penal code (which stipulated the death penalty for a large number of offenses, such as the theft of a handkerchief) could not be relied upon to control criminals. Rather, he argued, the nation needed to reform the criminal code to deal with the social origins of crime, and to create a more effective policing system. Secondly, Fielding made the pursuit of criminals more systematic in his own district. He created a small group of "thief-takers" in 1750. These men had agreed to continue as constables beyond the end of their regular volunteer service. Ordinarily, most citizens would have refused to trouble themselves with this sort of work, but Fielding probably convinced them to serve by a combination of an appeal to their civic pride and a reminder about the lucrative side of policing. Victims of crime paid substantial rewards for the arrest of thieves, and, since Fielding's "thief-takers" would concentrate on catching criminals, these officers would increase their economic opportunities rather significantly by agreeing to join Fielding's little group. Whatever their motives, Fielding's constables soon were among the few reliable officers who could be counted upon to pursue criminals vigorously.

When Henry Fielding died in 1754, his half-brother John succeeded him as Bow Street magistrate and served in that office for twenty-five years. John continued his brother's efforts to reform the penal code and his use of "thief-takers." By 1785 these officers had evolved into the Bow Street Runners, some of the most famous policemen in English history. Neither the campaign to educate the British public to the need for a new approach to criminal law nor the innovative use of constables had any immediate effect, however. Barbarous punishments and incompetent law enforcement remained typical throughout the eighteenth century. The Fieldings were important, though, because they were among the first people to begin the necessary process of rethinking the whole problem of how to create a police capable of dealing with the changes disrupting English society.

Patrick Colquhoun was another man destined to long, frustrating service in the early efforts to alter law enforcement. Colquhoun made his fortune in commerce while still a young man in his native city, Glasgow. His wealth gave him the means and time to turn his talents to a wide range of social problems. In 1792 Colquhoun accepted an appointment as a London magistrate, and for the next twenty-five years he concentrated his energies on the reform of the police.

Like the Fieldings, Colquhoun is best remembered for his writings on crime and law enforcement. His two best known works were *A Treatise on the Police of the Metropolis*, published in 1797, and his *Treatise on the Commerce and Police of the River Thames*, which appeared in 1800. The first volume is by far the most famous of the two;

within ten years it went through seven editions and established
Colquhoun as the foremost authority on police reform. His fame rests
upon the fact that he proposed the system which became the basis for
modern policing. Other reformers before Colquhoun had simply
tinkered with the traditional system of law enforcement which had been
in existence for five hundred years. Colquhoun saw the problem of
policing from a radically different perspective which revolutionized
the entire philosophy and structure of law enforcement.

The key to Colquhoun's ideas about the police is his belief that a specific government agency could, and should, regulate people's behavior.
This proposal contradicted tradition and constitutional scruples. It
undermined the ancient principle that the residents of local communities, through their voluntary service as constables and watchmen,
should supervise their neighbors' conduct. Furthermore, Englishmen
overwhelmingly feared that a police under governmental direction
would become an instrument of political repression, as were the French
police at the time. Colquhoun justified himself by demonstrating to his
readers that law enforcement in London was hopelessly inadequate to
the task of controlling crime. He assembled the first systematic, detailed analysis of crime, its origins, and its presumed costs. Then he
surveyed the agencies which were supposed to do something about
crime and pointed out their deficiencies. Finally, he argued that these
difficulties could be solved by separating the police and judicial duties
of those agencies; the police responsibilities could then be placed
under the direction of a single board. Policing, Colquhoun concluded,
had become a new branch of government which had three principal
functions: 1) the maintenance of public order; 2) the prevention and
detection of crime; and 3) the correction of manners and morals.
Colquhoun's ideas were a fundamental departure from the prevailing
version of policing. He rejected the centuries-old idea that the community should rely on amateurs to protect itself. Essentially, he favored a
paid, professional police recruited and maintained by a centralized
authority. Colquhoun was thus the first theoretician of policing who
recognized that the vast changes which had occurred as a result of
urbanization and industrialization over the last hundred years made a
radically new solution to the problems of law enforcement necessary.

Colquhoun's ideas about the three functions of the police represent
an early version of the theory of crime prevention. Others would
elaborate upon the basic components of this theory, but its essential
points would remain. Reduced to its simplest terms, the theory main-
tains that crime can be prevented by imposing governmental authority
 upon individuals who are likely to violate the law. This assumes, of
course, that such people can be identified before they commit a crime.
Colquhoun solved this difficult problem by pinpointing the origins of

crime as immorality and poverty (he was not the first to do so, but he was the first to present so much evidence to prove his assertion). He believed, and many people agreed with him then and afterward, that such behavior as drinking, gambling, and sexual laxity led to crime. The poor were too often tempted to commit crimes because they indulged in immoral activities more frequently than respectable people, or so it was widely thought. Furthermore, certain types of businessmen encouraged crime. Chief among these were pawnbrokers, junkdealers, and tavern keepers. If the police could deal with these problems, through their power to arrest malefactors and to license certain businesses, crime would decline in frequency.

*not revenue but control*

The theory of crime prevention implied an expanded definition of illegal behavior to include activities which seemed to contribute to crime, an increase in government authority, and a concentration of that authority in a particular agency. Few people in England were willing to implement Colquhoun's ideas because they were convinced that his proposals contained more dangers than advantages. He did not live to see his proposal adopted. As the eighteenth century ended, the structure of law enforcement remained basically unchanged. Social upheavals caused by urbanization and revolution in England and America had clearly demonstrated the inadequacies of the police, and important new ideas had emerged, but the overwhelming majority of people in both nations remained steadfast in their loyalty to the old ways. Further changes were required before that loyalty would be undermined.

## SUGGESTED READINGS

The English background to colonial law enforcement is briefly and cogently described in T. A. Critchley, *A History of Police in England and Wales 900-1966* (London: Constable and Company Ltd., 1967). Good descriptions of law enforcement problems in America's colonial cities can be found in Carl Bridenbaugh's two volume study: *Cities in the Wilderness: The First Century of Urban Life in America, 1625-1742*, 2nd ed. (New York: Alfred A. Knopf, 1964), and *Cities in Revolt: Urban Life in America, 1743-1776* (New York: Alfred A. Knopf, 1955). For more detailed analyses see: Kai T. Erikson, *Wayward Puritans: A Study in the Sociology of Deviance* (New York: John Wiley & Sons, 1968), and Douglas Greenberg, *Crime and Law Enforcement in the Colony of New York, 1691-1776* (Ithaca: Cornell University Press, 1976). For an extensive analysis of the changes which occurred in English ideas about crime and criminal law, the best work is Leon Radzinowicz, *A History of English Criminal Law* (4 vols.; London: Stevens, 1948-1968).

# 2

# Police Reform: 1829-1860

Changes in local law enforcement in England and America were caused by two powerful trends in both countries. The first of these trends was urbanization; the second, industrialization. Over a long period of time, these developments increased the standard of living for both western Europeans generally and for Americans. Such beneficial trends would seem to have little relationship to law enforcement, but in fact they made vast changes in the police necessary.

The need for changes in the police arose from the fact that industrialization and urbanization created a new kind of society. Old ways of thinking and behaving became obsolete, but the effort to replace them provoked a great deal of protest. Factories, for example, needed sober, punctual workers who could be trusted with machines. At the beginning of industrialization such workers did not exist in sufficient numbers because they were accustomed to less demanding schedules; they regarded drinking as an important recreation; and they feared machines which they thought would deprive them of jobs and destroy their status in society. In order to create what they regarded as a reliable work force, factory owners became enthusiastic advocates of many social reforms such as temperance. Workers resented these reform efforts and resisted them whenever possible. Likewise, urbanization promoted unrest by bringing together people from diverse class, ethnic, and (in the United States) racial backgrounds who resented each other. Conflicts between these competing groups over such issues as whose version of morality would dominate society were another source of trouble.

Crime, as distinct from collective protest, also appears to have increased in this period. Urbanization and industrialization both enhanced the material prosperity of many individuals and concentrated enormous numbers of less fortunate people who turned to crime to support themselves. Petty thievery abounded, and more serious offenses such as burglary, highway robbery, and swindling proliferated. The diversity and persistence of criminals frightened the inhabitants of cities who wanted their property and lives secured against these depredators.

Social change, unrest, and crime made the old system of law enforcement obsolete. Watchmen had never been effective in dealing with crime and violence; now their situation became even more impossible. Constables had overseen many activities which made urban life possible, but they were too few in number, too overworked, and too little interested in preventing crime to be effective in a rapidly changing society. A new kind of police was needed, one which would maintain order and pursue criminals in the altered circumstances of the early nineteenth century. In the three decades prior to 1860, reformers on both sides of the Atlantic set out to transform the nature of law enforcement. Although their efforts succeeded, the police forces they created were not comparable in spite of the fact that a single model—that of crime prevention—was the basis for reform in both countries.

## English Police Reform

Social problems in England after the end of the Napoleonic Wars in 1815 eventually led to the creation of the world's first preventive police force. Workers' protests against new machines, food riots, and an apparent increase in crime generally alarmed Parliament. The army had traditionally been the only force able to disperse rioters, but it was now having greater difficulty doing so because the mobs seemed more willing to resist. Army officers had always disliked using troops against Englishmen, and the mobs' resistance made them even more reluctant to undertake their suppression. Then too, soldiers were ill-suited to dealing with ordinary criminals. Frequent disorder and the army's inadequacies thus forced the Tories, England's ruling party, to consider alternatives. In 1822, when the prime minister appointed Robert Peel as home secretary (an official responsible for internal security), he ordered Peel to establish a police which would deal with rioting as well as with ordinary crime.

Peel did not succeed immediately. He quickly discovered two major obstacles in his way. The first obstacle was the average Englishman's fear that a police such as Peel intended would be used to undermine liberty. Parliament shared this fear and defeated Peel's first attempt to establish a new police. The second major obstacle was the belief that the only solution to the crime problem was reform of the criminal law to make it more humane. In the early nineteenth century England's criminal law was among the most brutal in existence. There were 223 crimes for which a person could be hanged. The law's savagery caused most important reformers to campaign for revisions on the assumption that more humane laws would be self-enforcing and would reduce crime. From their perspective, changes in the structure or philosophy of the police would therefore be unnecessary. These ideas blocked Peel's efforts to reform the police for seven years. In that time the criminal law was changed considerably. These changes were important in the long struggle to create a more sensible criminal code, but in the meantime Peel's plans for the police remained unfulfilled.

Peel finally achieved his objective in 1829. He had worked to build his power in Parliament during those seven years, and he had at last found a way to reform the police without arousing overwhelming opposition. Simply put, Peel used two tactics to achieve his victory. First, Peel narrowed his objective to reform only the metropolitan London police instead of trying to establish a police for the whole of Great Britain. He clearly intended to extend his reform to the remainder of the nation at a later date (which was in fact what happened), but he was momentarily more interested in getting reform started somewhere and London, as the nation's capital, was best suited to his purposes. Secondly, Peel submitted a bill to Parliament which was extremely vague about details. These tactics succeeded when Parliament passed the Metropolitan Police Act of 1829. Under this Act, the home secretary was to appoint two men as police justices (later, they were called commissioners) to command the new organization. These men were to recruit "a sufficient number of fit and able men" as police constables, and they were to be responsible for the overall administration of the police as well as for the conduct of their men. The English preventive police thus began, and have remained, a highly centralized organization administratively.

The success of London's preventive police was due entirely to the good sense of the men whom Peel chose to lead the new organization. Peel had decided that one commissioner should be a military man who would have a practical knowledge of discipline and organization; the other should be a lawyer whose knowledge would be invaluable in defining the appropriate limits of police power. Accordingly, Peel chose Colonel Charles Rowan and Richard Mayne, an Irish barrister, as the first commissioners. Both men turned out to be superb choices whose long service (Rowan served until 1850; Mayne until 1868) provided the continuity of command which enabled the London police to develop into a superlative organization. Rowan was an especially fortunate choice. As a young lieutenant in the early nineteenth century, he had served under Major-General Sir John Moore, an officer who may have been influenced by Colquhoun's ideas. At that time the British army was notorious for its soldiers' criminal behavior. Moore adopted crime prevention as a disciplinary experiment. He insisted that his officers show respect for their men and treat them firmly but justly. Moore believed, and experience proved him right, that soldiers treated in this fashion would be easier to control and more effective in combat. Rowan therefore learned an important aspect of crime prevention—mutual respect between the policeman and the people he serves—while in the army. As a police commissioner, Rowan's experience provided the basis for molding the soon famous behavior of London's "bobbies."

Mayne and Rowan worked out the organizational details of the new police together. They carved London into a number of divisions (seventeen at first, with more added later). The size of these divisions varied according to the amount of crime within each. Divisions which had a higher rate of crime than others had smaller boundaries, thereby enabling constables to cover their beats more frequently. Each division had a commander called a superintendent; each superintendent had a force of 4 inspectors, 16 sergeants, and 165 constables under him. Initially, this meant that the London police would consist of nearly 3,000 men. The commissioners also decided to put their men in a uniform (a blue coat, blue pants, and a glazed black tophat), and to arm them with a short baton (or truncheon) and a rattle (for raising an alarm). Finally, each constable was required to wear his personal number on his collar where it could be easily seen. Once these details had been arranged, the men had been recruited, and the force had received its instructions, the new police took to the streets in late September 1829.

The new police quickly discovered that they would have to overcome tremendous public hostility to their very existence. At the present time, when the English display considerable pride in their bobbies, it is easy to forget that the initial response to them bordered on hysteria and rage. Many people feared the new police would undermine liberty; others resented any interference in their personal freedoms or assumed rights; workers regarded policemen as enemies created to suppress their efforts to protect themselves from changes wrought by industrialization. All these fears and resentments took very concrete form in attacks on constables and in the public's refusal to condemn such assaults. Examples of abuse abounded in the early years. Aristocrats who resented efforts to regulate their coaches in street traffic ordered their coachmen to whip officers. If that failed, they had their eager servants drive over the offending patrolman. Juries and judges refused to punish those who assaulted the police and in fact often encouraged such behavior by their verdicts. The leader of a crowd which threw a constable on a spiked fence was fined a trifling sum. A man convicted of hitting a woman brought assault charges against the arresting officer. When the jury in this case found the officer guilty, he was sentenced to two months in jail. Defendants freed on some legal technicality by a hostile judge would often add injury to insult by suing for false arrest. Too frequently the arresting officer in these cases ended up in jail. No funds existed to pay the fines and court costs for officers who had done their duty and had found themselves incarcerated as a result. Policing London's streets was thus a dangerous and very lonely business in the early 1830s.

Since public hostility threatened the very existence of the police, Commissioners Mayne and Rowan moved decisively to counter it. The policies they adopted emphasized a willingness to listen to all complaints and a patient forbearance of abuse. Constables received no help from their superiors in the form of public declarations of support. Instead, the men were constantly cautioned to be respectful and yet firm in dealings with the public. The commissioners, in the meantime, invited anyone with a complaint to submit it to their office. Each complaint received a full hearing, and if it was justified by the evidence the offending constable was removed from the force without further ado. Rowan and Mayne did try to offset bitter and usually inaccurate newspaper accounts of police behavior by sending the offending editor an official version of an incident, but the newspapers were not obliged to print such stories and did so only at their own whim. The mild, in fact submissive response which the commissioners adopted toward the hostility and abuse their men were suffering did have a carefully designed purpose. They hoped to create public support for their officers by stressing the reasonableness of their conduct. This policy exposed individual patrolmen to many problems, but it gradually worked to the advantage of the police. Public hostility began to lessen as the moderate conduct of the police became more widely known through countless personal experiences with constables on a daily basis. This restraint, and the continued willingness of the commissioners to listen to any just complaint, shifted public opinion decisively in favor of the police after a famous riot at Cold Bath Fields in May 1833. In this riot one policeman was killed and two others severely injured. When a jury returned a verdict of justifiable homicide at an inquest over the officer's death, in spite of the overwhelming evidence of murder, the public reaction was one of disgust and strong support for the police. The commissioners had won the battle of public acceptance.

London's police reform was not immediately copied elsewhere in England. Local communities outside the nation's capital did not experience as much crime and disorder as did London. Consequently, cities such as Bristol and Manchester accepted the necessity for change very slowly. It took many years and several Parliamentary Acts before the London model for policing replaced a stubborn reliance on watches to protect the king's subjects. The Municipal Corporations Act of 1835 began the reform process which did not end until passage of the Local Government Act in 1888. Even by that late date the crime prevention model had not entirely succeeded in eradicating the older methods of law enforcement. But it had at least become the dominant approach to policing in England.

### The Social Background for Police Reform in America

The reform of the London police attracted favorable attention in America shortly after the bobbies began patrolling their beats. But crime prevention was not permanently adopted as the basis for police reform in the United States for many years. The single most important reason for this delay was the fact that the negative social consequences of urbanization and industrialization had not yet become as serious as they were in England. America's cities had only begun to grow. In the years from 1830 to 1860 they would acquire new residents so fast and in such large numbers that problems with housing, city services, crime, and poverty became acute. Industrialization had not yet become an important economic development; there were only a few factories scattered in small towns along the east coast. Once industrialization began in earnest in the 1840s, it would contribute significantly to social problems and unrest among American workers. Thus, police reform began in England rather than the United States because the British felt the need for a better police earlier than Americans did.

An absence of major problems caused by urbanization and industrialization does not mean that American society was free of strife. On the contrary, there were at least four important sources of trouble in the 1820s and 1830s which urbanization and industrialization aggravated: nativism, racism, social reform, and politics. All four caused a great deal of turmoil which occasionally turned violent.

Nativism, or prejudice against persons of foreign birth, became an important issue during the 1820s and remained so until the Civil War. Catholic immigrants (especially the Irish after 1840) were especially suspected of being incapable of loyalty to the United States. Native Americans thought Catholics could not understand the principles of democracy and would work to undermine our cherished institutions. Prejudice of this sort usually took the form of social and economic discrimination. Catholics found it difficult to obtain decent jobs and housing, and their children had to attend public schools in which reading from a Protestant Bible was part of the daily routine. But nativism did not always confine itself to these forms of discrimination. A number of riots can be traced to nativist origins, including the burning of a Boston convent in 1834, the Philadelphia riots of 1844, and the Louisville riot of 1855. In many cases property damage was extensive and several people lost their lives.

Racism could also be a deadly source of turmoil. Most blacks lived in the South as slaves, but several northern cities such as Cincinnati, Philadelphia, and New York contained small populations of free Negroes. These people lived in generally wretched conditions and were the victims of intense prejudice. They eked out minimal livings by taking the worst paid jobs available. Casual and organized violence made their lives even more miserable. In Philadelphia during the late 1830s and early 1840s, white thugs armed with knives frequently stabbed any black who had the misfortune to be walking on the same street. Race riots erupted on the slightest pretext. Between 1829 and 1850 Philadelphia had five major race riots which required military intervention.

Violence also derived from some aspects of social reform during the antebellum era. Many Americans supported a wide range of reforms which they felt were necessary to the well-being of society. Practically every thing, from eating habits to slavery, came under close and critical scrutiny. Two of the most important reforms, and ones which caused considerable turmoil, were the abolition of slavery and the temperance crusade. Opposition to the abolitionists was widespread in many areas of the North. Many whites feared that freeing the slaves would increase competition for jobs. Since the demand for the abolition of slavery also disrupted delicate political and economic relations between the North and the South, other whites opposed it as detrimental to the nation's well-being. Antagonism toward abolitionists frequently took the form of mob action, especially in the 1830s, and thereby contributed to the widespread rioting of that decade. The temperance crusade also angered many people, particularly immigrants and workers. The Germans and the Irish, for instance, regarded temperance as an assault upon their respective ethnic cultures, in which drinking was accepted as a normal activity. The fact that temperance advocates tended to be native Americans from the upper classes convinced opponents of this reform that they were being asked to sacrifice one of life's few pleasures to the convenience of their social superiors. For a change, however, the temperance crusade did not provoke mass violence. Instead, temperance was a critical political issue which influenced the outcome of many local elections. It also became a major law enforcement problem which significantly affected the development of American policing.

Politics became a source of social turmoil because urban politicians lacked stable party organizations which could provide a framework for settling public issues. In order to build stable organizations, the politicians had to appeal to the sympathies and prejudices of the voters in ways which would make these voters remain loyal to their parties. Thus a local party might adopt a platform favoring nativist principles; voters who favored those principles flocked to this party, while those who did not stampeded to another which announced its opposition to nativism. Parties also tried to create enthusiasm for their principles and candidates by adopting techniques which would create mass participation in their rallies. Parades were a favorite tactic which soon became a major source of violence. When the parades of opposing parties met in the street, riots followed. Elections were also a fruitful source of trouble. Rival parties often clashed at the polls, as their adherents struggled to stuff a ballot box or to prevent their opponents from doing so. During one election in the mid-1830s, street fighting between competing parties in Philadelphia culminated in a gun battle which only ended when one side burned down the building in which their opponents had taken refuge. Political conflicts became so violent because they reflected the bitter social antagonisms of their era. Democrats tended to be proimmigrant, antitemperance, and antiabolition. Whigs tended to be nativist, protemperance, and abolitionist. Fundamental social divisions thus created political battles of more than ordinary intensity.

The Industrial Revolution and urban growth, particularly in eastern and midwestern cities, intensified these bitter social issues and complicated the problems of maintaining public order. Now many thousands more people from different ethnic and social backgrounds crowded together competing for jobs, status, and privilege. Cities began to develop distinctive neighborhoods as people sorted themselves out along ethnic and class lines. Institutions which had once served the whole city now changed to reflect neighborhood aspirations and prejudices at the expense of the general welfare. Fire companies were one example of this shift. Once an important service which protected cities from a major danger, fire-fighting companies themselves became dangerous. Their members reflected the ethnic composition as well as the social and political views of their neighborhoods. Fire companies on the way to a blaze often ran into other companies from rival neighborhoods. Instead of proceeding to the fire, these rivals stopped to fight one another. Riots frequently developed from these battles and lasted for several hours. With no effective civil force available to deal with these conflicts, the rioters often fought until mutual exhaustion caused them to stop.

Threats to social order were only one problem facing urban residents. Crimes of a different sort also alarmed them. Highway robberies on poorly lit city streets attracted increasing concern. Pedestrians risked their lives as well as their pocketbooks walking home at night. Daring thieves prowled the business districts seizing anything from a pair of boots to a sack of gold coins as opportunities presented themselves. In an era when an attempt to collect accurate crime statistics had not even been made, it is extremely difficult to determine whether crime was actually increasing. We can say, however, that concern over property offenses had become widespread. Citizens arming themselves to defend their homes and persons was only one indication of this growing fear. Such measures had been unthinkable prior to the 1830s. Fear about this kind of crime, combined with dismay over the decay of social order, therefore made a powerful argument for police reform.

**American Police Reform**

When the movement to improve law enforcement did begin in the 1830s, the reformers' motives reflected the diversity of their concerns. Some wanted a new police which would restrain the behavior of "undesirable" citizens such as the Irish; others were concerned about the effect of disorder and crime on the safety of property and property values; and finally there were those who felt that the amount of crime, rioting, and general social conflict threatened the basis of civil society. It is impossible to say which group, if any, dominated the movement for a new police. All three shared the desire to alter existing police arrangements to cope with new needs, and representatives of each group could be found in every large city by the late 1830s. Their problem was how to convince a majority of their fellow citizens that police reform had become necessary to the future well-being of their communities.

This problem was not as easy to solve as many reformers first assumed. One central theme emerged as the crucial issue in every city: the reformers had to devise a police system which would conform to the ideology of republicanism. No reform plan could succeed unless it embodied the cardinal virtues of that ideology, especially its emphasis on decentralization of power (or checks and balances) and accountability to the voters. Any plan which advocated a police controlled by a single person, or a small number of people, immediately provoked cries of despotism. Similarly, proposals that policemen serve during good behavior, or that they wear a uniform (two features of the London police) aroused fears that the reformers wanted to tyrannize their fellow citizens. Uniforms were un-American in principle, and service during good behavior would encourage policemen to think they were not answerable to the public they served. Partisan politics made the reformers' task considerably more difficult. Local politicians wanted to be sure that their opponents would not use a new police to harass them at the polls by arresting their supporters. Such manipulations had already occurred with the existing police; the fear of a partisan police was thus based on experience. In sum, police reformers had to tread carefully around the sensitive issues involved in ideology and partisanship. Considering the obstacles, it is remarkable that they succeeded at all.

New York was the first American city to adopt a lasting version of a preventive police. While the exact details of New York's reform movement were not duplicated elsewhere, the general situation was fairly typical of the obstacles the reformers faced and the solutions they used to overcome their opponents. The campaign began in 1836 when New York's mayor sent the Common Council a report advocating police reorganization to better cope with civil disorders.. In rejecting the mayor's recommendations, the councilmen made it clear that republicanism was the basis of their refusal to act. Their own report concluded that: "The nature of our institutions are [sic] such that more reliance may be placed upon the people for aid, in case of any emergency, than in despotic governments." Police reform disappeared as a major issue until 1841, when a spectacular murder case once more revealed the deficiencies of local law enforcement. Mary Cecilia Rogers was the victim in this case. She left home to visit her sister on July 25; three days later her body was found in the Hudson River. This murder, which was never solved, caused a sensation. Local newspapers clamored for police action, and when the police displayed an unwillingness to investigate unless a sufficient reward was forthcoming, the press began to campaign for reform. The demand for a new police received so much public support that all political parties endorsed reform. Unfortunately, the politicians could not agree on a plan. The campaign for a preventive police only succeeded when the Democrats mustered enough power to dominate decisions regarding reform. In 1844 the New York state legislature, then controlled by Democrats, passed a law establishing a preventive police for New York City.

Under the provisions of the New York law, preventive policing came to America in a dramatically different form than that adopted in Europe. The most important difference was readily apparent: in the American version, the police were deliberately incorporated into politics. Two provisions of New York's reform law made the police part of the political process. First, the law provided that each ward in the city would be a separate patrol district. This meant that in order to gain public acceptance the police would have to be responsive to the law enforcement views of the people in the wards they patrolled. In this situation, uniform enforcement policies which dealt with city-wide problems would be impossible. One ward might favor keeping saloons open on Sunday, for example, but another might not. Controversies over police behavior, therefore, became inevitable as special interest groups fought among themselves to extend their version of law enforcement over the whole city. The process for selecting policemen was the second means by which they became involved in politics. New York's mayor chose the police from a list of names submitted by the aldermen and tax assessors of each ward. He then had to submit his choices to the city council for approval. This system applied the theory of republicanism to preventive policing. No one person had control over appointments, and the politicians who made the appointments were all accountable to the voters. In practice, however, this selection process gave most power over the police to the ward aldermen. Those politicians had no interest in finding capable men to serve as policemen. They regarded the new police as a great opportunity to reward their friends and supporters regardless of their qualifications. Patronage politics was thus built into preventive policing at the outset and quickly became another source of controversy.

Other provisions in the law indicated that the legislators had little understanding of how to create an effective preventive police. They authorized a force of no more than 800 men, a number which would make intensive patrolling difficult, especially since a police district's boundaries had no relation to the geographic concentrations of crime in the city. The law did provide for the appointment of a chief of police, but he was to have no power to appoint policemen, to assign them to districts, or to remove them from duty. All those responsibilities were reserved to the mayor and city council. Thus there would not be a strong executive who could hold the new police to a common standard of conduct. Finally, the law did not require the police to wear a uniform; instead, they were to carry a badge or other emblem which they could use to identify themselves. Citizens would therefore find it very difficult to locate an officer when they had need for one.

In spite of these problems, the new force did have some resemblance to a preventive police. All police functions, from maintaining order to arresting criminals, had finally been centralized in a single body of men. Competing groups, such as watchmen and constables, were disbanded. The new police would patrol the city around the clock, not just at night or at their own convenience. Pay scales were high enough to attract competent recruits (although the politicians' control of nominations guaranteed that competence was not always a primary consideration). These were important advantages over the old police, and they at least provided the basis for further improvements when and if the public would demand them.

Police reformers in other cities did not adopt every feature of New York's plan. But there were enough similarities to say that New York served as a kind of model for the campaigns to establish preventive policing elsewhere. New Orleans and Cincinnati adopted plans for a new police in 1852; Boston and Philadelphia did so in 1854, Chicago in 1855, and Baltimore in 1857. By the 1860s, preventive policing had been accepted in principle, properly modified to meet American conditions, in every large city and in several smaller ones. This was an important achievement.

## Critical Issues in American Policing

Several issues critical to the success of the new police emerged quickly, however, and helped determine their future development. The original American model of a police founded on the principles of crime prevention had several failings aside from the fact that politics was to play so large a role in the departments. Three important problems confronted the first police officials in the early years of policing, between 1845 and 1860: 1) a controversy over the adoption of uniforms; 2) a concern about arming the police; 3) and the issue of appropriate force in making arrests. The uniform was an important issue for a variety of reasons. First, the lack of a uniform undermined one of the principal ideas associated with crime prevention. In theory, people would be deterred from committing crimes when they knew that an officer was nearby. This was the uniform's purpose—it made a patrolman visible. Without this visibility, so the theory went, people would be more inclined to commit crimes. Other considerations also affected the uniform issue. The victim of a crime, for example, usually wanted to find a policeman in a hurry. How was he to do so if the police dressed, and therefore, looked just like everyone else? Uniforms would also help compel some officers to do their duty. In one case, a patrolman sitting in a saloon calmly looked the other way when a fight began. Since no one knew he was an officer, he could shirk his duty without suffering any consequences. These, then, were some of the reasons why many people insisted that the police should be uniformed.

Policemen themselves had other ideas. A uniform smacked of subordination and tyranny to many of them. These officers denounced uniforms as un-American liveries which would destroy their sense of manliness and democracy. Other patrolmen took a more practical, though still negative, approach to this question. They claimed that a uniform would actually hinder their work. Thieves would be able to see them and escape before the officer could reach the scene of a crime. One patrolman went so far as to claim that even wearing his badge prevented him from making arrests because criminals could see the sun reflecting from it, warning them of his approach. Feelings on this issue ran fairly high among the police. In New York, the patrolmen hired a lawyer at one point and threatened legal action to nullify an order to wear a uniform.

Opposition from the ranks thus made the uniform issue difficult to resolve. The tactics which eventually succeeded in uniforming the police varied from one city to another and depended upon the intensity of opposition as well as the means available to overcome it. Officials in New York took advantage of the fact that their police served four year terms of appointment. When those terms expired in 1853, the city's police commissioners announced that they would not rehire any man who refused to wear a uniform. The commissioners remained firm in their determination through a subsequent storm of protest, and New York became the first city with a uniformed police. This innovation took much longer to appear in Philadelphia. Mayor Richard Conrad ordered his police to wear a regulation hat in 1854, and even tried to encourage compliance by appearing in the standard headgear himself. His officers refused to follow suit, however, and this attempt at a minimal uniform failed. Four years later another mayor, Alexander Henry, tried psychology. He decided to take advantage of the Reserve Corps' pride in their distinctiveness. The Corps consisted of the most physically imposing men in the department, and they were detailed to act as an anti-riot squad. Henry pointed out to these officers that a uniform would make them look even more distinctive, and prescribed a blue coat, pants and patent leather cap for their use. The Corps reacted favorably, but the remainder of the force did not. Henry finally had to adopt stringent rules in 1860 to obtain compliance with his order to wear a uniform. With some last grumbling, the Philadelphia patrolmen submitted. Elsewhere progress came more easily. Both in Boston (1858) and in Chicago (1861) the police seemed less inclined to protest and uniforms were adopted in those cities with little incident.

Arming the police was a far more sensitive issue than the dispute over uniforms. The personal safety of officers and citizens alike was at stake, and few problems could equal the threat of death for dramatic impact. Considering the seriousness of this issue, it is surprising that the public debate over it was never very intense. Police officials, newspaper editors, and private citizens did have opinions on this matter, and in general they viewed an armed police with considerable suspicion. But their arguments against allowing the police to carry firearms somehow lacked conviction. After pointing out the usual problems with firearms, such as the difficulty in regulating the policemen's use of weapons, and after some forlorn remarks to the effect that the London police had no need for guns, officials and private citizens alike concluded that an armed police was most undesirable and probably unavoidable.

However unhappy the critics of an armed police might be, they had to face one unavoidable fact. Americans, unlike the British, had a long tradition that every citizen had the right, even the duty, to own firearms. Guns were part of the American culture. Nativism, racism, and antagonisms among immigrant groups complicated the problem of gun use and control considerably. Beginning in the 1840s, people in cities began to use firearms against one another systematically for the first time. Street fights, riots among firemen, and various other sorts of social conflict became occasions for the use of pistols (and occasionally muskets). When the newly organized preventive police began patrolling the streets, they were armed only with nightsticks. During the late 1840s and early 1850s, newspapers began to carry stories about officers shot in the line of duty. A few of these incidents appear to have been ambushes, but most occurred when a policeman intervened in a fight in which one of the assailants was armed with a pistol.

The problem facing the police had now become critical. Patrolmen never could be sure when a rowdy might have a gun, yet the officer knew he had to intervene in disorder quickly or risk having a small dispute between a small number of people grow into a serious problem. Tactical considerations, such as when and how to use force, became more complicated in these circumstances. Officers who misjudged these questions could pay a severe penalty. The solution to these difficulties emerged during the 1850s as individual policemen began to carry firearms regardless of official orders and public opinion. In some cases, as in Philadelphia, the city councils authorized their police to carry pistols, but such authorizations only recognized what was becoming standard, if informal practice. The public accepted an armed police because there appeared to be no other alternative at the time. One of the most significant changes in American policing thus developed from the conditions which officers confronted on the city streets.

One of the most admired characteristics of the London police was, and is, their restraint in using physical force to make arrests. American policemen, however, have been notorious for their readiness to use force, and this trait has attracted a great deal of criticism over the years. The attitudes toward, and the use of firearms in the United States helps explain our police's willingness to employ force, but the presence of guns does not completely account for it. There were at least two other reasons why policing in this country has often been so physical. The explanation for this behavior on the part of the police lies first in American attitudes toward law and law enforcement and second in the social turmoil of the mid-nineteenth century.

American attitudes toward law and law enforcement are full of contradictions. Many citizens believe that laws against certain kinds of behavior are necessary, but that those laws should not be enforced against them. (Traffic regulations are good examples of this attitude.) Some people want to use the law as a way to regulate conduct which they think is offensive; but there are others who oppose using the law in this manner because they are not offended by that same behavior. (Laws against drinking or keeping saloons open on Sundays are examples of controversial legislation.) In too many cases, then, there is no consensus that a particular law, or a group of laws, should be uniformly enforced. This becomes an extremely difficult problem for an officer who is, for instance, under orders to arrest drunks when he is patrolling a neighborhood where drinking and drunkenness are seen as normal activities. The officer knows that if he arrests a drunk who then resists him, he cannot rely on bystanders to assist him because they disapprove of his actions. But he cannot back down from making the arrest; such an act would make him look ridiculous to onlookers who are already inclined to disrespect him anyway. Faced with these circumstances many patrolmen in the mid-nineteenth century resorted to force as a means of establishing their personal authority over the people they policed. In effect, law enforcement was often reduced to a question of whether a particular officer had the physical strength to dominate a situation requiring his intervention.

The social turmoil of the era between 1840 and 1870 also helped explain the use of force. Violence had become commonplace, and many people who supported police reform did so in the expectation that a more effective police would reestablish order on the streets. These people did not always care overly much exactly how the police accomplished that goal. If a few heads got broken in the process, that was a cost they were willing to pay. This was especially true during the 1850s, though it has usually been the case since that time as long as excessive force was used against certain classes of people but not against others. Charges of police brutality appeared most often during the 1850s and 1860s when a patrolman made the mistake of clubbing a "respectable" citizen who blundered into an encounter with an "undesirable" drunken Irishman (or someone equivalent). In effect, then, excessive force was implicitly encouraged as a means of obtaining more peaceful cities.

Although no one probably intended it, the use of force became a permanent legacy once the police discovered how useful it was in solving many of their problems. Violence, after all, did decline, but it did not disappear in the social life of American cities. Uncertainty whether an offender was armed, and a continuing lack of consensus over the enforcement of some laws, perpetuated the policeman's need to rely on his physical prowess as a means of dealing with incidents on the streets.

### English and American Policing in Comparison

America's version of preventive policing thus developed quite differently from its British cousin. The contrast between the London bobby and the American cop appalled many people in the United States who had hoped to duplicate the polite, presumably efficient Britisher in a New World setting. But those who were disappointed or uneasy over the differences between the new police in each country failed to understand that the English model for crime prevention could not work in the United States. It could not for three reasons: the politics of the English and American policing were extremely different; the law enforcement policies which each police adopted differed dramatically; and the social environment in which each police worked contrasted sharply.

 Politics affected the organization and the behavior of the police in both England and America. The difference in political influence became apparent, however, in the effect which politics had. In England, politics contributed to the success of the new police; in America politics severely hindered police effectiveness. London's police commissioners, Rowan and Mayne, answered for the conduct of their men to only one politician, the home secretary. That official consistently supported them in their efforts to establish a disciplined police force free from outside interference. London's police therefore had a highly centralized command structure in which the commissioners had the authority and responsibility necessary for the success of their work. By contrast, an American chief of police had many masters. So did his patrolmen. Mayors and aldermen interfered often and without thought about the consequences in matters of appointments, discipline, and law enforcement policies. In this situation there was no single standard of behavior which would have helped the patrolmen and the public to understand what was expected of the new police. A great deal of the public's disappointment with the police, and the police's inability to overcome their negative image, can be traced to the ways in which American politicians mismanaged their law enforcement responsibilities.

But politics does not explain everything about the differences between the police in England and America. The second important area in which contrasts in style became apparent had to do with law enforcement policies. In general, law enforcement was much more uniform in London than in American cities. Temperance regulation provided a classic example of the difference. If a law said all taverns had to close by midnight on Saturday, Commissioners Rowan and Mayne expected their officers to see that the law was obeyed. In the United States, however, saloonkeepers with political connections could use their influence with the patrolman's superiors to avoid closing laws. Temperance reformers unhappy with this situation could occasionally force the police to close saloons which had been violating the law, but the saloons did not stay shut for very long. The seesaw battle between reformers and saloonkeepers became a major source of problems for the police. No matter what they did, someone was angry at them. The absence of standard policies led to a situation in which people with an interest in questions of morality constantly tried to manipulate the law and the police to achieve their own ends.

The social environment was the final reason why the British and American police developed in such different ways. Policemen in both countries encountered violence against them when they first began patrolling the streets. But the attacks on English constables decreased considerably within a few years while assaults on American officers remained at a rather high level. The reason for this trend in the two countries seems to be that American cities had more volatile problems than those in London. London was already an extremely large city; most American cities were just becoming modern metropolises. It may be that Londoners of conflicting views and from competing classes simply had learned to live together more effectively than had American citizens who had not had so many years to familiarize themselves with the demands of urban life. Violence was therefore more typical in America because people had not yet discovered other ways to deal with their problems. The attitudes toward the ownership and use of guns further complicated matters. Policemen simply had to expect gang members, thieves, and assorted rowdies to be armed and willing to shoot them. Faced with this fear, American patrolmen felt compelled to rely upon force as a normal part of their ability to control the streets. London bobbies were fortunate that coercion was an extraordinary tactic.

Contrasting conditions thus created different traditions in England and America during the formative years of preventive policing. The bobby learned to enforce laws uniformly by the impersonal authority which resided in his official position as a lawman. American patrolmen learned that laws could be manipulated to serve the interests of various powerful groups and that they had to rely upon their personal authority and ability to impose their will on a populace which regarded them with suspicion and hatred. Thus the reform of law enforcement which had become so necessary due to the consequences of urbanization and industrialization produced two very different police forces.

## SUGGESTED READINGS

T. A. Critchley, *A History of Police in England and Wales, 900-1966* (London: Constable and Company Ltd., 1967) is a good general survey of England's policing. For developments in America, the two standard histories of representative departments are Roger Lane, *Policing the City: Boston, 1822-1885* (Cambridge: Harvard University Press, 1967) and James Richardson, *The New York Police: Colonial Times to 1901* (New York: Oxford University Press, 1970). Wilbur Miller, *Cops and Bobbies: Police Authority in New York and London, 1830-1870* (Chicago: University of Chicago Press, 1977) is an excellent study of the differences between American and British police development. John C. Schneider, *Detroit and the Problem of Order, 1830-1880: A Geography of Crime, Riot, and Policing* (Lincoln: University of Nebraska Press, 1980) is an important study of the problems of urban social order.

# 3

# Varieties of Criminal Behavior: The 19th Century

**B**y the middle of the nineteenth century most people generally assumed that the reformed police now had the ability to deal with the crime problems of America's cities. The adoption of prevention as the basis for law enforcement, combined with the expansion and reorganization of departments, presumably gave the police the tools they needed to cope with criminals. And yet these expectations were only partially fulfilled. Criminals continued to plague city residents in spite of the efforts of the new police. Irate taxpayers accused the police of failing to fulfill their mandate. They believed that the original concept of a preventive police was still sound, but that corrupt politicians and policemen had undermined it.

This view of the problems confronting the police was simplistic. It ignored the role which urbanization (reinforced by industrialization) played in complicating law enforcement during the nineteenth century. Urbanization did not cause crime, but it did create an environment which provided more opportunities for criminal behavior and it did make the task of controlling crime much more difficult.

At no time in American history have our cities expanded as rapidly as they did in the nineteenth century. New York, which had a mere 60,000 residents in 1800, contained nearly 4,000,000 people by 1900; Chicago, an insignificant village in 1837, numbered some 2,000,000 inhabitants by the end of the century. Many cities often doubled their size every ten years. Practically all of this growth came as a result of basic changes sweeping Europe and the United States. New methods of farming, which emphasized large production units and the use of machinery, forced millions off the land. Industrialization simultaneously increased the demand for workers, thereby attracting huge numbers of these displaced people to the burgeoning cities of America. Whether a native-born American or an immigrant, all these people sought more satisfying living conditions. Their goals helped determine where these people settled. Since opportunities were more limited in the South at the time, the overwhelming majority of this mass migration headed toward the cities of the North and Midwest. New York, Massachusetts, Pennsylvania, and Illinois, for example, received nearly half of all the foreign immigrants who arrived during the century. Even larger numbers of native-born Americans settled in the cities of those states.

This massive influx of new residents affected urban law enforcement in three ways. First, it increased the geographic size of cities enormously as new housing and business areas opened to accommodate these people. This meant that the physical effort involved in patrolling a city increased beyond anyone's expectations. No police force could maintain a suitable presence on the streets at all times. Budgetary problems complicated the effort to protect cities. Throughout the century cost-conscious politicians kept the number of officers as small as possible. During the frequent economic down-turns which occurred, departmental strength suffered as mayors sought ways to reduce city payrolls. Thus the sheer size of the cities, and their economic problems, jeopardized one of crime prevention's cardinal principles: pervasiveness.

Secondly, urbanization encouraged specialized use of land within cities. Expanding businesses needed convenient locations. Prosperity and changing tastes prompted many people to seek more spacious homes. The poor crowded into the inner city neighborhoods where they could afford the rents. In sum, more distinct downtown, suburban, and slum areas emerged. Opportunities for crime varied within these districts. Careless merchants and homeowners made tempting targets in the business and middle class areas. The tensions of slum life created numerous situations where violence often erupted. Crime thus expanded with urban growth.

Finally, the process of urbanization threw thousands of strangers together. Irishmen, blacks, Germans, Scandinavians, Italians, Poles, and Jews, to mention just a few groups, crowded into cities where they lived cheek-by-jowl. The initial contacts between these groups sometimes were anything but friendly. Ethnic rivalries, class distinctions, and different levels of political influence mixed in the urban neighborhoods to produce a fruitful source of crime. These differences created situations in which uniform law enforcement policies became impossible. Criminals would learn to exploit these situations.

The types and amount of crime did not remain constant throughout the nineteenth century. In general, violence was more common in the early period of urbanization than later. As people adjusted to urban life, they learned to settle their differences by means other than violence. Property crime became more frequent over time. Thieves may not have increased in number (that is nearly impossible to determine) but they did become more skillful. A single thief, or group of them, could presumably commit more successful crimes by the end of the century. But the shift toward more property crimes did not necessarily mean that the total amount of crime increased.

Continuous changes in the urban environment thus enhanced the possibilities for crime throughout the nineteenth century. A bewildering variety of criminals plagued urban residents, but the types of crime which occurred can be related to the basic developments which were transforming the cities. From this perspective, three categories of criminal behavior emerge. Ethnic rivalries and the growing need for orderly behavior in public places were responsible for much of the street crime at the time. The opportunities for theft which emerged in conjunction with downtowns and suburbs attracted the attention of numerous part-time criminals and professional thieves. And the conflicts over law enforcement policies provided illegal entrepreneurs with possibilities for profit which they might not otherwise have had. These three categories do not conform readily to legal definitions of crime, but they do provide a classification which is helpful in describing the nature of criminal behavior in ways which make the problem facing the police more easily understood.

## Street Crime

Criminal behavior on the streets mirrored the patterns of settlement and economic growth within nineteenth century cities. The poor were gradually being concentrated in the inner city wards, close to the bustling downtowns which were constantly pushing into decaying residential areas in search of more space. Many in the upper classes, having discovered the delights of large homes on roomy lots, eagerly sought even better accommodations at increasing distances from the inner city. And the massive influx of new residents provided a further incentive for continuous urban expansion.

Street crime occurred most often in the slums and business areas of these burgeoning cities. Many of these offenses violated the increased demand for regularity and predictability in public places. Both qualities had become hard to achieve in the chaos of urban growth, but both were crucial to the continued orderly development of cities. Traffic violations pointedly demonstrated the nature of this problem. The movement of goods and people within the metropolis was a basic necessity which various kinds of behavior constantly jeopardized. Horsecar drivers, for instance, frequently raced one another through the streets, paying no attention to the discomfort of their passengers or the danger to pedestrians. Wagon drivers and coachmen often disputed rights-of-way, sometimes to the point of assaulting one another. Pedestrians wandered haphazardly across the streets. At busy intersections, it was every man for himself as dozens of drivers sought to force their way through a maze of competing vehicles.

Seeking to counter the rising disorder of the streets, city councils passed numerous ordinances establishing new guidelines for correct behavior. Fines and other penalties, coupled with more stringent licensing requirements, were used to induce compliance with these regulations. But compliance took time to develop; thousands of people unaccustomed to these kinds of laws provided enough work to keep as much as one third or more of a city's police busy writing citations. Eventually, new technologies (such as street lights and the internal combustion engine) would solve some of these traffic problems—and create new ones. For most of the nineteenth century, though, violations of city ordinances were among the most common crime committed.

Drunkenness was another, indeed the most common, street crime. This offense also violated public order, but in addition it involved basic social conflicts which made it one of the most volatile issues of the day. The debates which raged around this offense reflected fundamental dis-agreements about the nature of drink. Self-appointed moralists, usually Anglo-Saxon Protestant in background, were convinced that drunken-ness caused crime and should therefore be suppressed. Various ethnic groups arrayed themselves against this view, arguing that drinking was simply a form of recreation. Immigrants frequently owned or operated saloons because these businesses required little initial capital and because they had a ready source of customers within their own neighborhoods. Successful saloon keepers often held political office or had friendly contacts with local politicians. The attack on alcohol and public drunkenness therefore struck at immigrant cultural prac-tices, economic opportunities, and political connections.

While the debate over law enforcement policies dragged on, thou-sands of tipsy citizens roamed the streets. They had innumerable opportunities to drown their sorrows or celebrate their good fortune. Practically every downtown street intersection had at least one saloon, and usually more. Unlicensed saloons proliferated in the slums, where a barrel of rotgut whiskey and a crude table usually sufficed to draw a steady stream of customers. Drunks created various problems. They offered tempting targets to wandering juveniles and thugs looking for easy money; they frequently needed help in finding their homes; they sometimes became quarrelsome and caused fights in saloons and on the streets; and, during the winter, they occasionally endangered their health or lives by falling asleep in alleys and gutters. No matter which view of liquor law enforcement prevailed at any moment, this behavior posed practical problems for the police.

Social tensions rooted in religious, racial, and ethnic differences also contributed to street crime. Immigrants, blacks, and native white Americans lived together in a confusing hodgepodge of slum neighborhoods. No ethnic group completely dominated a particular urban area; so-called ghettos of Irishmen, Jews, or Poles always contained a majority of people from other ethnic backgrounds. Blacks were perhaps the only exception to this rule. As a consequence of this ethnically mixed residential pattern in the slums, these areas seethed with tensions. Irish Catholics despised Irish Protestants; Germans disliked Poles (and vice versa); Americans distrusted Catholics; and everyone abused the blacks. Throughout the nineteenth century the conflicts generated by mutual suspicion, misunderstanding, and bigotry caused countless crimes. Physical assaults, either on a random basis or in more concerted form, abounded, especially in the middle decades of the century.

An interracial street assault in New York's famous slum neighborhood, the Five Points. *Courtesy Library of Congress.*

Assaults occurred practically every day, often without provocation. On the south side of Philadelphia, for example, Irish immigrants living close to blacks consistently attacked their neighbors during the early 1840s. Black men and women walking along a sidewalk might suddenly be stabbed by a passing juvenile. Irish Catholics, on the other hand, had to be careful not to wander onto certain streets where their Irish Protestant enemies might set upon them without warning. The use of firearms made these incidents even more dangerous. Prior to the 1840s few people carried guns. But the rising social tensions of the antebellum era, combined with a fear that the police could do nothing about crime, prompted many citizens to carry firearms for the first time. And they quickly learned to use their weapons to settle disputes. Juveniles shot one another during altercations; adults used pistols on ordinary criminals as well as ethnic, religious, and political rivals. The carnage of the Civil War seems only to have abated, not eliminated, this practice. Ordinary people thus had the motives, means, and willingness to use force on their neighbors throughout the century.

Gang warfare added another, sometimes spectacular, dimension to the problem of assaults. At a time when society provided few diversions for youngsters, juveniles who sought the company of their peers usually congregated on street corners. This habit was common throughout any city, and some of these informal gatherings evolved into gangs. For the most part these groups caused only minor annoyances. They pelted pedestrians with foul language and snowballs, and fought rivals for control of a particular street corner. These activities were not very dangerous to any of the participants. But there were exceptions to this general situation. Some very large gangs developed, particularly in the slums. These groups organized themselves not simply to dominate a local street corner but rather to defend their neighborhoods against aggression from rivals, equally large gangs of opposing ethnic, religious, and political backgrounds. These gangs typically attached themselves to volunteer fire companies which were also organized as neighborhood institutions. Together, the gangs and their fire companies waged almost literal war on their rivals. Arson became frequent during the middle decades of the century, as gangs set fires to attract their enemies. When the opposing fire companies arrived, supported by their own gangs, they ran into ambushes which often erupted into riots. The introduction of the professional fire departments, coupled with the switch to preventive policing, helped put an end to excessive gang violence. These developments did not, however, entirely eliminate gangs because the basic social reasons for their existence did not disappear as long as ethnic tensions persisted and gang-age juveniles remained numerous.

Riots were the most spectacular form of violence which plagued nineteenth century society. People who had not yet adjusted to the complexities of the new urban-industrial society, and who objected to the ways in which their lives were being affected, frequently vented their anger and frustration by taking to the streets. They resented having to live in close proximity to groups they had always hated; they had little tolerance for the increasing influence which city governments and factory owners exerted over them; and they had very few nonviolent ways to defend themselves from the negative effects of broad social and economic developments. Rioting was thus a form of protest against some group or some change which the rioters regarded as a threat to their way of life.

All sorts of people participated in riots. The most respectable and the least respectable elements in urban society often agreed upon a choice of targets in a riot, regardless of how little else they might share in common. This was especially true in riots involving race or religious questions. During the 1830s and 1840s numerous anti-Negro riots erupted in Philadelphia, Cincinnati, and other places. Mobs led by respected local citizens attacked the Negro sections of their towns with considerable ferocity. Religious intolerance and antiimmigrant feelings surfaced in such affairs as the destruction of the Ursuline Convent outside of Boston in 1834, the Nativist Riots in 1844 in Philadelphia, and "Bloody Monday" in Louisville in 1855. These are only a few examples of the many riots which occurred during the nineteenth century. Although rioting hardly became an everyday affair, riots were frequent enough to remind Americans that violence could erupt when important issues went unresolved.

## Theft

The expanding cities offered numerous opportunities to steal goods and money. Large numbers of businesses, conveniently concentrated in the downtowns and along major thoroughfares leading to the suburbs, made tempting targets. The suburban homes of the comfortable middle and wealthy upper classes were filled to the bursting point with the material splendor of a successful, expanding economy. A variety of circumstances made much of this wealth vulnerable to thieves. In an era when credit for individual shoppers did not exist, people habitually carried cash with them for their daily needs. Businessmen, with only rudimentary ways to protect their cash and merchandise, compounded their security problems by carelessly displaying goods and leaving valuable commercial papers or money lying about their offices. With so much so readily available, the only question was when thieves would find ways to take advantage of these prolific opportunities.

Most thefts from both businesses and homes involved small losses. The nature and extent of these crimes indicate that the perpetrators were usually juveniles and adults whose economic circumstances

A typical street theft. Homeless boys shoplifting at a clothing store.

tempted them into occasional thefts. The family wash might disappear if the housewife left it hanging too long. Brooms, shovels, and various other household items were also taken frequently. Some more daring thieves took advantage of the prevailing custom of hanging coats, hats, and umbrellas on a clothes tree located just inside the home's main entrance. They merely opened the door, stepped inside, grabbed whatever was within reach, and retreated to safety. Brass door fixtures, a popular decoration at the time, presented yet another opportunity. Juveniles simply unscrewed the fixtures and walked off with them. Hardware and clothing stores were favorite targets of these thieves. The shop owners inadvertently encouraged thefts by displaying samples of their goods on the sidewalk in front of their stores. It required little effort to walk by and grab something from these displays. Plate glass display windows appeared in many cities well before the Civil War. Jewellers seemed to favor this method for attracting customers, and many thieves found this innovation irresistible. Window smashing was for a time a common form of robbery. The thief merely threw a rock through these windows, grabbed a handful of merchandise, and ran off before the owner could react. Since this procedure was noisy, the thieves improved their technique by using glass cutters. Now the victims often failed to notice their losses until hours afterward.

Petty criminals did not steal these small items for their own use; they took them because they needed money. Hence these thieves had to have some way to convert such articles to cash. This vital procedure was in fact extremely easy because some businessmen depended upon the acquisition of miscellaneous kinds of property for their livelihoods. Junk dealers, used clothing merchants, and pawnbrokers paid a fraction of every item's worth to a steady stream of people who brought these articles to them every day. These businessmen asked no questions about the ownership of this property, and conducted their affairs with a minimum of police supervision. Indeed, it was not until the middle of the century that even feeble efforts to regulate these businesses began. Genuinely effective regulation remained a goal, not a reality, for decades thereafter. Petty thieves thus had a secure market for their goods.

Professional thieves were a small but dedicated minority among the so-called criminal classes of America's cities. Their skill, persistence, and choice of victims distinguished them from lesser criminals. Unlike the casual thief who stole whatever he chanced upon, professional criminals planned their activities carefully. They also developed more organized operations which depended upon cooperation among a group of thieves, and they became adept in the use of various tools required in their work. Planning, technical skill, and organization enabled professional criminals to engage in a wide variety of illegal activities. They did not devote their lives to one particular aspect of crime, even though they might be better at one line than another. Instead, they applied the basic principles of their craft to whatever opportunities they found interesting and lucrative.

Pickpockets did not have to worry about changes in business practices during the century. With thousands of people habitually carrying cash and wearing valuable jewelry, they only needed to develop a system for robbery on the streets. Once such a system evolved, it remained unchanged because victims had virtually no defenses against it. As with sneaking, the basic ingredients for success emphasized organization, skill, cooperation, and distraction. Pickpocket "mobs" usually worked in threes. One man, the "stall," bumped the victim to gain his attention and to stop him momentarily. The second thief, known as the "wire," expertly relieved the victim of his wallet, watch, or stickpin—whichever was most accessible. Once the valuables were removed, the "wire" immediately passed the loot to a third accomplice standing next to him. If the victim realized he was being robbed and grabbed the "wire," he was unable to substantiate his accusation because the loot had disappeared. Pickpockets applied their methods to the countless opportunities they found on the crowded streets, in hotel lobbies, at railroad depots, and on street cars. Good pickpockets made a tidy income. Eddie Jackson, one of Chicago's best wires, earned $1500 a week in his prime during the 1880s.

Banks naturally attracted the attention of professional thieves. Prior to the 1870s, these businesses were remarkably easy targets of a technique known as sneaking. Bank tellers stood behind simple counters. An unlocked gate at the end of the counter admitted customers to rear offices, and the safe, which stood directly behind the counter, remained open during business hours. To rob such a bank, thieves used three or four men depending upon the circumstances. Waiting until a lull in business, when only one teller was on duty, one thief would engage the teller in some elaborate transaction. A second man stationed himself to mask the teller's view of the gate. The third thief slipped through the gate, walked quietly to the safe, and filled his pockets with cash and negotiable paper. He then retraced his steps while his partners kept the teller occupied. All the gang then withdrew, being careful not to arouse suspicion. With its many variations, this sneak technique worked well for years, not only in banks but also in such businesses as brokerage houses. Later in the century changes in the business procedures (such as locking the gates and moving the safe into the rear of a bank or office) frustrated this simple design for robbery.

To the despair of their victims, burglars, and particularly safe-crackers, habitually displayed extraordinary skill in their work. These thieves maintained a technical superiority over their opposition until the end of the century. The lack of burglar-proof safes lay at the heart

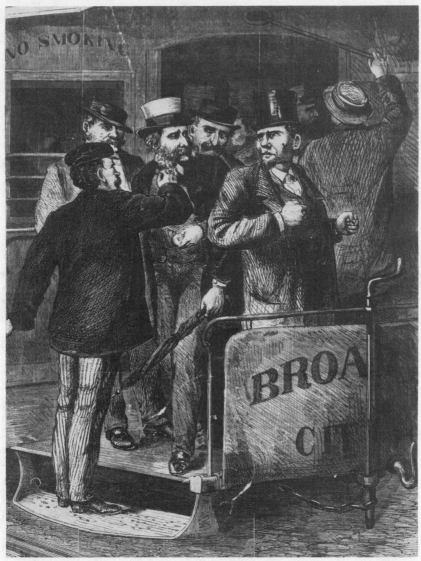

Lessons for the uninitiated. Pickpockets at work on the city railroad cars, New York.

of this superiority. Neither bankers nor businessmen could find a safe manufacturer whose product could withstand the attention of an experienced, well-equipped burglar. These criminals carried a strange assortment of tools designed to capitalize upon the destructive power of the mechanical principles of screws and levers. The "roundabout," for instance, was a device capable of cutting a circular hole through a safe door. This instrument was extremely effective prior to 1860, when many safes were still made of iron. When safe manufacturers adopted steel as their basic metal for construction (during the 1860s), burglars turned to diamond bits set in crank shafts of their own design to bore into doors. These tools thus enabled safecrackers to rob just about any bank or business, regardless of size. In these circumstances, safe-crackers made a great deal of money. Burglars in New York, Massa-chusetts, and Kentucky looted banks of over a million dollars each in three separate incidents between 1869 and 1876. The most famous robbery occurred in 1878, when thieves plundered the Manhattan Savings Bank of New York of $2,747,700 in cash and bonds.

The technical virtuosity of burglars forced their victims to rely upon defenses based upon a multi-layered safe design and the element of time. Since no metal then known could withstand a determined burglar, manufacturers resorted to building safes which had a number of layers of steel, iron, stone, and wire mesh. Although a burglar could cut through a single sheet of any of those materials, he did not have enough time in the course of the night to finish his work when he encountered this kind of construction. Only in this way did the burglar's potential victims nullify his technical superiority. Not every business or bank, however, could afford the expense of such a defense. After 1880, major banks were secure, but smaller banks and most offices were not. Their security depended upon further improvements in less expensive safes, but better designs and metals did not become available until the 1890s. Safecrackers in the meantime had very lucrative careers.

Confidence men formed yet another group of inventive and ingenious criminals. These thieves practiced a number of games which would today be classed as "short cons," although the distinction between "short" and "big" cons had not yet emerged. One particularly effec-tive con, called the drop game, appeared very early in the nineteenth century and remained a favorite ploy for many decades. In this con the first thief would accost the victim on the street, and while talking to him suddenly "discover" a wallet lying at the victim's feet. While the two men examined the wallet, a second thief would appear and declare that the victim was entitled to half the contents, which usually consisted of a single, large-denomination bill. After a brief protest, the first con man would agree to divide the spoils; the victim would be induced to hand over cash in return for the wallet; and the two con men sauntered off leaving the victim holding a counterfeit bill. Another game, known as "watch-stuffing," developed in the 1840s and 1850s. In this con a cheap watch was plated to resemble gold, and the con men peddled these trinkets to gullible pedestrians.

Somewhat more elaborate cons evolved at mid-century. One of the most notorious of these, the green-goods game, was initially very simple. A con man printed a large batch of circulars in which he offered to sell counterfeit money at discount prices to people willing to cheat their friends and neighbors (small businessmen seemed particularly prone to accept these offers). After mailing the circulars, the con man merely waited for the responses. Victims who responded to these circulars by sending money received packages of sawdust for their trouble. By the 1870s this game had become more complex. Victims came to see the con man. This change required the con man to have partners who performed various tasks such as meeting the victim, bringing him to some pre-arranged spot, and escorting him back to his train. Now victims were shown a satchel full of genuine money which they duly paid for. As soon as the victim had handed over his cash, one con man distracted him momentarily while another member of the gang switched satchels. The victim left carrying a bundle of cut paper. If he discovered the fraud, the con men threatened to expose his larcenous intentions if he prosecuted them. In spite of numerous exposés, the green-goods game remained a reliable, lucrative con until the 1890s.

Except for con men who always dealt in cash, most professional thieves needed fences to dispose of the property they stole. The quantity and value of their loot meant that these criminals could not rely upon ordinary junk dealers or pawnbrokers to handle their goods. Most small businessmen did not have the resources to deal safely with large amounts of expensive jewelry, clothing, and bonds. In order to convert their spoils to cash, therefore, many professional thieves turned to a few fences who had developed extensive operations by mid-century. One of the most famous of these receivers was Frances (Marm) Mandelbaum of New York City. During the course of her career, which stretched from about 1860 to 1884, Marm Mandelbaum epitomized the critical role which major fences played in the lives of professional thieves. Her store, originally a haberdashery, became a depository for stolen goods of all descriptions which she sold off through a national network of business contacts. Thieves regularly met at her place to plan their activities. When necessary, Marm extended credit to her friends and arranged police protection. All these services made her an influential figure in the underworld and a character of considerable notoriety in legitimate society. Eventually fleeing to Canada to escape prosecution, Marm ended her days comfortably esconced in Toronto. Her departure did not, however, undermine the business of theft. Others promptly filled her place and continued to provide the services criminals required for successful careers.

## Illegal Enterprise

Urbanization not only intensified social tensions and expanded the opportunities of professional thieves, it also created demands for entertainment appropriate to the tastes and wealth of the new urban society. Recreational opportunities were initially very limited, especially for women, but male-dominated ideas about interesting diversions soon transformed two extremely lucrative urban businesses, prostitution and gambling. Both activities were as old as human civilization, but new conditions in the burgeoning cities created a situation in which each had to change to meet the increasing demand for its services.

Cultural differences, based on ethnicity and class, contributed to the expansion of these activities and complicated police efforts to control them. Some ethnic groups were more tolerant of vice than others. This situation became a fruitful source of controversy, as members of one point of view sought to impose their ideas on everyone else. Native-born Americans were especially concerned about the increases in gambling and prostitution. They sought to control these activities in order to make other ethnic groups conform to their social values.

Prostitutes and gamblers discovered that customers for their services tended to concentrate in the business areas of the nation's cities. Thousands of entrepreneurs and their employees ministered to the needs of an expanding economy each day. Visitors from across the country poured into every city and sought lodging in numerous hotels scattered around the downtown areas. All these people sought diversions from the day's cares, and a number of different forms of entertainments emerged to succor them. Restaurants and theaters catered to some needs; prostitutes and gamblers to others. The most elegant brothels and gambling houses thus located quite openly in the "bright-light" districts which developed within and on the fringes of downtown. Their proximity to the large numbers of people who worked in or visited the business districts ensured their success.

For the madames who ran the brothels, recruiting new employees became one of the most important business problems. Most prostitutes worked an average of only four years. Furthermore, each brothel had to keep offering its customers fresh faces in order to retain their share of the trade in a highly competitive enterprise. This combination of short careers and the need for novelty required brothel owners and managers to be constantly on the lookout for new recruits. They solved this problem by relying in large part on the attractions they could offer to some women. Thousands of young, single women flocked into the cities looking for legitimate work. Not all of them found suitable jobs, and those who did frequently earned extremely low wages. Prostitution, on the other hand, paid extremely well. A woman working in a good or elegant brothel could expect to earn fifteen to thirty dollars a week, a pay scale which compared very favorably to wages ranging from two to five dollars a week in factories and domestic service. Many women found these higher incomes sufficiently attractive to become brothel inmates.

Brothel owners initially seemed to rely upon direct contacts with prospects in their recruiting. Madames would literally sit on their front steps and talk with likely inmates who happened to walk by. As the demand for fresh faces increased, however, madames began changing their methods. Privately run employment offices, known as intelligence agencies, became an important source of new women. Madames placed advertisements in these offices announcing "openings" in their businesses. Women who answered these announcements often agreed to join a brothel's staff, and in these cases the intelligence agency collected a fee for locating employees for the madames. In the 1870s and 1880s, continued demand for women may have prompted more elaborate organized recruiting efforts. Procurers seem to have emerged who, in some rare instances, secured new inmates by bringing them in from outside the city.

Business problems, such as recruiting, and the immense profits to be made in prostitution, eventually attracted the attention of men who had considerable organizational talent. During the 1890s and thereafter vice rings developed to control and exploit the business of prostitution. These rings had powerful political connections which helped insulate them from police interference. James Colosimo was the leader of one such ring in Chicago. He began his career as a sanitation worker in the 1890s. Colosimo first displayed his organizational abilities by molding his fellow workers into an effective voting bloc which supported Chicago's first ward aldermen, "Bathhouse" John Coughlin and Michael "Hinky Dink" Kenna. The first ward contained an area called the Levee, one of Chicago's largest concentrations of saloons, gambling houses, and brothels. Shortly after becoming a trusted precinct captain for his aldermen friends, Colosimo became involved in prostitution. He married Victoria Moresco, a Levee brothel owner, and began to organize his own vice ring. By 1903 he and his associates had emerged as important procurers in the intercity recruitment of prostitutes. Already a wealthy man, Colosimo next opened a restaurant which quickly became one of the most famous Levee gathering places for important people in politics and entertainment. Until his murder in 1920, Colosimo combined vice and politics to create a highly successful career as one of Chicago's foremost underworld figures. He typified the ways in which other individuals managed to build lucrative careers in prostitution at the turn of the century.

A trend toward more complex organization also characterized the history of gambling at the time. Until the 1840s professional gamblers were flamboyant individualists who plied their trade on steamboats, at county fairs, and in the back rooms of saloons. They moved about a great deal, living from day to day on their skill in games such as three card monte (a card version of the shell game) and poker. Between 1840 and 1880, gambling was transformed into an important urban business by two developments: the shift to faro as the basic game in gambling houses, and the emergence of horse racing as a major form of entertainment. Intrigued by the possibilities for profit in these two developments, many gamblers abandoned their former life-styles to become prominent citizens with strong ties to their local communities.

Faro became the single most popular card game in America during the middle decades of the nineteenth century. Its popularity derived from the belief that it offered the bettor the fairest odds among all such games. The equipment for faro included a cloth with a card deck embossed upon it, chips for betting, and a metal box from which a single card was dealt per turn. Bettors placed their chips on the embossed cards. The dealer drew the top card from his box and paid anyone who had bet on it; then he drew the next card and collected from anyone who had placed chips on it. This completed the cycle and everyone was free to reconsider his wager. Gamblers quickly devised various ways to manipulate the deck within the dealing box. Small, needle-thin metal picks built into these boxes, for example, could be activated by hand pressure to push out the card beneath the top one (the gambler had previously memorized the order of the cards so that he knew what was coming up next). Someone who had placed a large bet on a card (and bets sometimes amounted to thousands of dollars) inevitably lost by this trick. Thus, in spite of its reputation for fairness, faro quickly became one of the surest ways to cheat at cards.

Attracted by the prospect of high profits from a steady flow of customers, gamblers began opening faro houses in the downtown entertainment areas. Their "dens" ranged in elegance from dingy rooms on the second floor above a saloon to palatial houses which offered their customers wine, hard liquor, and a sumptuous buffet. The more important gamblers employed rather large staffs of dealers, doorkeepers, waiters, and even chefs. They also developed partnerships, both with fellow gamblers and with ordinary businessmen, to operate these establishments. The partnerships helped ensure against ruinous losses by spreading the responsibility for paying off lucky customers, and they also enabled gamblers to create cash pools which supported a large amount of betting on a continuous basis. Some partners gradually expanded their operations from a single faro house to several. As in any other business, the partners split the profits on the basis of each gambler's contribution to the corporate fund.

Long considered one of the most reputable forms of entertainment, horse racing was also transformed at mid-century by the demand among city dwellers for exciting diversions. Some imaginative sportsmen introduced sprints, a race format which quickly became standard throughout the country because more horses could now run in more events in a shorter span of time than ever before. Backed by some of the nation's most prominent citizens, and encouraged by the support of city residents, racing entered into an era of expansion and prosperity. In order to accommodate the growing interest in racing, major sports figures and their friends built several new tracks: Saratoga (1864), Jerome Park (1866), Monmouth Park (1870), Pimlico (1870), the New Orleans Fairgrounds (1873), and Churchill Downs (1875).

Gamblers quickly became crucial to the betting public's enjoyment of racing. Pool selling was the prevailing method of wagering at the time. In this system each horse in a race was "auctioned" to a crowd of bettors, and the money thus collected was held by the auctioneer (pool seller) until the race had been run. Once the results had been announced, the pool seller paid off the winner and retained a small (5 percent) commission for himself. Since many thousands of bettors did not have the time to attend races personally, gamblers opened poolrooms in the downtowns of every city to accommodate these customers. Poolrooms received the results of each race by telegraph. Bettors simply had to drop into a poolroom for a few minutes before a race, place their wager, and await the nearly instantaneous outcome. When New York's legislature outlawed pool selling in 1877, gamblers, with the full support of track officials, introduced bookmaking as a substitute. Poolrooms continued to sell pools and make book for the remainder of the century, in spite of the fulminations of outraged moralists.

Faro houses and poolrooms were extremely profitable, highly visible, and definitely illegal. This fact complicated the gambler's life. In order to protect his investments and continue his operations, he had to develop ways to forestall interference in his affairs by either the police or crusading moralists. The structure of urban politics enabled some gamblers to acquire a large measure of immunity for their activities because the ward system required the election of aldermen who represented the interests of every neighborhood in a city, and the downtowns were one such area. Gamblers had certain resources which they could turn to political uses in these downtown wards. Their employees constituted a sizable body of men who could be relied upon to vote for the candidate favored by their bosses. Furthermore, gamblers controlled large amounts of money, a commodity in demand to finance party operations during elections. Gamblers used these resources either to help local politicians or to run for, and hold, political office themselves. Whichever approach they used, gamblers thus acquired the influence they needed to protect and perpetuate their business activities.

John Morrissey's career illustrates the close ties which evolved between legitimate society and gamblers during the nineteenth century. While a young man living in upstate New York, Morrissey developed a reputation as a tough street fighter. Moving to New York City in 1849, he quickly established himself as an important sports figure and politician. Morrissey won the United States prize-fighting championship from Yankee Sullivan in 1853; by that date he was also a valued member of Tammany Hall who commanded many of the "shoulder-hitters" (street toughs organized to intimidate political opponents during elections). His prestige as a fighter made him an idol among New York's Irish, giving him an independent power base which he later used to good advantage. In 1859 Morrissey formed a partnership with a local gambler to open his first faro house. Eventually, the partners operated sixteen gambling dens, and Morrissey began casting about for new investments. He established an elegant faro house at Saratoga, New York, and began cultivating friendships with prominent men who vacationed at this fashionable resort. With the help of his new friends, Morrissey built Saratoga racetrack in 1864; shortly thereafter his gambler friends opened the first poolrooms in New York City to receive race results from Saratoga. Morrissey's prestige, popularity among his own countrymen, political power, and social connections now enabled him to run for political office. He served two terms in Congress (1866-70) and one in the New York State Senate (1874-76). While pursuing a career in public office, Morrissey continued to be an influential figure in gambling. He helped introduce pari-mutuel betting and bookmaking to the public, participated in the first attempt to create a national gambling syndicate (which failed), and maintained his investments in faro. By the time of his death in 1877, Morrissey had demonstrated how gambling had become closely intertwined with the worlds of sports, politics, and high society.

Street crime, theft, and illegal enterprise challenged the capacities of the police, in spite of their enhanced numbers and new preventive approach to law enforcement. Underlying socioeconomic developments such as urbanization made crime a persistent problem by introducing continuous dislocations and changes which expanded the opportunities for criminal activities. The history of gambling offered a classic example of the ways criminals seized upon change to restructure their behavior in order to increase their profits. Their close ties to politicians and prominent sportsmen would of course become particularly important in the later history of law enforcement. The police had no control over these developments, but some people expected them to deal effectively with criminals nonetheless. Quick to find fault with the police, and slow to understand the nature of crime, they soon proposed additional changes which would, presumably, improve police efficiency.

## SUGGESTED READINGS

The study of crime during the nineteenth century has not yet received much attention. Our knowledge of the American underworld is still largely limited to the delightful but journalistic studies by Herbert Asbury. Among Asbury's best books are: *The French Quarter: An Informal History of the New Orleans Underworld* (New York: Alfred A. Knopf, Inc., 1936) and *Sucker's Progress: An Informal History of Gambling in America from the Colonies to Canfield* (New York: Dodd, Mead & Co., 1938). These works should be supplemented by David R. Johnson, *Policing the Urban Underworld: The Impact of Crime on the Development of the Police in America, 1800-1887* (Philadelphia: Temple University Press, 1978), and Roger Lane, "Crime and Criminal Statistics in Nineteenth Century Massachusetts," *Journal of Social History*, II (1968), 157-163. For comparative purposes, students should refer to J. J. Tobias, *Urban Crime in Victorian England* (New York: Schocken Books, 1972), Kellow Chesney, *The Victorian Underworld* (New York: Schocken Books, 1972), and Howard Zehr, "The Modernization of Crime in Germany and France, 1830-1913," *Journal of Social History*, VIII (1975), 117-41. For an important study of the decline in violent behavior, see Roger Lane, *Violent Death in the City: Suicide, Accident, and Murder in Nineteenth-Century Philadelphia* (Cambridge: Harvard University Press, 1979).

# 4

# Entrepreneurs, Reformers & the Emergence of Professionalism: 1870-1920

**T**he police departments which had emerged by the 1870s accurately reflected the strengths and weaknesses of nineteenth century America's approach to local law enforcement. In keeping with the widespread belief that power should not be concentrated in too few hands, large numbers of politicians had a direct role in controlling the police. Individual neighborhoods, represented by those politicians, influenced arrest policies. Patrolmen, recruited from those neighborhoods, shared much of the outlook of the people they policed. Various problems balanced these strengths. Uniform enforcement policies did not exist. The lack of training, especially in the law and legal procedures, meant that policemen had only the vaguest notions about collecting evidence or safeguarding a citizen's rights. An officer's personal discretion dictated when or if to arrest someone. In these circumstances, the effectiveness and behavior of the police varied considerably, not only from one city to another, but also within a particular city. Law enforcement was thoroughly decentralized, thoroughly democratic, and thoroughly chaotic.

Some people welcomed this situation; others did not. The first group, which might be described as the urban entrepreneurs, included men who benefited from the character of American law enforcement. Politicians, crooks, and corrupt policemen were prominent among this group. Those who despaired over the way the police had evolved were, not surprisingly, the critics. Indignant moralists alarmed about vice, wealthy Americans appalled by lower-class influence over policing, social scientists concerned about the problem of crime, and honest cops angry at political interference in their work struggled to change the police.

Between 1870 and 1920 the entrepreneurs and the critics fought for control of law enforcement. At the beginning of this era the entrepreneurs had a clear advantage. But social and economic changes, combined with a growing intolerance for vice and crime in general, would eventually threaten their dominance and give the critics their chance to seize control. By the end of this era, the reformers had won some major victories and were on the verge of decisively altering the nature of policing. These fifty years were therefore crucial to the emergence of the modern police department.

Whipping-post stocks in city jail, ca. 1890. *Courtesy of St. Louis Police Library.*

## Urban Entrepreneurs and Policing

The development of preventive policing coincided with the emergence of a new political system which was destined to govern most of the nation's large cities well into the twentieth century. By the 1840s, rapid urbanization had begun to undermine local government's ability to deliver vital services. At the same time, the need and demand for adequate services were expanding faster than the government's ability to respond. Garbage collection, street paving, and fire protection were just some of the requirements for an orderly urban environment, but by mid-century no city could claim to be providing them in an efficient way.

Recent immigrants to the cities, including both foreign and native-born citizens, had the greatest need for help from local government. Living in the central wards of every city, these people had the most problems and the fewest resources for coping with their new environment. Middle- and upper-class property owners had the social and political influence which ensured that their needs would receive due consideration. But the lower classes' huge numbers and pressing problems attracted the attention of ambitious politicians too. These people would be an important source of power if properly organized and led.

Since republican ideology and the ward system effectively decentralized urban politics, the solution to the problems of governing cities had to evolve from within the neighborhoods. The diffused nature of political power, lower-class needs, and local politicians' ambitions combined in the boss system. Beginning in the 1840s, individuals appeared in many inner-city wards who gradually accumulated political power. They started their careers by joining important neighborhood institutions like volunteer fire companies and gangs. After being elected leaders of such organizations, these men pledged their followers' votes to local politicians. Once they had demonstrated that they could deliver votes, their power increased considerably. They became respected politicians whose organizations enabled parties to gain or remain in office. Party leaders rewarded these local bosses with patronage jobs, contracts for urban services, and opportunities to make money for themselves and their friends. The boss system thus benefited political organizations, individual politicians, and their lower-class supporters in the neighborhoods.

The police were absolutely critical to any boss' ability to perpetuate his political power. In the nineteenth century elections were often turbulent affairs in which parties used every conceivable trick to defeat their opponents. Many of these tactics were illegal, but politicians used them as a matter of course in their determination to win. Since the police had the responsibility for maintaining order and upholding the law at polling booths, bosses and their allies had to control the patrolmen who guarded the polls. Officers had to know whose tactics to ignore or suppress, whose rowdies to support or arrest. Without the friendly aid of the police, victory at the polls was well-nigh impossible.

Bosses had several ways to ensure that policemen heeded their wishes during elections. First, they controlled appointments to the police force. At a time when civil service was nonexistent, everyone in city government owed his job to some politician. Patronage was one of the most important sources of a boss' power because it enabled him to reward his supporters in concrete ways. And a position as a policeman happened to be one of the era's most desirable jobs. Walking a beat required no special skills, a fact which appealed to lower-class urbanites who could not obtain well-paid jobs in industry. Patrolmen also earned fairly high wages and they had steady employment, two things which other workers did not always enjoy. Applicants therefore besieged bosses with their pleas for appointment, giving those politicians the ability to insist on loyalty to their organizations as a prerequisite to joining police departments.

The command structure of the departments also contributed to political control of the police. A commission consisting of important politicians (or their supporters) ran practically every large city police force in the late nineteenth century. These commissioners consulted the ward bosses about nearly all departmental matters. The chief of police was usually a mere figurehead who had no real power unless he was an important politician himself. In that case his political influence gave him some leverage in running affairs. Furthermore, precinct and ward boundaries usually coincided. This arrangement meant that local commanders owed their positions to the ward boss and answered to him for their behavior. As long as they enjoyed his support, commanders had practically a free hand in the daily operations of their precincts. Even desk sergeants played key roles in the politicized command structure. They often had the authority to dismiss someone from custody and used this power to correct such mistakes as the arrest of a boss' supporters by an overzealous patrolman. These arrangements made it possible for politicians to issue instructions to the police regarding law enforcement at the polls. Any officer who ignored these orders did so at his peril.

Finally, bosses did not necessarily have to rely upon either their patronage power or their control of the command structure to ensure compliance with their wishes. Most police officers were genuinely enthusiastic partisans at elections. Of course their jobs depended upon the outcome, and that was certainly a paramount consideration in their behavior. But elections were not simply a matter of which party won. Elections also determined important social issues such as whose moral code, which ethnic groups, and whose religion would temporarily prevail. Irish and German Catholic patrolmen, for example, faced the prospect of a defeat for their culture—including their preferred drinking habits—religion, and class as well as losing their jobs. Policemen therefore could lend their wholehearted support to electioneering tactics which, however illegal, promised a victory for their way of life.

Politicians were not the only group who used a decentralized police to further their careers. Other entrepreneurs also regarded America's approach to local law enforcement as an important asset in their struggle for power and wealth. Their success varied according to the particular circumstances, but they all drew inspiration from the widespread attitude that a person should make the most of what he had or could get. This exploitive, self-serving approach to life was not confined to any particular class or activity. It seems to have been a consequence of the expansive, opportunistic character of American society at the time.

Within this general context, entrepreneurs could rely upon at least three other considerations which worked to their advantage. Guardians of the public's virtue insisted that certain behavior had to be eliminated. They focused their attention on drinking, whoring, and gambling. Laws enacted to suppress those activities were especially useful to corrupt entrepreneurs because they provided a legal framework for extorting money from people who offered those amusements to the public. Secondly, saloonkeepers, prostitutes, and gamblers regarded bribery as a normal business expense. It was far easier, and perhaps less costly in the long run, to pay for protection rather than campaign against tiresome but persistent moral crusaders. Finally, the average policeman was rather tolerant about these vices. Most officers regarded them as inevitable, and more to the point, they frequently participated in them. Brothel madames paid for favors such as quelling a rowdy guest by offering a patrolman one of her girls. Policemen patronized neighborhood poolrooms to place small bets and consumed many free drinks in saloons. Thus many officers engaged in what amounted to petty corruption themselves, probably in the conviction that their behavior was neither extraordinary nor harmful. In these circumstances, they would acquiesce in any arrangements which their superiors made to protect vice.

These conditions transformed command positions in police departments from offices of public trust to opportunities for personal profit. Men who sought these posts too frequently did so as entrepreneurs rather than as public servants. They earned appointments as police chiefs, captains, lieutenants, and sergeants by working hard for important politicians and, in some cases, by buying these offices outright. In some cities, such as New York, both political service and hard cash were required, but this was not always the case.

Although corruption was characteristic of all departments, the actual details for acquiring wealth varied. New York may have had the most systematic arrangements. By the late nineteenth century politicians had established a standard fee for every appointment, from patrolman to captain. An applicant for the lowly job of walking a beat had to pay $300, aspiring captains $15,000. These fees provided an additional incentive, if any was needed, for profiteering. New York's precinct captains occupied the best positions to exploit their offices. Each captain was, for all practical purposes, the master of his domain. He selected one of his detectives to be his personal bagman. Once a month this officer made the rounds of every saloon, gambling house, and brothel in the precinct to collect their tribute. Each business paid a fee which varied according to its size and receipts. At the turn of the century the police assessed poolrooms between $100 and $300 a month; whorehouses between $50 and $150; and gambling houses $50 to $300 a month. The city's saloons contributed an estimated $50,000 to $60,000 a month to the police and politicians. Most of this money went to the commanders and their political sponsors. Bagmen kept perhaps 20 percent of each month's collection and turned the remainder over to their superiors.

Captains grew rich in this system. The career of Alexander S. Williams, one of New York's most notorious police entrepreneurs, illustrated the possibilities. Williams joined the department as a patrolman in 1866. His connections with important Republican politicians enabled him to secure a captaincy in 1872. During the next several years Williams earned a noisome reputation for brutality and well-deserved nickname, "Clubber." By 1887 he had had 358 formal complaints filed against him and had been fined 244 times. Yet he remained on the force. In 1884 Williams moved, as he put it, from "salt chuck" to "tenderloin" when he became precinct commander of New York's fashionable red-light district. Diligent attention to graft collections quickly made him a wealthy man. An investigation of the department in 1894 revealed that Williams owned a house in one of the city's best neighborhoods, an estate in Connecticut, and a steam yacht. These disclosures led to his resignation within a year, but he had accumulated sufficient funds in police work to live in comfortable disgrace.

Until World War I, corruption was not as systematic in Chicago, where the boss system was less well developed, as it was in New York. Entrepreneurs who hoped to enrich themselves had to develop political bases of their own, or establish close ties with the few available ward bosses. Although these requirements placed formidable obstacles in the path of rapacious individuals, some managed to overcome them. Jacob Rehm is one example. Rehm demonstrated his political clout as early as 1858 by campaigning successfully for election as city marshal.

Thereafter he held a series of important political posts, including deputy superintendent and police commissioner. His big break finally came in 1872 when the temperance issue sundered local politics. Rehm helped organize the People's Party, whose candidates campaigned for a wide-open town. When his party won, Rehm received a suitable reward with his appointment as police superintendent. Not a man to mince words, Rehm announced that he had accepted his new position in order to make money. For the next three years he did just that. Gamblers and prostitutes paid for protection on a regular basis, and Rehm became an important figure in the Whiskey Ring (a national conspiracy to defraud the federal government of tax revenues). When finally exposed in 1875, Rehm resigned with his fortune made.

Precinct commanders and police superintendents did not monopolize the opportunities for graft. Detectives also displayed a fine entrepreneurial talent, though in different ways. Throughout the nineteenth century detectives were primarily engaged in the recovery of stolen property. Their incentive to perform well derived from the special role they played in the recovery process. Essentially, detectives acted as negotiators between thieves and their victims. This situation gave them an ideal chance to make money. Victims paid rewards for the return of their goods; criminals paid bribes to avoid arrest. A calculating detective decided what to do in a particular case on the basis of who offered him more. There were other ways to earn a tidy income as well. Relations between detectives and thieves had frequently evolved to the point where they simply split the proceeds of crime on a regular basis. Pickpockets, for example, worked particular streetcar lines consistently. Detectives exacted a standard percentage of each mob's earnings every week for the privilege of working unmolested. Victims who complained too loudly had their property promptly returned because neither the detectives nor the thieves wanted any disruptions in their business arrangements. Other detectives developed close ties with confidence men, exchanging protection from arrest for part of each con game's take. Criminals thus worked hand in hand with detectives to bilk the public at every opportunity.

Systematic corruption devastated the reputation of the police, but its effect on their actual performance is less clear. Entrepreneurs confined their attention to those areas where there was money to be made. Not every precinct offered lucrative opportunities for graft, and protecting vice and helping at elections hardly exhausted the wide range of activities in which the police engaged. A large amount of policing was utterly mundane, occasionally dangerous, and only incidentally remunerative. In their day to day patrol work, many policemen seem to have attempted to carry out their duties conscientiously. The problem in assessing their success is that we need to remember the context in which patrolmen worked. In general, they accepted political obligations and vice protection as normal in policing. By recruiting officers from the neighborhoods, every department ensured that it contained a variety of attitudes toward law enforcement. This policy created pluralistic standards defining what was or was not acceptable behavior. Finally, the ignorance of law and the emphasis on individual discretion gave each patrolman enormous freedom to devise his own version of law enforcement. Thus policing seemed chaotic because its underlying unity emphasized a tolerant attitude toward behavioral and moral variety.

Severe limits on a superior officer's ability to supervise his patrolmen enhanced the apparently chaotic nature of policing. Once a man left the station house, he was his own boss. The single most important characteristic of a policeman on his beat was not that he might be corrupt, but that he was alone. Communications systems which enabled a precinct commander to contact his men did not exist until late in the century. When call boxes became available, department supervisors installed them slowly. Chicago was the first large city to have such a system, beginning in 1880. Other cities did not make extensive use of call boxes until the 1890s. A lack of control over patrolmen was implicit in the absence of contact. Station house personnel did not know what was happening on the streets until the beat officers told them. Victims of crime, or persons needing assistance, did not go to the precinct houses (unless they lived close by); normally, they sought out the patrolman. The decision to intervene in a problem rested almost entirely with that officer.

Department officials did have one important way to exert some influence over the daily activities of their men. They defined a good patrolman in terms of the number of arrests he made. An emphasis on statistics to measure performance may have been inevitable in a situation where officials could not control a policeman's behavior. But this reliance upon numbers also helped support the pluralistic style of law enforcement. Officials did not have to inquire into *how* a patrolman maintained order or prevented crime on his beat in order to assess his performance. The use of statistics was also useful in demonstrating to the public that the police were doing their jobs. Chicago Police Commissioner Mark Sheridan put this point precisely in 1873 when he said: "The police are efficient; they made 28,000 arrests last year." Statistics therefore justified the taxpayers' support of their local departments and gave officials an easy standard for gauging a patrolman's effectiveness without jeopardizing their pluralistic approach to policing.

Policemen found it relatively easy to demonstrate their productivity. They constantly encountered drunks while making their rounds, and often arrested them. Drunkenness in fact constituted at least half of the total arrests for any year in practically every department. A wide variety of misdemeanors accounted for the bulk of the other offenses in the annual reports. Felonies usually formed a small category, typically representing only 10 to 15 percent of all arrests. Considering the wide variance in standards of social behavior, and the minimal controls over the conduct of officers, it is somewhat surprising that they arrested as many people as they did. Patrolmen did settle many disputes and problems without hauling someone off to the station house. They often intervened in brawls, quieted family quarrels, escorted drunks home, and admonished careless drivers without making an arrest. In these cases they might be said to be maintaining order at

A nineteenth century traffic jam. One of the perennial, mundane problems of policing. *Courtesy Library of Congress.*

the expense of strict law enforcement. But the large number of misde-
meanor arrests also indicates that officers enforced the letter of the law
when, in their judgment, that became necessary. Although the historical
record is mixed, it would seem that many policemen acted more re-
sponsibly than their critics claimed, often combining common sense
with official powers to suit particular circumstances.


## Reformers and Policing

The decentralized, neighborhood-oriented model of policing seemed
to enjoy undisputed dominance in the late nineteenth century. But
important changes caused by urbanization and industrialization began
to challenge that model. Traditional ideas about political power, the
nature of local government, and the functions of the police encountered
severe criticism because the old ways of doing things in cities appeared
to be increasingly inadequate. As the criticism grew more widespread,
disparate groups with conflicting ideas began to coalesce in spite of
their differences. Their discontent with the dominant model of policing
provided a basis for cooperation, and the evolving urban-industrial
social order offered new ideas and sources of support for implementing
a different approach to law enforcement.

Urbanization helped undermine the standard model of policing by
overwhelming its principal advocates, city politicians. As long as they
managed to deal with the consequences of urban growth, their power
remained basically intact. Events threatened their dominance very
rapidly, however. By the 1890s the population and land areas of many
cities had grown so vast that local politicians seemed unable to govern.
The political system had not been designed to cope with the extraordinary demands placed upon it by urban expansion. State laws restricted the funding capacities of local governments, forcing them to
borrow to pay for services which were inadequate before they were
completed. Decentralized power within the cities encouraged duplication of effort, waste, and, of course, outright corruption. In these
circumstances housing shortages, crime, disease, and population con-
gestion appeared to be intensifying rather than diminishing. Law enforcement, which was only one aspect of a far broader set of problems,
would inevitably be affected by the wider debate over urban problems.

Alarmed by the apparently chaotic growth of cities, many Americans
sought to determine its causes and offer solutions. No one suggested
that growth was in itself bad, since urban expansion was widely regarded as a "good thing." By ignoring the fundamental reason for the
origins of the cities' problems, critics could focus their attention on
more superficial explanations. Given the middle- and upper-class backgrounds of these critics, it is hardly surprising that they pinpointed

the boss system as a major cause for the disturbing lack of effective government. These politicians, according to these critics, sought power and profit for themselves and their followers at the expense of the public's welfare.

Various solutions to the problems of urban expansion suggested themselves once the source of the trouble had been located. Since bosses and their immigrant supporters were responsible for the current mess, it followed that their power should be broken. Men who had the public's welfare at heart should hold key offices and implement policies which would benefit everyone, not just some city residents. In practice this meant that the social and cultural values of the middle and upper classes ought to dominate urban government. Those values stressed uniform standards of conduct, honesty in elected officials, and a reliance on rules rather than customs in regulating public affairs. A tolerance for varying standards of morality and behavior would thus disappear when and if these critics assumed power.

Outraged moral crusaders and citizens might temporarily defeat a particular boss, but as long as the political system remained unchanged they would not retain power very long. Many critics of urban government therefore sought ways to change the system in order to reduce political participation by "undesirable" elements. This goal drew upon the lessons of industrialization for ideas and support. Good management and disciplined workers were vital to America's economic success in the late nineteenth century. The many men who participated in creating prosperity, or who benefited from it, naturally assumed that their methods had wider application. If factory workers could be prodded into habits of punctuality and sobriety, if waste and inefficiency could be eliminated by the use of expert knowledge, and if men could be entrusted with sufficient power to manage huge enterprises profitably, perhaps other problems could be solved with the same techniques.

Many urban residents eagerly embraced the lessons they saw in a successful industrial revolution. They sought to alter the structure of local government to achieve the same rationality, centralization, and uniformity which were the hallmarks of a well-run business. This approach to the problems of urbanization required change in the distribution of power. Although most Americans remained suspicious of concentrated authority, the boss system weakened traditional fears about too much power resting on one person's hands. That system, it was argued, could only be defeated by giving power to a few responsible officials who would act in the public's best interest. In order to ensure that politicians did not respond only to special interests (i.e., ward leaders, lower-class immigrants, and criminals), they would run for office in city-wide elections—an arrangement which increased the voting power of the middle and upper classes considerably.

In sum, the traditional attitudes toward political power and the structure of local government underwent important alterations in the late nineteenth century. Discontent with various urban problems climaxed in the Progressive Movement (1896-1917) which achieved many fundamental changes in American society. The progressives drew the various criticisms of city life into a program which emphasized three basic ideas: honesty and efficiency in government; increased authority for public officials; and the use of experts to deal with specific problems. Police reformers, who were only a small part of the general effort to grapple with urban life, used these basic ideas for many of their own programs.

In the years before progressivism coalesced into a major social movement, people concentrated their energies on three approaches to reform. Moral crusaders were perhaps the loudest and most persistent group of police critics. They drew their support from substantial numbers of native-born, white, Anglo-Saxon Protestants who shared their disgust over urban vice conditions. Drinking, gambling, and whoring, in their opinion, threatened America's moral fabric, undermined local politics, and destroyed the integrity of law enforcement. Obviously, such behavior could not be tolerated. But these reformers could not eradicate vice because they did not control the police. Their efforts to acquire that control provided some lively moments in many cities, however.

The Reverend Charles Parkhurst's campaign to cleanse the New York police illustrates the methods and frustrations of the moral crusaders. Parkhurst had impeccable credentials to lead a crusade. He was the president of the Society for the Prevention of Crime and the minister of the Madison Square Presbyterian Church. Early in 1892, Parkhurst launched a vigorous attack on police corruption and vice in New York City. After two years of demands for change, this crusade finally culminated in the most famous investigation of the police in the nineteenth century when the state legislature created the Lexow Commission to inquire into police affairs. Throughout 1894, investigators exposed police interference in the electoral process, payoffs for appointments and promotions, and connivance with criminals. But in the course of the commission's work Parkhurst and his followers lost control over the inquiry. Republican politicians used the commission for their own purposes. Dismissing the reformers' demands, the Republicans ensured themselves a role in police patronage and election fraud by passing a law which established a bipartisan Board of Police Commissioners to run the department. Parkhurst's attempt to change law enforcement policies and eliminate vice came to nothing. This inability to control the outcome of investigations typified the dilemma of moral reform prior to the progressive era.

Similar frustrations plagued another group of critics who wanted to improve the quality and effectiveness of the police. These people advocated civil service commissions to eliminate political influence in appointments, higher standards of literacy and health for new recruits, and educational programs to teach patrolmen their duties. Parenthetically, but not accidentally, the adoption of these ideas would help exclude many foreign immigrants and lower-class Americans from the departments. Like the moral crusaders, this group of critics came from the ranks of respectable society. Their experiences with industrialization made them intolerant of the dominant political system and with the decentralized model of policing. Scientific management and expert knowledge would, according to these people, solve a wide range of social problems. They were appalled not only by the lack of uniform law enforcement standards, but also by inferior quality officers, police inefficiency, and the lack of discipline.

In order to disseminate their ideas, these police critics sometimes joined other reformers to form organizations which would campaign for change. The National Prison Association, founded in 1870, was one important example of this tactic. Its Standing Committee on the Police endorsed the goals of a nonpartisan police, civil service, and training programs for officers. Progress, however, came slowly. New York adopted civil service in 1883, as did Chicago in 1895, but politicians in both cities made sure that they controlled the commissioners who supervised these new bureaucracies. Political influence therefore continued to be crucial in appointments. Reformers had better luck in Cincinnati when the state legislature created a new, nonpartisan, Board of Police Commissioners in 1886. The new commissioners initiated an ambitious program of military drill and discipline, regular physical examinations, and seventy-two hours of classroom instruction in reading, writing, spelling, and the intricacies of the police manual. No other department at the time implemented so many reform ideas, and Cincinnati's example was not duplicated elsewhere for many years.

A small number of policemen, especially commanding officers, constituted the last group of critics seeking change. These men viewed the problems of law enforcement from a different perspective than their fellow critics. Vice, for example, was inevitable in their opinion. As long as gamblers, prostitutes, and drunks did not disturb individuals or neighborhoods, these officers tolerated their behavior. Nor were they particularly troubled about such matters as the social, religious, or cultural backgrounds of patrolmen. They apparently did not share the view of moralists and others that only literate, white Anglo-Saxon Protestants made good officers. But they did have grievances. In particular they resented the way politicians interfered in the daily affairs of their departments and they deplored the lack of effective police work against criminals. They proposed to solve these problems by increasing the crime-fighting abilities of their departments.

Police chiefs of course had very little leverage for achieving reforms because they were political appointees. Any policies or behavior they adopted which threatened the status quo would result in their dismissal. Under these circumstances, police officials confined themselves to activities which could not be viewed unfavorably. They sought to create, rather tentatively, a basis for intercity cooperation by exchanging some information about criminals and their depredations. During the 1890s, police administrators encouraged the use of the Bertillion system of criminal identification. This system was cumbersome, involving a number of physical measurements of a criminal, but at least it was a step toward maintaining more accurate records. Serious efforts to improve police work became more systematic in 1893 when a large number of chiefs founded the National Police Chiefs' Union. This organization, which evolved into the International Association of Chiefs of Police (IACP) by 1901, was the most important forum for reform-minded policemen at the time. Its increasingly wide-ranging convention programs indicated that policemen would not be content to let others dictate the nature of changes in policing. This development would have important consequences as reform coalesced into a powerful national movement.

Progressivism helped transform the disparate strands of police reform into a more coherent movement. This does not mean, however, that major improvements in policing swept the nation in the years prior to World War I. Important changes did occur, but not on a scale which reformers desired or politicians feared. Rather, progressivism seriously weakened the national dominance of the decentralized model for policing by introducing changes in the structure of politics and by organizing the various ideas about police reform into a fairly consistent intellectual position. The latter achievement was perhaps the more important in the long run. By weaving together various proposals the progressives eventually handed the police a valuable tool for asserting control over their own affairs after 1920.

Structural changes in local politics which affected law enforcement occurred in an erratic pattern across the nation. By 1915, for example, 204 police departments, including most of those in the largest cities, had been placed under civil service. This reform was a kind of halfway step in the process of separating politicians and policemen. In many cases, politicians found ways to get around the superficially imposing regulations regarding appointments. But the reformers insisted upon creating elaborate procedures within the civil service which probably diluted a politician's ability to discipline an officer. Perhaps the most important consequence of this reform was that police applicants might have to be politically active to secure an appointment, but they did not necessarily have to continue their activity once on the force. Their job security now depended upon other measures of their performance besides party loyalty, a change which patrolmen appreciated and supported. Another change which had similar results involved the shift to more powerful chiefs of police. After 1901 the commission form of departmental governance fell rapidly out of favor. By World War I some 75 percent of the largest police departments were commanded by a single administrator who had considerably expanded control over the daily affairs of his organization. The chief was no longer a mere figurehead, but he was also not very secure in his power because he served at the pleasure of the mayor. Political interference in policing therefore persisted in altered form while the police chiefs gained greater prestige and a freer hand in departmental administration.

While some police reformers struggled to achieve long-standing goals, others began to develop an entirely new approach to policing. This more venturesome group sought to make policing a profession. Although these people did not at the time have the same definition of professionalism which prevails today, they did grasp its essentials. They understood that a profession is devoted to the pursuit of a particular goal; that its hallmarks are expertise and training; and that its members presume to an exclusive ability to deal with a special set of problems. All of these characteristics had become familiar to the progressives through existing models such as medicine and academia. Reformers had extended the range of professions themselves in various urban reforms which had required the development of experts like city planners and managers.

Late nineteenth century police critics who had advocated training for the police and the removal of politics from departmental affairs obviously contributed to this trend to create a professional police. But something new was added after 1900: a redefinition of the primary police mission. During the nineteenth century the police had performed a wide range of loosely related duties. They had acted as boiler inspectors, street cleaners, and charity workers to mention just a few of their many responsibilities. Miscellaneous assignments such as these detracted from the effectiveness as well as the image of the police as an agency designed to deal with crime. Now, some progressives, joined by police chiefs eager to enhance their departments' prestige, began to insist that crime fighting was the sole function of the police. The fact that this assertion was not true did not matter. By narrowly defining the central goal of policing, it became possible to identify this occupation with the powerful and prestigious ideology of professionalism. It gave the police a new sense of mission. And it justified a wide range of proposals which by themselves might not otherwise have survived.

August Vollmer was the leading proponent of policing as a profession. He began his career, modestly enough, as marshal of Berkeley, California, in 1905. As a small town housing a major university, Berkeley had none of the political characteristics which would have hamstrung a typical reformer. It was a homogeneous community in which the principal police officer did not have to deal with complex law enforcement questions and in which he had the authority to implement ideas virtually without hindrance. Vollmer's fortunate circumstances gave him free rein for his innovative ideas. A vocal exponent of the claim that the police were primarily crime fighters, Vollmer set out to train his small department as rigorously as possible in the most modern methods he could find. As a first step, he opened the Berkeley Police School in 1908. The curriculum included criminal evidence law, first aid, and, a harbinger of Vollmer's fascination with technology, photography as an aid to crime detection. Eight years later, in 1916, Vollmer joined with some university faculty members to create a permanent three year training program in which scientific methods of criminal investigation played a central role. In 1917 Vollmer became the first president of the Board of Managers for California's new Bureau of Criminal Identification and Investigation. Knowledge, technique, and bureaucratic centralization were fast becoming the hallmarks of Vollmer's drive for police professionalization.

As his fame spread, Vollmer became a national spokesman for the creation of professional police departments. He was not the only advocate of this idea, however. The IACP, beginning with Richard Sylvester's long term as president from 1901 to 1915, emerged as a major forum for propagating the new faith. Its program included recommendations to centralize authority within departments, to rationalize the administrative structure, and to improve the quality of police personnel. Prodded by Vollmer's example and the IACP's program, police departments across the country began to implement changes. Police academies appeared, although in too many cases the curriculum and standards were a farce. Literacy, health, and intelligence requirements began to inch upward until they were markedly higher in the 1920s than they had been in the 1890s (although there were wide variations in the general quality of recruits).

Expertise usually leads to compartmentalization, and the early efforts to professionalize the police were not an exception. Reformers advocated special squads to handle particular problems, and they were more successful than they perhaps expected. Political opposition to such squads was minimal, and the police liked them because they had prestige. Under these circumstances, special squads proliferated for vice, alcohol, narcotics, robbery, homicide, auto theft, and other offenses. Whatever their practical effect, these squads were an important part of the image which the police were trying to cultivate as professionals who understood how to fight crime.

Reformers did not achieve all their goals in the progressive era. The attachment to decentralized, democratic urban government proved too strong in the long run, a fact which hindered many reform ideas which depended upon greater political centralization for their success. And where change did occur, politicians learned to adapt. Police chiefs might become more powerful, but they still answered to the mayor. Police academies might introduce recruits to some training, but the exams could be rigged. By 1920, then, much remained to be done. Piecemeal changes, slowly accumulated since 1870, had made some difference, but not nearly enough to destroy the nineteenth century's conception of policing. There was one extremely important difference between the situation in 1870 and that of 1920 however. Reformers had finally developed an ideology which had a power and appeal equal to the ideology of decentralization. Professionalism, once applied to the police, offered enormous possibilities for continued, and ultimately, radical, change. The emergence of this ideology therefore marked a major turning point in the long struggle to create a different model for policing.

## SUGGESTED READINGS

Contemporary sources offer one of the best ways to compare the sharply divergent attitudes of Americans toward their police in the half century after 1870. John J. Flinn, *History of the Chicago Police from the Settlement of the Community to the Present Time* (repr.; Montclair, N. J.: Patterson Smith, 1975), was originally published in 1887. Flinn's *History* is an uncritical paen of praise for the Chicago police, but it demonstrates the pride which many people felt regarding the achievements of a decentralized, democratic approach to law enforcement. Raymond B. Fosdick, *American Police Systems* (New York: The Century Co., 1920) is, on the other hand, one of the classic critiques of that approach by a leading reformer. Two more recent interesting books which attempt to place the struggle for police reform in a broader context are: Samuel Walker, *A Critical History of Police Reform: The Emergence of Professionalism* (Lexington: Lexington Books, 1977); and Robert M. Fogelson, *Big-City Police* (Cambridge: Harvard University Press, 1977). Gene E. Carte and Elaine H. Carte, *Police Reform in the United States: The Era of August Vollmer, 1905-1932* (Berkeley: University of California Press, 1975) contains some useful information on Vollmer's career. The best recent work on the role of politics and reform in law enforcement is James F. Richardson, *The New York Police: Colonial Times to 1901* (New York: Oxford University Press, 1970).

# 5

# Federal
# Law Enforcement:
# The 19th Century

The principles of republican political theory created an important dilemma in the history of American law enforcement. Power was divided between the states and the federal government, with most of the everyday problems of maintaining law and order reserved to the states. Since crime was, in the vast majority of cases, a local phenomenon, this arrangement made a great deal of sense. Local authorities would presumably have the knowledge and ability to deal effectively with criminals. But some crimes did have implications for national development. Mail robbery, mail fraud, and counterfeiting, for example, had the potential to affect America's orderly growth by disrupting economic and social communications and by undermining a standard currency.

Local police departments were not equipped to handle these offenses. They simply had no authority over federal property; whatever happened on or to this property was none of their concern. On the other hand, the constitutional mandate for federal law enforcement was extremely vague. The Constitution specifically mentions only two crimes, counterfeiting and treason. An absence of any reference to a national police created the problem of who would protect federal property and enforce federal laws. Starting from insignificant beginnings early in the nineteenth century, the federal government gradually created a fairly respectable capacity to enforce its laws. This achievement emerged from circumstances which bore little relationship to local police reform in the cities.

Compared to the tremendous controversy and close scrutiny which accompanied the reform of local policing, the national government's efforts to deal with crime evolved in relative obscurity with a minimum of debate. The absence of any significant interest in the creation of federal law enforcement agencies is extraordinary. Public indifference may have been due to two things. First, the executive branch of the national government, which enforces federal laws, was extremely small and had little direct impact on the daily lives of most people during the nineteenth century. An unobtrusive government was unlikely to stir much interest in its affairs. Secondly, the structure of the executive branch obscured the emergence of federal policing activities. Each department which exercised some control over domestic affairs (Treasury, Post Office, etc.) had particular law enforcement problems which were not necessarily shared by the other branches. Furthermore, their problems did not appear simultaneously; rather, they evolved as each department evolved. Federal law enforcement therefore developed haphazardly, with no central supervision, in response to specific needs. In these circumstances, the national government's policing activities probably seemed unimportant to the general public.

The absence of public concern over federal law enforcement was not the only difference between the development of local and national policing. Federal officials never attempted to implement the theory of crime prevention as the basis for their policing activities. Detection was the fundamental approach to federal law enforcement from the outset. Necessity in part dictated this approach. The executive branches of the government did not have the funds or manpower available for a comprehensive program of crime prevention. Such an effort spread over the vast territory of the nation would have been inconceivable in the nineteenth century. Neither political tradition nor theory would have allowed the attempt. Then too, the crimes which concerned federal officials could not easily be prevented. Mail fraud, for example, succeeded so often because a fake enterprise was extremely hard to identify. Any suspicions had to be investigated thoroughly due to the sensitive nature of fraud accusation. Counterfeiters worked in secrecy, not on the streets, and had fairly extensive organizations. Federal agents had to spend a great deal of time collecting information and tracking suspects before enough evidence could be gathered for an arrest. These circumstances made detection an obvious choice for dealing with federal offenses.

Finally, nineteenth century federal law enforcement's structure differed from its local counterparts. Urban police departments were separate organizations charged with maintaining public order and safety in broadly defined terms. Federal officers had neither a separate identity nor a general assignment to uphold the law. Rather, they worked within a particular government bureaucracy where they investigated specific crimes. The Treasury Department, for instance, did not have a detective corps which was responsible for enforcing all the laws related to revenue. Instead, it had special agents (a common title for government detectives) assigned to two of its branches, the Customs Service and the Bureau of Internal Revenue, and the department also controlled the Secret Service. Each of these law enforcement details worked at separate tasks instead of combining their efforts. The federal law enforcement effort was therefore fragmented from its inception.

The problems inherent in the haphazard creation of federal policing did not become obvious for many years. In the meantime some agencies began to build the rather formidable reputations for effectiveness which became a hallmark of federal law enforcement. During the nineteenth century the two most important exemplars of this development were the post office inspectors and the Secret Service.

### Crimes Against the Mail

In the nineteenth century no federal agency had more contact with the general public than the Post Office. Mail was widely recognized as an important means of promoting communication and economic development. No one seriously disputed the need for federal supervision of this vital service. Shortly after the new national government began operations in 1789, Congress passed several laws which made interference with the mails a criminal offense. The Post Office was thus among the very first federal agencies to develop a potential need for a policing ability.

Potential need quickly became practical reality. Almost from the outset, a variety of criminals pounced on the mails to enrich themselves. Some of these offenders were outright thieves; others were criminals by virtue of public opinion and legislation. The definitions of criminal behavior at the federal level changed over time, reflecting a similar tendency in local law enforcement. In general, the Post Office was continually concerned about robbery and embezzlement throughout the century. After the Civil War the department broadened its concerns to cope with offenses against public morals, fraud, and swindling. Thus the tendency for federal policing to expand its activities emerged fairly early (though in a small number of agencies) and became one of the key legacies of this period.

A large part of the Post Office's crime problem could have been eliminated if Americans had not insisted upon using the mails to transact their cash business. The mail had not been intended as a cash carrier. Americans simply assumed that they could use it in this way. By mid-century the mails carried most of the cash which circulated across the country. So much ready cash proved too tempting to some postal employees. Dishonest clerks and postmasters were the bane of the service. Letters passed through so many hands that thieves easily hid their activities beneath the sheer volume and large size of the department.

Postal employees enjoyed a relative monopoly on these thefts for approximately the first thirty years of the department's existence. Then, around 1820, competition began to develop. Mail stages traveled without guards, and they carried large sums of cash in their mail pouches. These facts made them a favorite target among highwaymen, and stage holdups became common for the remainder of the century. After the Civil War these highwaymen extended their activities to railway express cars, probably because the amount of mail in a single car increased the chances of a large haul. Burglars also began to devote some attention to post offices in the late nineteenth century. These buildings, scattered by the thousands throughout the nation, rarely had watchmen and typically used flimsy safes. Too many post offices were an open invitation to theft, and burglars obliged, stealing stamps, blank money orders, and cash. They sold the stamps and money orders to fences in large cities who peddled these items to local businessmen looking for ways to reduce their expenses.

By mid-century the habit of using the mail for business began to attract swindlers and confidence men. Lotteries, for instance, had long been accustomed to selling tickets by mail. A nationwide campaign to suppress lotteries after 1830 had driven most legitimate operators out of business by 1860. Some imaginative criminals bilked a gullible public which gambled in spite of the law by advertising gift lotteries through the mail. They blanketed the nation with circulars offering tempting prizes like valuable farms, silverware, and racehorses. These circulars instructed interested persons to send a dollar (sometimes less) to a certain address in order to be eligible for a drawing. Many people complied, and that was the last they heard of the lottery. Variations of the gift lottery scheme proliferated during the 1860s and became a major source of income for criminals for the remainder of the century.

Advertisements for employment opportunities offered another avenue to wealth for swindlers. Enterprising individuals bought a large supply of envelopes, paid a printer to produce a few thousand standard job descriptions, sent out a random mailing, and settled back to collect their responses. Hundreds of people answered these fraudulent ads, often sending as much as five dollars to pay the "agent's" fee. This swindle seems to have been a favorite ploy among amateur thieves and petty criminals rather than hardened professionals.

Finally, some thieves catered to the enormous popularity of gambling by developing schemes to victimize "country cousins" who did not have the time or opportunity to satisfy their betting urges in their local communities. Since a man's mail was private, no one need know about the wonderful opportunities for huge profits which a friendly "commission agent" promised in his circulars. These agents invented two principal forms of swindling: the "bucket shop" and the racing "tip" sheet. Bucket shops pretended to buy and sell stocks for their victims. Shop operators became adept at milking suckers for considerable sums before announcing (by mail, of course) that recent speculations had gone badly and that the business was bankrupt. These shops appeared in the 1870s and were quite common until World War I. Companies offering racing tips emerged in the late 1890s and shortly thereafter became a national scandal. The techniques of these businesses copied the bucket shops with great success, and many thieves made quick fortunes before declaring a convenient bankruptcy.

Coping with all these criminals would have been taxing enough in the best of circumstances. But the Post Office also found itself in the forefront of an even more difficult battle, the crusade against obscenity. Pornography and other materials relating to sex blossomed in an age of cheap printing techniques and new medical knowledge. The public was deluged with information, advice, and practical aides to contraception and abortions just after the Civil War, and the flood continued for decades thereafter. Dime novels proliferated, and not all of them depicted the noble adventures of Buffalo Bill and Wyatt Earp. Middle- and upper-class Americans, especially those of Anglo-Saxon, Protestant backgrounds, thought they knew pornography when they saw it. They waved aside the problems of definition in a rush to legislate morality. Obscene ideas turned out to be surprisingly widespread, however. Respected ministers, frustrated middle-class women, and assorted voyeurs, wrote extremely explicit letters to neighbors, family members, friends, and acquaintances. The massive volume of this mail indicated that a sizable number of Americans were unaware that they lived in an age of Victorian prudery. When Congress enacted legislation aimed at obscene mail in 1873, it handed the Post Office an extraordinary law enforcement problem.

**Postal Inspectors**

The variety of all these criminal offenses confronted postal officials with serious difficulties. But for more than four decades after Congress established the Post Office, the postmasters general had no authority to hire employees to deal with crimes. This situation forced the postmasters general to adopt temporary measures. Initially, they assigned a few assistants to investigate problems as they occurred. As long as these assistants dealt with theft by other employees, this arrangement worked moderately well because the assistants' knowledge of mail service routines enabled them to uncover irregularities.

An increase in the volume of mail and the development of highway robbery in the early nineteenth century undermined these early arrangements. Regular employees were too few in number, too overworked, and too unfamiliar with the ways of the underworld. Postmasters general switched to another temporary expedient, hiring men from outside the department. Called special agents, these men not only investigated crime, they also performed a wide variety of miscellaneous inspection duties. They recommended the removal of incompetent postal employees, evaluated the effectiveness of the mail service, and suggested alterations in routes to increase efficiency. To the extent that these duties combined order maintenance with the detection of crime, these special agents most resembled the constables who patrolled the cities at this same time. And like the constables, they were few in number. Postmasters general probably employed no more than a dozen special agents at any one time before the 1830s.

Congress finally responded to the growing need for more effective law enforcement in 1836. In a law which reorganized the whole Post Office, the postmaster general received authorization to hire full-time special agents. The provisions of this legislation granted broad authority to investigate any aspect of the mail service to these agents, and gave them arrest powers. Congress' motives for this long overdue reform are obscure. It may be that in the course of the department's general reorganization some congressman concerned about mail depredations managed to insert this change into the final bill. Whatever the origins, the results were quietly revolutionary. These special agents became the first formal police force within the executive branch of the federal government.

Postmaster General Amos Kendall organized the new special agents into an Office of Inspection under the control of an assistant postmaster general. Various bureaucratic changes between 1836 and World War I did not alter the basic approach to law enforcement, but there were some important organizational innovations. The most significant change occurred in 1875. Prompted perhaps by the need for greater efficiency as the volume of criminal problems increased, the postmaster general created the Division of Postal Inspectors and Mail Depredations. Shortly thereafter he divided the nation into six inspection districts, distributed his inspectors (as they were now titled) among these districts, and placed an inspector-in-charge in each area to supervise its business. A chief-inspector administered this new system from Washington. At approximately the same time, recruiting methods also underwent important changes. Previous to the 1880s, inspectors had been recruited from outside the Post Office. Now they came from the ranks of railway mail clerks, an elite corps within the department. Intradepartmental recruiting seems to have provided an opportunity to create an exceptionally capable group of detectives who were experts on postal laws, discreet, highly motivated, and extremely honest (a quality notoriously lacking among city detectives at the time).

Postal inspectors needed to have all these qualities because of the sensitive nature of their work and because Congress vastly expanded the scope of their activities after the Civil War. Inspectors investigated robberies, embezzlements, and counterfeit stamps as well as the efficiency of the Post Office in general. Accusations against employees had to be well-founded. In an era when all government servants were patronage appointees, important Congressmen were extremely suspicious that the Post Office's detectives used criminal charges to attack an important source of their power. Inaccurate or incompetent investigations could cause political controversies which would destroy the effectiveness of the inspectors. Hence they had to be cautious for the sake of the Post Office's relations with Congress. Caution also applied to their expanded duties, beginning in 1865 when Congress began to defend public morals with a law against sending obscene material through the mail. This initial legislation was strengthened several times. In 1868 Congress passed another law which prohibited mailing circulars and letters concerning lotteries. Then in 1873 Congress expanded the definition of obscenity. Finally, in 1890 the Post Office obtained authority to issue fraud orders against various types of businesses. Inspectors now had the power to destroy businesses and to cause ordinary citizens acute embarrassment. Was a soap manufacturer engaging in a lottery when he offered his customers a chance to win a large quantity of his product? Should an inspector prosecute someone who wished a personal enemy eternal damnation? A too rigorous interpretation of the laws would stir opposition, invite controversy, and probably hurt a large number of innocent people. And yet there were people using the mail to abuse and frighten their neighbors, just as there were businessmen engaged in blatant violations of the lottery laws. Inspectors needed considerable discretion and judgment to steer a reasonable course through the problems they faced enforcing morality.

These considerations made careful work the hallmark of the Post Office's detectives. They developed the habit of making thorough investigations as systematically and as unobtrusively as possible. J. Holbrook, a special agent in the 1850s, used methods which convey some of the meticulous care these men adopted. In a case involving the theft of several letters containing money, Holbrook disguised himself as a traveler. This permitted him to survey the mail route, observe the routines of the postmasters, and learn the habits of local postal employees in casual conversations with local inhabitants. When he noticed that a venerable postmaster happened to own a coat somewhat too grand for his income, Holbrook arranged a trap to test his suspicions. He sent a packet containing marked bills along this mail route, confirmed that it had disappeared upon its arrival at the suspected post office, and caught the old postmaster with his wallet full of the marked money. Such detective methods seem to have been fairly typical throughout the century.

Obscenity cases caused the Post Office considerable notoriety, primarily because of Anthony Comstock, a zealous moral crusader who seems to have been convinced that God had appointed him as a personal agent against pornography. Comstock played a key role in persuading Congress to enlarge the scope of its obscenity laws in 1873. Thereafter he served as a postal inspector without pay in New York City. Unlike other inspectors, Comstock preferred spectacular tactics to mundane detective work. He especially liked to lead raids on pornography dealers, abortionists, and swindlers. In the course of these affairs, Comstock smashed doors, seized property, and personally arrested malefactors, all with a maximum of publicity. Comstock prided himself on the terror he assumed he caused among these criminals. He seized huge amounts of "devices" for contraception and abortion, as well as thousands of swindlers' circulars, and burned everything he confiscated. In the meantime other inspectors took on the greater burden of dealing with obscure individuals who ran afoul of the obscenity laws. More often than not, they traced obscene letters to ordinary people whose fantasies and hatreds had motivated their explicit missives. Local communities where these perpetrators lived frequently rewarded the inspectors with disdain and rage. A great deal of effort typically came to naught when local juries refused to convict these offenders. The effect of the inspectors' efforts to safeguard the public's morals is therefore difficult to determine. It may be that they merely contributed to the development of a new, controversial issue in American society: the definition of obscenity and the role of the law in suppressing it.

In the course of their investigations the postal inspectors developed vaguely defined but nonetheless important relationships with local police departments. This trend had no formal basis in law, and the Post Office apparently did not encourage it by administrative policies. Rather, cooperation probably arose from practical considerations of mutual interest and overlapping jurisdictions. For example, although special agents had no legal authority to attack gift lotteries in the 1850s, they passed information about them to city policemen who did have jurisdiction. Several states after 1870 had laws against obscenity and confidence games, and postal inspectors seem to have developed the habit of trading information about these criminals with local authorities. An informal basis for cooperation thus emerged in the nineteenth century.

Although postal inspectors appear to have been unusually dedicated and adept, they were engaged in an endless and overwhelming task. Their workload increased all out of proportion to their abilities and numbers. A Congress which was suspicious of their political intentions and determined to economize kept the size of the inspection force extraordinarily small. In 1870, when some 3,000 complaints were filed with the Post Office, a staff of 48 special agents may have had some hope of clearing their dockets. But in 1900 a flood of 198,000 complaints requiring investigation simply swamped the inspectors who numbered less than 100. They responded to this situation by concentrating on only the most important cases.

Within the confines of that smaller caseload the inspectors did fairly well. They were particularly good at ferreting out dishonest postal employees, an accomplishment which did much to sustain public faith in the safety of the mails. Inspectors also did tolerably well tracking down mail robbers. By the 1890s these thieves had begun to leave the mailbags in railway express cars alone to avoid federal intervention in their crimes. Some failures matched these achievements. Post Office burglaries continued to be a major problem, as did enforcement of the obscenity laws. On balance, though, the postal inspectors had created a solid record for efficient, effective policing—a precedent which encouraged emulation.

### Counterfeiting

The federal government created the Secret Service to protect the nation's currency. In effect, these officers acted upon the same principle as the postal inspectors: they safeguarded a vital service to the public. The standardized currency which developed initially as an emergency measure during the Civil War became an important stimulus to the nation's economic growth afterward. When the secretary of the treasury first proposed to issue a paper currency in 1861, however, he did not suggest that he would also need to protect this money with a new police force. That lesson would only come with experience.

With the exception of the paper money issued by the Continental Congress during the American Revolution, the central government had not attempted to issue currency prior to 1861. The United States Mint had produced coins which only a few counterfeiters had copied because the effort involved was too great for so little return. It was far easier and much more lucrative to copy state bank notes which were the basic circulating medium in a currency-starved economy. As a result, the Treasury Department had very limited practical knowledge of the extraordinary talent, resourcefulness, and organization of the nation's counterfeiters.

Counterfeiting appeared in America during the 1690s, as soon as paper money began circulating in the colonies. In spite of horrendous penalties, including hanging, this crime flourished prior to the Revolution. The Continental Congress' desperate need for money enhanced counterfeiters' opportunities beyond measure. They made a significant contribution to the destruction of the public's faith in the nation's currency during the 1780s by circulating huge amounts of bogus continentals. State governments gave counterfeiters further opportunities by authorizing their own currencies. It is highly likely that a large proportion (perhaps as much as a third to a half) of every currency in circulation by the late eighteenth century was spurious.

The counterfeiters could keep such large amounts of bogus money in circulation because they were both numerous and well organized. With the possible exception of slave smugglers in the early nineteenth century, no group of criminals was so well prepared to carry out its activities. Their success rested upon the fact that every state granted hundreds of charters to local banks, each of which had the authority to issue currency of their own design. A nearly endless variety of notes made it impossible for anyone to know all these pieces of paper. Gangs simply had to collect a few samples of bank notes in those states where they intended to pass counterfeits and mass produce copies. This part of their task required some place where they could work without fear of discovery. Counterfeiters preferred rural locations for their copying operations, and usually selected isolated sites away from well-traveled routes. Some gangs even retreated into the Canadian forests to establish their manufacturing plants.

Once their products were ready for marketing, counterfeiters used at least two distribution systems. In the first, gang members went into areas where the fake notes usually circulated. Posing as travelers or salesmen, these men passed small quantities of their bogus money until they had exhausted their supply. They then returned to the plant with their profits. Wholesaling provided a second means of distribution. Other criminals often knew the locations of the counterfeiters' plants, or they knew some of the gang. These thieves bought large amounts of their counterfeiter friends' product at discount prices for hard cash. Legitimate businessmen, who used counterfeits to increase their profits, also ordered batches of bogus notes from representatives of these gangs. In the early part of the nineteenth century counterfeit money thus moved by these means along fairly fixed distribution routes from Canada into the southern states via the eastern seaboard.

Victims of these criminals usually demanded better defenses against their depredations. Bank officials responded by adopting more complex designs for their notes to frustrate counterfeiters who would not have the skill or patience to duplicate elaborate patterns. These counter-measures did help thin the ranks of the counterfeiting fraternity, but not the amount of bogus money. Some of these criminals in fact had the engraving skills required to copy the more complicated designs. Others turned to new technologies to defeat their opposition. Lithographic and electroplating techniques made the copying chore rather easy, and made detection even harder. As a result of their technical expertise, counterfeiters evaded the efforts to curtail their activities and in fact prospered. By 1859 there were more than 4,000 different counterfeits in widespread circulation, and contemporary observers estimated that half the money in use was fake.

The federal government's decision to issue a paper currency thus coincided with the heyday of counterfeiting, a situation which did not bode well for the success of the new money. In fact, the appearance of a national currency initially expanded the counterfeiters' potential market area because it was legal tender throughout the union. Counterfeiters promptly enlarged their regional operations to take advantage of national opportunities. They quickly proved their technical mastery by successfully copying the best work of the government's most adept designers and engravers. Local police, who had never coped effectively with these criminals, now displayed a complete inability to deal with their expanded and sophisticated operations. The secretary of the treasury thus faced a major problem: he did not have the ability to protect the national currency.

## The Secret Service

Considering the size of the task involved, the secretary's first efforts to suppress counterfeiting were rather inept. In 1864 he offered rewards for the conviction of these criminals and hired a few private detectives to make arrests. William P. Wood, then warden of the Capitol Prison and a fairly unsavory character with contacts in the underworld, was the most important detective the secretary engaged. Wood rounded up thirty-four counterfeiters in less than a year by exploiting his personal contacts among criminals. These measures proved inadequate, but not insignificant. By employing private detectives, whose methods were sometimes illegal, the secretary inadvertently but decisively shaped the initial development of the Secret Service.

Early in 1865 the secretary recommended the formation of a permanent force to deal with counterfeiting. Lincoln's assassination delayed consideration of this idea, but in June, William Wood was appointed the first chief of the United States Secret Service. The new organization's personnel and regulations were remarkable. Most of the first agents, who numbered about thirty, had been private detectives. As for the agency's guidelines, a federal official said: "Our policies and rules can take shape as your work progresses.'' Given the notorious behavior of private detectives in general, and of William Wood in particular, this announcement was an open invitation to abuse. The Secret Service thus began operations with a mandate to maintain the public's confidence in the nation's currency by any means which produced results.

Whatever his ethical defects, Wood knew his business. He distributed his agents among eleven cities, giving them the opportunity to develop and maintain an extensive knowledge of local criminals and their activities. This would not have been possible if the agents had all remained in Washington. Wood thus created a national law enforcement network which could collate local information, minimize duplication of effort, and concentrate resources fairly effectively. This was not, however, an elaborate bureaucracy. Wood's small staff and the fact that many agents were his friends meant that he could operate a highly personalized organization which he dominated.

Wood's agents applied their detective methods and knowledge of criminals to their new jobs with considerable success. Infiltrating gangs of counterfeiters and developing a system of informers appear to have been their two favorite tactics in the early days of the Service. Agents would become acquainted with a suspected counterfeiter and gain his (or her, in some cases) confidence. Then the agent observed the suspect's behavior and friends long enough to learn the gang's operations. Finally, he offered to buy a large amount of the gang's product. If the counterfeiters accepted his offer, the agent stationed some help nearby, closed the deal, and made the arrests. Once a counterfeiter was in custody, the agent attempted to turn him into an informer by proposing to exchange a reduced sentence for information. These deals were not always honored, however, even when they resulted in additional arrests.

The Secret Service also used surreptitious entries to ferret out counterfeiters. Agents watched a building where they suspected a gang worked until they learned the times when it was vacant. Leaving a lookout to warn of any problems, they picked door locks, examined the contents of a shop, and departed before anyone returned to work. The agents apparently used surreptitious entry to confirm their suspicions rather than to gather physical evidence. Having ascertained the details of a gang's operations, they then resorted to other ploys to close the case.

These tactics were effective. Wood's agents captured more than 200 counterfeiters in the first year of their operations, a record so impressive that their methods escaped criticism altogether. In fact, when Wood retired in the early 1870s, his successor specifically commended the tactics of the agents because of their success. Official praise served to perpetuate these methods; they became an accepted part of the Service's approach to law enforcement. When the Service recruited men who had no detective experience, as it did later in the century, the new agents were trained in tactics which had become standardized through long use. John Wilkie, who became chief of the service in 1897, tried to introduce reforms, including a prohibition on stool pigeons, but he did not immediately succeed in undermining traditional methods. He did, however, improve the general quality of the agents by refusing to accept men solely on the basis of their political connections.

In the late nineteenth century the Secret Service nearly became a general, but unofficial, policing department for any executive agency which needed law enforcement assistance. The Service's vague mandate and loose regulations did not specifically prohibit its agents from expanding their investigations. Furthermore, the Service's aggressive, successful tactics recommended themselves to other agencies which were having problems enforcing their own laws and responsibilities. When Congress established the Department of Justice in 1870, for example, it did not authorize the attorney general to employ his own staff of lawmen. Congress appropriated money to employ temporary agents in 1871, but it still refused to allow the Department to have its own full-time investigators. The attorney general therefore frequently used Secret Service men. Most of the work they did for him involved enforcing internal regulations. They checked the accounts and records of the department's clerks and attorneys, and reviewed the marshal's vouchers for expenses. From these mundane beginnings, the Secret Service gradually expanded its aid until it helped most of the federal agencies which needed investigators. Secret Service agents helped track down confidence men in cooperation with postal inspectors; they inquired into smuggling problems for the Customs Service; and they investigated the traffic in illegal aliens for the Bureau of Immigration. This help did not attract much attention beyond the confines of the agencies which relied on the Secret Service, probably because the amount of this activity remained relatively small and noncontroversial until after 1900.

Controversy finally erupted during Theodore Roosevelt's second term as President. Apparently under direct orders from Roosevelt, the Secret Service investigated a series of land fraud cases for the Department of the Interior. The results were spectacular. In Oregon, these investigations uncovered enough evidence to send a former United States land commissioner, a United States congressman, and a United States senator to jail. Simultaneous inquiries in Colorado produced equally damaging accusations against several prominent politicians there, but local juries refused to convict the malefactors. Undeterred, the Service continued its probes in Oklahoma, Louisiana, and Georgia, arousing a storm of controversy as local politicians scrambled to protect themselves from prosecution. Their anguished demands for an end to these "persecutions" reached into Congress, where powerful Republican leaders sternly asked what business the Secret Service had harassing loyal party members. Roosevelt refused to halt the investigations or to curb the Secret Service in spite of intense pressure to do so. Congress therefore took the matter into its own hands by passing a law in 1908 which required the Service to confine its activities to protecting the President (a responsibility it had acquired in 1901) and to pursuing counterfeiters.

Although politics prompted Congress to restrict the scope of the Secret Service's activities, that decision simply conformed to the basic approach to federal law enforcement which had become well entrenched before 1908. Decentralization, which derived from republicanism, influenced the structure of federal as well as local policing. There was a difference, however, in the reasons why decentralization triumphed in federal law enforcement. Crime shaped the development of both local and national policing, but the federal government dealt with a much narrower range of criminal activities than did urban police departments. The amount of crime worrying federal officials was therefore less than that which occurred in cities. Furthermore, law enforcement was divided among several departments of the national government, thereby diffusing the impact of crime on federal activities.

Federal law enforcement in the nineteenth century thus approached its task from a narrow perspective which stressed detection and a lack of coordinated effort. The Secret Service's aid to other agencies, while important in filling gaps and demonstrating the possibilities inherent in cooperation, made no immediate impact on the structure of federal policing. Departments which borrowed Secret Service agents were merely trying to make maximum use of scarce enforcement resources rather than deliberately attempting to create a centralized national police. The successes of the postal inspectors and Secret Service agents, in the face of considerable difficulties, did, however, provide the basis for more innovative experiments after 1908.

## SUGGESTED READINGS

The history of federal law enforcement is virtually unexplored. Personal reminiscences and journalistic accounts of the postal inspectors and Secret Service agents offer colorful and interesting insights without providing any systematic examination into their activities. J. Holbrook, *Ten Years Among the Mail Bags: or, Notes from the Diary of a Special Agent of the Post-Office Department* (Philadelphia: H. Cowperthwait & Co., 1855) is a delightful and lucid recollection of the methods and problems which faced postal agents at mid-century. Likewise, Don Wilkie, *American Secret Service Agent* (New York: Frederick A. Stokes Company, 1934) contains some interesting references to the Secret Service's methods at the turn of the century, but Wilkie's enthusiasm must be judged from the perspective that his father happened to be chief of the service. The best journalistic studies of federal law enforcement are: Walter S. Bowen and Harry E. Neal, *The United States Secret Service* (Philadelphia: Chilton Co., 1960) and John N. Makris, *The Silent Investigators: The Great Untold Story of the United States Postal Service* (New York: E. P. Dutton & Co., 1959). Wayne E. Fuller, *The American Mail: Enlarger of the Common Life* (Chicago: University of Chicago Press, 1972), an excellent book on the history of the Post Office, contains a chapter on the postal inspectors which is one of the few systematic studies of the subject. Lynn Glaser, *Counterfeiting in America: The History of an American Way to Wealth* (New York: Clarkson N. Potter, Inc., 1968) is somewhat anecdotal but valuable for its comprehensive survey of counterfeiting.

Frontier justice. A group of vigilantes prepare to hang some captives.
*Courtesy Library of Congress.*

# 6

# Law Enforcement in the American West

For most Americans the history of Western law enforcement is a chronicle of fascinating episodes in which courageous marshals faced dissolute outlaws in stand-up gunfights on the streets of famous cowtowns like Dodge City, Kansas. Steel nerves, quick hands, and skillful pistol work quickly settled the issue of whether law and order would triumph over evil. The legend of good men vanquishing bad ones in brief, violent confrontations has dominated our understanding of Western law enforcement for nearly a hundred years. But it is just that: a legend. Like any legend, it has a kernel of truth to it. There were some extraordinarily adept gunslingers like John Wesley Hardin and "Doc" Holliday who occasionally duelled with their enemies on the streets. Spectacular as such fighters were, they vastly distorted the truth about the process of imposing order in the vast territory between the Mississippi River and the Pacific Ocean during the late nineteenth century.

During most of the late nineteenth century, law enforcement in the West assumed a confusing variety of forms because of one crucial problem: the absence of well-developed, standardized government. Large parts of the West were under federal control; others had been organized into new states; and still other areas remained, at least nominally, under Indian control. While an area remained a territory, law enforcement was entrusted to a United States marshal and his deputies. A small town within the territory might appoint someone as a local policeman, but he had no legal authority to deal with criminals since the town itself had no legal standing as long as it remained unincorporated. Once a state (or states) emerged from the territory, the state legislature had the power to deal with crime by appointing county sheriffs. But some parts of the new state might not have enough people living there to justify creating a county immediately. Thus some areas even within the new states might not have legally constituted peace officers. Citizens in these places had to petition local courts, or their legislature, to incorporate counties and towns. In the meantime, the ability to enforce laws remained ambiguous. Indian reservations, and the Indian Territory (in present-day Oklahoma) further complicated matters because only the Indians, with occasional help from the United States Army, had law enforcement rights in these areas. As settlement progressed, and standardized government slowly emerged, the confused status of various law enforcement problems was clarified. But in the interim criminals had considerable freedom of movement. Simply fleeing to the federal territories usually ensured their safety because they could not be extradited.

### Sources of Crime

The absence of standardized government meant that there was no uniform way to control the problems which caused crime and disorder in the West. Although the particular kinds of crime which occurred differed in some respects from those committed "back East," Western crime stemmed from the same sources. There were in fact three basic causes of crime: social, economic, and political conflict. In some cases, all three causes became intertwined, but each also contributed in their separate ways to the crime problem. Social conflict, for example, erupted from antagonisms between ethnic groups. Contrary to popular misconceptions, the West attracted a wide variety of peoples. Anglo-Americans jostled with Mexicans, Indians, Chinese, freed blacks, Australians, Englishmen, Scandinavians, and a smattering of other ethnics in competition for land and wealth. Competition bred prejudice (or reinforced it), and sometimes resulted in harassment or violence. Mexicans, Indians, and the Chinese suffered especially from this situation. Spanish land grants were often ignored and Mexican families thus lost their homes. The Chinese, who made up a large part of the work force which built the transcontinental railroads, suffered from mob attacks and many individual abuses. Indian claims, of course, went unheeded by everybody. All this created a great deal of bitterness which became a fruitful source of disorder.

Economic conflicts arose when competing groups wanted to use the West's resources in different ways. The classic example of this problem was the clash between cattlemen and sheepherders, both of whom wanted unlimited access to grazing lands. In fact, sheep and cattle can graze successfully together, but no nineteenth century cattleman believed that. Cowboys therefore harassed sheep-men unmercifully. An unarmed herder had little chance to stop ranch hands from raiding his camp and slaughtering his sheep. Resistance usually meant death or maiming from gunshot wounds. The war between sheep and cattle-men continued until the early 1900s, but it was not the only source of economic competition which bred crime. Large cattle companies re-garded small ranchers as vermin to be stamped out. They even went so far as to argue that small ranchers were rustlers—otherwise how could they have acquired their herds? This peculiar logic justified several murders before peace between the two groups was achieved. Finally, another form of economic conflict developed in employee-employer relations, especially in the mines. The lone prospector did exist, but he was a peculiarity rather than a typical figure. Mining was a big busi-ness which required large amounts of capital and a competent work force. Strife between miners and the corporations often ended in vio-lence at a time when labor unions were widely regarded as un-American and employees were treated as little more than a kind of property. One of the most famous examples of this violence occurred at Ludlow, Colorado, in 1913. When workers at a mine owned by John D. Rocke-feller struck for higher wages, strikebreakers attacked the miners' tents, shooting several women and children. In the ensuing battle, 200 militiamen fought with 400 miners. When the smoke cleared, 74 people lay dead. This was only a more spectacular case of the deadly forms which economic conflict could generate.

Political controversies also contributed to the chronicle of crime and disorder. The bitterness of the slavery issue (which also had social and economic implications) provided a good example of this problem. During the 1850s, settlers from the North and the South fought battles over whether Kansas would be a free or a slave state when it joined the Union. Many men, on both sides, developed skills with firearms and learned a callousness toward life which would serve them well when they turned to outlawry after the Civil War. Jesse James was one such character. James became a member of "Bloody" Bill Anderson's Southern guerrillas during the war. Among other actions, James par-ticipated in the famous raid on Lawrence, Kansas, in August 1863. Anderson and William Quantrill, one of the most notorious guerrillas of that era, joined forces in this attack which left 200 men, women, and children dead and the town reduced to ashes. James Butler "Wild Bill" Hickok was another notorious graduate of the Kansas bloodshed. He rode with a guerrilla band composed of northerners during 1856 and 1857, before moving on to seek his fortune farther west.

With the sources of crime and disorder rooted in the fabric of Western society, peaceably inclined settlers were hard pressed to find ways to enforce the law effectively. This situation was made even more difficult because many peace officers were themselves deeply involved in the conflicts which convulsed the West. United States marshals and their deputies, for example, obtained their offices through their political contacts. Enforcing the law could, and did, mean that these marshals represented a temporarily dominant political faction who abused their power to advance their own fortunes. Arbitrary law enforcement provoked resentment and resistance, thereby complicating an already complex problem. In spite of the difficulties, Westerners did manage to establish peace. They did so by relying upon a combination of four groups who, at various times, assumed responsibility for law enforcement. These groups were: private citizens, United States marshals, businessmen, and town policemen.

### Law Enforcement by Private Citizens

Private citizens usually became involved in law enforcement by joining a posse or by helping to repel an immediate danger. These contributions were made on a temporary basis. The demise of the Dalton gang provides one example of this. When the five members of this outlaw band rode into Coffeyville, Kansas, on October 5, 1892, they expected to encounter little resistance to their plan to rob two banks simultaneously. The town was small and the single police officer could not be expected to offer much resistance to one of the area's most notorious gangs. Moreover, the Daltons had grown up in the town, knew its layout well, and also knew which routes offered the easiest escape. Unfortunately for them, however, some local citizens noticed what was happening in the banks. Instead of cowering behind the nearest cover, these people armed themselves, took up positions around the banks and began firing. The gang members dashed toward their horses, fatally shooting several townsmen along the way. But the run over open ground in a hail of lead proved equally fatal to them. Four of the five men died on the street, and the fifth, Emmett Dalton, was so badly wounded that he did not recover for months.

The spectacular demise of the Dalton gang was only one instance of how private citizens contributed to law enforcement. Another, much more complex example emerged in the form of vigilance committees. Vigilantes were not a Western invention, but the lack of established authority and systematic government made them seem a natural solution to many of the problems plaguing the region. Between 1849 and 1902 there were 210 vigilante movements. California provided the model for these movements while Montana experienced the most deadly vigilante episode.

Popular tradition usually holds vigilantes in high regard. True, they were a bit abrupt in their methods, and they had no legal right to hang people, but by-and-large vigilante committees performed valuable work ridding their communities of dangerous criminals. This simplistic view overlooks the fact that vigilantes were not always people intent on administering justice to criminals. Frequently, they were more interested in imposing their conception of order on their neighbors. Vigilantes settled fundamental social, economic, and political conflicts by violence. The people they hanged or chased out of town were frequently those who challenged the vigilantes' ideas about local government.

San Francisco's experience with vigilance committees illustrates these points. Located at the gateway to the goldfields, many San Franciscans became wealthy provisioning thousands of immigrants pouring into the state to seek their fortunes. The city grew rapidly from a few hundred people in 1846 to over 30,000 by 1850. Growth, however, brought problems as well as benefits. The city's actual and imagined wealth attracted large numbers of gamblers, prostitutes, and assorted thieves who quickly established a flourishing underworld. Corrupt courts and an inadequate police made matters worse by failing to control these criminals. Burgeoning opportunities for plunder and a practically nonexistent government combined to make San Francisco something of a thieves' paradise.

This situation provided the background for San Francisco's first vigilance committee in 1851. Local merchants and their friends banded together to deal with the city's crime problem. But this committee was motivated less by a desire to administer justice than by a conviction that too much crime was bad for business. These vigilantes feared that their city would develop such a noisome reputation that immigrants would refuse to settle there and invest their money in San Francisco. Spurred by this fear, about 700 vigilantes descended upon local criminals. In one month they arrested 90 men (half of whom had to be released for lack of evidence). Of those actually punished by the vigilantes' courts, only 4 were hanged. One man was whipped and 14 others were banished from the city. The vigilantes' activities received widespread public approval, and, for a while at least, crime did decline.

During the next five years, however, conditions deteriorated somewhat as criminals once more became fairly active. While some people found this deterioration disturbing, even more citizens resented the ways in which their local government had changed. A political machine, run by Democrats and supported by hundreds of Irish immigrants, had gained control over the city's public affairs. In 1856 the businessmen decided to take charge once again, but this time they intended to do far more than merely chase a few criminals out of town. They sought to secure the merchant community's economic and social power by seizing local political power.

Another murder triggered the 1856 vigilance movement. Several people who had participated in the 1851 vigilance committee issued a call for action. The response was overwhelming. Nearly 8,000 citizens joined the vigilance committee, making this the largest such movement in American history. The vigilantes elected William T. Coleman, a prominent merchant, as president. Coleman insisted upon absolute authority to run the committee and received it. He organized the vigilantes into paramilitary companies and established a headquarters protected by sandbag ramparts. Once ready for action, the committee's representatives forcibly removed prisoners from the local jail. This illegal act placed the vigilantes in blatant defiance of the regularly established government, and California's governor ordered them to disband. He also called out the state militia to enforce his order, but the militiamen ignored the governor and joined the vigilantes instead. Secure from outside intervention, the vigilantes proceeded to their work. During the summer they conducted numerous illegal searches, arrested a large number of people (mostly Irishmen), and held rigged trials. By the end of August, 25 men had been deported and 4 others had been hanged. Approximately 800 San Franciscans, frightened by these activities, left town permanently.

The committee next turned to politics, forming the People's Party to participate in the fall elections. At the conclusion of those elections the vigilantes' party had won the mayor's office and over half the seats on the board of supervisors (aldermen). They also controlled the sheriff, the chief of police, the tax assessor, and the United States marshal. Once installed in office, the vigilantes' representatives proceeded to adopt measures highly favorable to the business community. In sum, the 1856 vigilance movement created a political machine which served businessmen's interests for over a decade. The battle against crime had taken a very peculiar turn. In fact, unlike the situation after the 1851 vigilance committee completed its work, crime did not decline after 1856.

San Francisco was not the only place where vigilance movements served other motives besides a desire to punish criminals. A rural vigilance movement with ulterior motives occurred in Wyoming in 1892. This episode, known as the Johnson County War, was distinctive primarily because it demonstrates that vigilantes did not always succeed. In fact, the Johnson County War was a dismal failure and the vigilantes were saved from their own folly only by their considerable political influence.

The Johnson County War developed from the conflict between large cattle companies and small ranchers. All cattlemen grazed their herds on public lands during most of the late nineteenth century. They were so accustomed to this practice that they regarded the public domain as their own, even though they had no legal rights to these lands. But large cattle company owners resented the small rancher who pastured herds on "their" land. During the early 1890s, Wyoming's major cattlemen tried to squeeze small competitors out of business by violence and brute political power, using the Wyoming Stock Grower's Association as a front for their maneuvers. At the same time, the association tried to solve the problem of rustlers. But local juries often failed to convict persons accused of rustling, thereby frustrating this effort. The failure to prosecute rustlers successfully may well have been due to the large cattleman's belief that every small rancher was a rustler, regardless of any proof to the contrary. From this perspective, the behavior of local juries simply indicated that they were in a league with the rustlers. This kind of biased thinking soon led to violence.

Wyoming's major cattlemen focused their wrath on Johnson County in 1892. Juries there had been particularly obstinate, and the county's small ranchers were active in organizing a new association to compete with the Stock Grower's. The violence began with the lynching of two small ranchers, a man and a woman, whom the Stock Grower's Association regarded as thieves. Next, two more men were murdered from ambush and their assailants escaped. After these preliminaries, the large cattlemen assembled a quasi-military expedition to make an organized raid on Johnson County. Gunmen from as far away as Texas were hired for this expedition, equipped at their employers' expense, and promised a $1,000 bonus for their work. Arrangements were made to assassinate the sheriff in order to prevent any unseemly conflict with the law.

The expedition began well. Two of the men marked for elimination were trapped in a ranch house and killed. One of the murdered men, Nat Campbell, was to have led the small ranchers' next roundup for a cattle drive separate from the one controlled by the Stock Grower's Association. His death thus struck an important blow at the association's competition. But this victory quickly turned sour. The gun battle at Campbell's ranch had been witnessed by local residents who rode away to warn their neighbors. Alerted by these reports, the sheriff issued a call for volunteers to repel the raiders. As dozens of angry citizens swarmed into the county seat, the sheriff's would-be assassin deemed discretion the better part of valor and disappeared. Over 300 men answered the call to arms and, led by their sheriff and the local minister, the posse went looking for the erstwhile vigilantes.

In the meantime the Stock Grower's hired gunmen had become discouraged by the cold weather and reports of a posse. They sought refuge at a friendly ranch, sent out a messenger with a plea to the governor for help, and fortified their position. When the posse arrived, they found the raiders entrenched behind some formidable breastworks which would cost many lives to take. After some careful examination of the situation, the sheriff decided that the vigilantes could be dislodged by a judicious load of dynamite run up against the fortifications on a wagon. The arrangements were duly made, and just as the wagon was due to be turned loose the United States Cavalry arrived. Wyoming's governor had received the vigilantes' message and used his power as the state's chief executive to ask the federal government for aid in supporting a nonexistent insurrection. The cavalry commander, fortunately, understood the truth of the situation and acted as a mediator instead of attacking the posse. Crestfallen at this turn of events, the vigilantes agreed to surrender, but only to the army. Once in protective custody, the raiders escaped the posse's wrath and the Johnson County War ended ignominiously. None of the gunmen was ever punished for his part in the raid, nor were any of the leaders called upon to answer for their acts. But their attempt to cloak economic suppression in the guise of vigilante justice had failed spectacularly.

As the examples from San Francisco and Wyoming indicate, vigilance movements frequently concealed complex motives behind a facade of community concern over crime. This was not always true. Some vigilantes dealt summary justice to genuine thieves and had no broader ambitions. But the fact that some citizens did use violence to achieve personal goals or to advance the economic and political power of their social groups demonstrates the dangers of leaving law enforcement in private hands.

**Federal Law Enforcement**

Vigilance movements occurred most frequently in the early years of settlement and tended to disappear as regularly appointed peace officers appeared. United States marshals were among the first such lawmen to arrive in frontier areas. Congress had created the position of marshal in the Judiciary Act of 1789 to give federal courts officers who could perform police duties. Since United States marshals enforced federal, not local, laws, they had jurisdiction over few criminal matters because the national government in the nineteenth century was not very involved in fighting crime. Marshals could act in cases of theft of the mails, crimes against railroad property, murder on federal lands, and a few other problems, but the vast majority of their responsibilities dealt with civil matters arising from federal court activities. In spite of these limitations, marshals played an important role in law enforcement. While an area remained a federal territory, they were the only authorities available to deal with criminals. Once a territory became a state (or several states), local lawmen assumed most of the burden of pursuing criminals. In these changed circumstances United States marshals still had a contribution to make through their power to appoint deputies. Policemen in towns, and county sheriffs, normally had juris-diction only within their immediate localities. Criminals could avoid pursuit simply by leaving the local lawman's jurisdiction. If a local lawman was also a United States deputy marshal, however, he could continue his pursuit across jurisdictions. Presumably this power only applied to offenses against federal law, but lawmen apparently did not always pay scrupulous attention to the distinction. Lawmen who held multiple offices were a necessary improvisation at a time when there were too few men available to guard the vastness of the West.

The marshal's position was not free of problems however. Two dif-ficulties were especially important. First, the United States marshal obtained office through political preferment instead of merit. Those who became marshals need not have any law enforcement experience, but powerful friends were absolutely essential. Political partisanship inevitably led to other problems. Both disappointed applicants from his own party and opponents from the other party harassed the success-ful candidate with charges of inefficiency and corruption to discredit him. Marshals thus had to spend considerable amounts of time guarding their political fences—time which would have been better spent on their official duties. The anger directed against marshals was partly based on envy. Marshals did not earn a salary; they made their livings from fees and occasional rewards. The rewards usually amounted to very little, but the fees marshals collected were considerable, usually totaling several thousand dollars a year. This fee system was the second major difficulty with the marshal's office. Chasing criminals did not make much sense economically, since fees from civil processes and related activities provided marshals with far more income. Further-more, the fee system easily lent itself to abuses. Unscrupulous marshals could manipulate their power to increase the amount of civil business which passed through their offices. Congress did not act on these problems until 1896, when the President signed a law providing regular salaries for marshals and making major changes in the fees system.

Most of the criminals with whom the marshals dealt were rather ordinary people who never acquired the fame of more notorious out-laws. Liquor smugglers and gunrunners supplying the Indians with con-traband posed one of the most persistent problems for the marshals. Mail robbers were another group which taxed the slender resources of federal law enforcement. Isolated mail carriers offered an easy and potentially lucrative target at a time when many people sent cash through the mails. Small town post offices were burgled frequently, especially by tramp thieves who became known as "yeggmen." An occasional murderer completed the motley cast of criminals who might run afoul of the marshals.

Train robbers tended to be the most famous outlaws whose activities violated federal laws. These men acquired their fearsome reputations in part because of the spectacular nature of their crimes. But they also gained notoriety because the American public, and especially Western settlers, admired their choice of targets. Railroads were probably the single most hated industry in the nineteenth century. They made enormous contributions to the nation's development, but in the process railroad owners acted with such callousness and rapacity that they alienated the very people they served. Unfair rate schedules and corruption of politicians were only two of their more notorious activities. Hence outlaws who robbed the railroads could be, and in many cases were, regarded as quasi-heroes who gave more evil men what they deserved. The public's admiration for their behavior became the basis for the romantic legends which surround the lives of the men who rode with Jesse James, the Younger brothers, Bill Doolin, the Dalton brothers, and others.

Unfortunately for the legends, train robbery had few romantic traits. Jesse James, for example, introduced the idea of wrecking a train to rob it. His gang first employed this dangerous technique to a train in Iowa on July 21, 1873. Wrecking did not imply a very high regard for the safety of a train's passengers or crew, and, in fact, these outlaws usually displayed little concern for innocent bystanders. A less innovative, but equally effective technique was to wait for a train to stop to take on water at some isolated place. While some of the gang covered the engine crew to prevent the train's departure, other members ran to the express car and demanded entry. Resistance from express messengers prompted a fusillade of shots occasionally supported with dynamite. Once the express car's safe had been rifled, the outlaws departed quickly for the safety of some hideaway. These heavily-armed gangs were usually more than a match for any posse which pursued them.

Full-scale battles between these outlaw gangs and posses were extremely rare, primarily because the gang members usually scattered after a robbery. This tendency gave federal officers an opportunity to track them down singly, a process which required a great deal of hard, ordinary police work. By carefully collecting and checking information, marshals learned the habits and favorite haunts of many outlaws. Rewards for this kind of information speeded the process of locating these men. Although federal lawmen had very limited funds for this purpose, railroad companies and other businesses willingly provided the money required. Once the system of soliciting and paying for information became well established in any particular territory, the marshals had only to await their opportunities.

Occasionally, the marshals had their work done for them. Jesse James was shot in 1882 by one of his own gang who found the reward too tempting; the Daltons' bravado ended in disaster at Coffeyville; and the Younger brothers found Northfield, Minnesota, extremely inhospitable. But lawmen could not depend on such incidents to deal with every outlaw. The elimination of the Wild Bunch, a gang led by Bill Doolin, illustrates the hard work and danger involved in federal law enforcement. Doolin's band operated in the Oklahoma Territory during the early 1890s, holding up trains and banks. The gang's members were fairly well-known in the territory because they had all worked as cowhands and in other jobs before turning to outlawry. Friends from their legitimate past had no particular desire to inform on them and occasionally aided the gang by supplying them with horses, food, and shelter. Doolin even married the daughter of a local postmaster, leaving his wife with her father while he made his raids. The gang's practice of dispersing finally led to its piecemeal demise. Information on the whereabouts of various members gradually accumulated in the hands of the territory's marshal and his deputies, and these lawmen assembled several posses to run the men to ground.

Most of the Wild Bunch died in shoot-outs which illustrated that gunfights in the best tradition of Western romance occurred very rarely. Few lawmen, and still fewer outlaws, felt compelled to issue formal challenges to a stand-up fight. It made more sense to seek as much cover as possible, and it made even more sense to have some supporters along to increase the odds in one's favor. Furthermore, handguns were not the weapons of first choice. Lawmen quickly learned that a double-barrelled shotgun outclassed any Colt .45 no matter how fast a draw an outlaw was supposed to be. Thus, when Deputy Marshal Heck Thomas finally located Bill Doolin at his father-in-law's home in August 1896, Thomas assembled a five-man posse to bring in the outlaw. Arriving at Doolin's hideout, Thomas checked with his two informants to make sure Doolin had not departed. Once assured that their man was still there, Thomas placed his men along both sides of a road leading past the small cluster of buildings. Shortly thereafter Doolin emerged and walked down the road. When called on to surrender, Doolin started shooting; a blast from Thomas' shotgun ended the fight and Doolin's career. The remainder of the gang met equally ignominious ends in encounters with overwhelming numbers of lawmen.

Careful, often tedious police work by Heck Thomas and other federal marshals did help bring the problem of Western outlaw gangs under control. Cooperation among federal and local lawmen; the cultivation of informants; and the use of overwhelming numbers against isolated gunmen succeeded where personal heroics would have failed. The marshal's most significant contribution to solving the West's crime problem was to provide a sound basis for cooperation among the various law enforcement agencies as they developed in each new state. Without such a basis, peace officers would have had a far more difficult time establishing order in the West.

## Local Law Enforcement

Local law enforcement developed simultaneously with settlement. Territorial status did not deter newly arrived immigrants from promptly organizing a police force, even though these officers had no legal standing. The need to have someone available to deal with criminals was far stronger than any concern about legalities. Generally the settlers in an area would hold a public meeting at which they would create a "government" complete with popularly elected officials. These men would either appoint a police force or ask the meeting to elect one. Peace officers chosen in these meetings began work immediately, depending upon the community's desire for order to back them up if anyone questioned their authority. These temporary lawmen might become official policemen after a town or a county received legal recognition.

Once a territory had been organized into a state, local law enforcement became the responsibility of county sheriffs and town (or city) policemen. Sheriffs were important politicians who usually obtained office because they represented the dominant social and economic groups in the local area. As with federal marshals, sheriffs spent only a small portion of their time chasing criminals. The county's principal law enforcement officer had a variety of duties which might include collecting local taxes, inspecting cattle brands, administering punishment to convicted felons, and serving civil processes. Because of the sheriff's great power and the variety of his responsibilities, many of the West's most famous personalities were willing to serve in this office. Hickok and William B. "Bat" Masterson were only two examples of gunmen who found time to act as sheriffs.

Although Hickok and Masterson had deadly reputations, they were not necessarily the best sheriffs in the West. That honor belongs more properly to men like John Slaughter, sheriff of Cochise County, Arizona, for two terms between 1886 and 1895. Slaughter owned one of Arizona's biggest ranches in the area south of Tucson. Unlike more notorious gunfighters who tended to avoid the more dangerous aspects of their work, Slaughter approached his job with determination and a sense of how to conduct good police work. He often used his deputies to infiltrate local criminal hangouts, thereby obtaining a steady flow of reliable information. He was also an extremely ruthless individual who apparently had little faith in the courts. Whenever Slaughter went after an outlaw, he never returned with a live prisoner. Furthermore, he always worked alone. His neighbors simply had to take his word that Slaughter had been forced to kill his man—an explanation Slaughter offered some twelve times while sheriff. Systematic work combined with deadly efficiency made Cochise County a far more peaceful place during Slaughter's years in office.

Law enforcement in towns and cities generally bore a strong resemblance to policing in eastern cities. Townspeople in places like San Antonio, Denver, and San Francisco adopted the police organization and procedures they knew existed in Chicago, New York, or Boston. The police forces were usually much smaller, but other details were the same. Each department was commanded by a chief-of-police (frequently called the city marshal during most of the nineteenth century) who had a number of patrolmen and an occasional detective under his charge. These men usually wore uniforms; they were political appointees; and the mayor and aldermen interfered in police matters just as they did in larger cities. With rare exception, the police forces received little attention in the romantic tradition of Western law enforcement because they were so ordinary compared to the more famous lawmen known to most Americans.

The famous lawmen, of course, guarded the streets of the West's rowdy cowtowns. Places like Abilene, Dodge City, and Ellsworth, Kansas, had reputations as tough, dangerous towns even in their own day. Stories of spectacular gunfights between cowboys and famous men like Wyatt Earp, Bat Masterson, and Wild Bill Hickok were and remain standard fare in popular literature. Unfortunately for the reputations of these men, their behavior as city marshals bore only an occasional resemblance to their legends. Hickok killed two men while marshal of Abilene. One of them happened to be a special policeman who was coming to his assistance; the other was Phil Coe, a gambler of some notoriety. Masterson killed no one while living near Dodge City, and Earp (who was never actually a marshal) may have killed one man. In fact, during the entire period when the cattletowns were in their heyday, from 1870 to 1885, a total of only forty-five violent deaths from all causes can be found. This was a remarkably low figure for towns which supposedly regarded homicide as a routine matter.

This low death rate reflected the realities of cattletown life. Businessmen dominated these towns. They had property to protect and they hoped that their little settlements would eventually become large cities. Property and ambition dictated the kind of law enforcement the cattletowns received. The business community sought lawmen who would prevent disorder from occurring, who would not be too zealous in the use of force, and who would suppress violence quickly with a minimum of fuss once it did occur. These goals required men who were tough characters; they did not have to be well-known gunfighters, however. Men with military backgrounds or some familiarity with firearms were preferred candidates for cattletown policing. The lack of a sufficient quantity of qualified men who were willing to serve, however, caused a steady turnover in these local police forces.

Thomas J. Smith and Henry N. Brown illustrate the fortunes and misfortunes of the search for competent lawmen in these small towns. Smith had been a New York City patrolman and a railroad detective-troubleshooter before he became Abilene's marshal in 1870. Although he wore a brace of pistols for emergencies, Smith never used them during his short term of office. Instead he used his fists to enforce the law. Texas cowhands accustomed to settling arguments with firearms were confused by Smith's tactics, but they obeyed him nevertheless. Smith was just the sort of man who could fulfill the requirements of the business community. He did not kill anyone, and he did not antagonize the cowboys whose money meant life to Abilene. Unfortunately, Smith was brutally murdered within a year by a local settler. Henry Brown was an example of the idea that the best person to catch a thief was another thief. A former member of Billy the Kid's gang, Brown accepted the post of city marshal at Caldwell in 1882. Caldwell residents found him a little too quick with a gun, but his reputation helped pacify many cowboys. The town actually enjoyed two years of peace under Brown's protection. Old habits proved hard to break, however. One day in 1884 Brown rode out of town with his assistant marshal and two other men, robbed the bank in a nearby town, and killed two bank officers. Shortly thereafter Caldwell's marshal was lynched by a mob.

As these two examples indicate, town marshals came from a wide variety of backgrounds and had mixed success enforcing the law in ways which businessmen favored. Too much violence among cowboys was bad for a town's reputation, but too much violence by lawmen was bad for a town's economy. City marshals successfully balanced the requirements of order and economics more often than local citizens had any right to expect, but the whole problem was finally resolved by the state legislature. Kansas farmers, tired of huge cattle herds trampling their crops, pressured the legislature to ban trail herds. They succeeded in obtaining this ban in 1885. This law ended a famous era in the West's history. The cattle industry moved farther west, into Colorado, Wyoming, and Montana, but the towns in those states never achieved the notoriety of the Kansas cowtowns. Changes in raising and shipping cattle in the late 1880s greatly reduced the problems of town law enforcement, and the trail-riding cowhand and gunfighter-lawman passed into legend.

The physical environment and the underdeveloped nature of society briefly gave western law enforcement a character all its own. And the legends which emerged from that brief period helped shape American perceptions about law and order. "Frontier Justice"—with its assumptions of quick, infallible solutions to complex problems—became a powerful symbol for people frustrated by the complexities of real-life police work. But beneath the legends Western peace officers were quickly influenced by the growing trend toward police reform after 1900.

## SUGGESTED READINGS

The history of Western law enforcement is so encrusted with legend that students should first develop an understanding of general Western history before attempting to sample the vast literature on this subject. A good general history is Robert V. Hine, *The American West: An Interpretive History* (Boston: Little, Brown, 1973). Frank R. Prassel, *The Western Peace Officer: A Legacy of Law and Order* (Norman: University of Oklahoma Press, 1972) is a valuable overview, and Joseph G. Rosa, *The Gunfighter: Man or Myth?* (Norman: University of Oklahoma Press, 1969) is a careful examination of an enduring legend. Glenn Shirley, *West of Hell's Fringe: Crime, Criminals, and the Federal Peace Officer in Oklahoma Territory, 1889-1907* (Norman: University of Oklahoma Press, 1978) is a good example of the more traditional approach to lawmen and outlaws, while Robert R. Dykstra, *The Cattle Towns* (New York: Alfred A. Knopf, 1968) is a superb book on a legendary topic.

# 7

# The Triumph of Reform: Police Professionalism 1920-1965

**P**olice departments changed dramatically between 1920 and 1965. The nineteenth century police had emphasized a flexible approach to law enforcement as a way of dealing with the diversity and conflicts of urban society. This approach had allowed local politicians to dictate police policies, department organization, and personnel selection. After 1920, new reformers campaigned successfully to alter the philosophy, organization, and personnel of police departments across the nation. An emphasis on uniform standards replaced the previous reliance on flexibility. Uniform enforcement policies drastically reduced the role politicians formerly had in police affairs because the new emphasis undermined the politician's role as mediator between behavior and the law. Changes in departmental organization also diminished political meddling. Reformers replaced the old, decentralized precincts with highly centralized bureaucracies. Ward politicians therefore had less influence over the administrative decisions which affected their communities. At the same time, centralization increased the power and importance of police chiefs. Finally, the reformers were able to increase the quality of policemen by imposing more rigorous educational and physical standards, and by introducing more effective training. The combined changes in the philosophy, organization, and personnel of the police created a new approach to law enforcement which was significantly different from the nineteenth century's approach.

All of these changes were the consequences of a single idea: the desire to make policing a profession. There was, and is, considerable debate over whether policing can ever be a profession, but the reformers responsible for transforming the police after 1920 had no doubts. They thought that policing *ought* to be a profession, and set out to make it one. In order to achieve that goal, the reformers sought one thing above all else: autonomy. Freedom from outside interference in departmental affairs was absolutely vital. Protected by this freedom, police officials would have the ability to correct many of the defects in their organizations and personnel which prevented the public from regarding policing as a profession.

The new reform campaign owed a great deal to three separate developments: 1) the influence of European achievements on law enforcement; 2) changes in society and politics in American cities after 1920; and 3) the emergence of a new kind of police reform movement. Each development made fundamental contributions to the emergence of a professional police in the twentieth century. In fact, professionalization would have been impossible without them and the quest for police autonomy would have failed.

### European Achievement: Criminalistics

Europeans pioneered in the application of scientific methods to police work. Their progress in this area was due to the special characteristics of continental police administration and to the impact of science on late nineteenth century life. With few exceptions, the national government in each European country controlled the police departments of every large city. Policemen served their central, not their local, governments, and had far greater powers to interfere in the lives of ordinary people than was the case in England or America. Department officials belonged to the national civil service, and therefore had no political allegiances within the cities which would interfere with their duties. Furthermore, these officials did not obtain their jobs after years of service as patrolmen. They were university graduates who usually had training as army officers or lawyers before they became police officials. As professional civil servants who had broad theoretical knowledge about law enforcement, these men were committed to efficient, effective policing.

As university graduates, these officials had been exposed to a wide variety of advances in science. By the middle of the nineteenth century sciences such as biology, zoology, and geology had captured the attention of most informed Europeans. Major theories, such as Charles Darwin's ideas about natural selection, undermined the dominant explanations about the nature and progress of mankind. Whatever one thought of the new theories, there was no denying that science and scientists suddenly enjoyed tremendous prestige. Their work caused a major change in the way people thought. European police officials joined in the general enthusiasm for the scientific method. They read widely in many areas, such as anthropology, biology, and chemistry, for solutions to practical problems in law enforcement. In effect, these officials became amateur scientists seeking to advance knowledge within their particular profession.

Among the practical problems facing police officials at the time, none were more important than the investigation and prosecution of crime and criminals. Both problems had become critical because there were almost no guidelines for identifying suspects, assembling evidence at a crime scene, and presenting cases in court. Criminals often escaped detection or punishment through police ineptitude. The two most important men who worked on these problems were Alphonse Bertillon and Hans Gross. During the 1880s these two men founded the modern police science of criminalistics.

Bertillon (1853-1914) became the more widely known of these two amateur police scientists. He was born to a middle-class French family whose father, a doctor, dabbled with statistics and anthropology. These subjects influenced Bertillon's own intellectual development and gave him some preparation for his first job in the Paris Prefecture of Police. Shortly thereafter promotion to records clerk marked the beginning of a brilliant career.

His new job required Bertillon to record the descriptions of all prisoners being held by the Paris Police. It did not take long for him to develop a contempt for the chaotic system in use at the time. His familiarity with the ideas and methods of anthropology made him aware of the appalling state of the basic information in these files. Uniform standards for describing and identifying criminals simply did not exist.

Bertillon remedied this situation. In 1878 he began devoting much of his time to developing a more systematic descriptive method. His goal was to identify individual, repeat offenders so that the judicial system could deal with this class of criminals more effectively. After years of work, Bertillon finally made his first positive identification of a recidivist in 1883. Further research perfected his methods, and in 1885 he published *Identification Anthropométique (Anthropometric Identification)*, a landmark in the development of criminalistics. For the first time in the history of law enforcement, the police had the ability to identify individual criminals by means of their physical characteristics.

The Bertillon System had four components: precise physical measurements; precise notations on the location of distinguishing features like scars; a photograph; and, later, fingerprints. In an effort to simplify

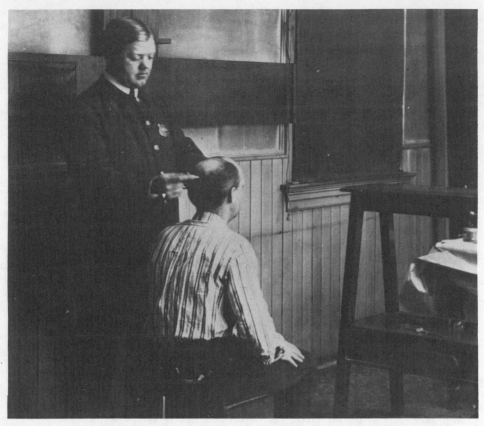

A demonstration of how to take Bertillon measurements. St. Louis World's Fair, 1904. *Courtesy of St. Louis Police Library.*

Bertillon measurements of a prostitute. *Courtesy of the Missouri Historical Society.*

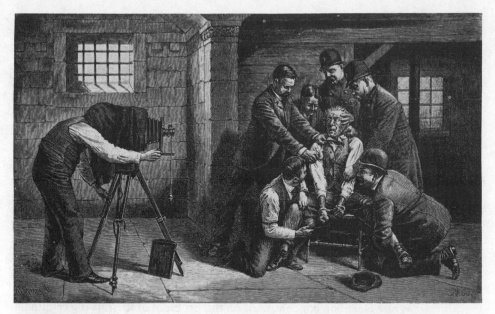

Criminals were not particularly happy about the developing science of identification.

And policemen seemed equally unenthusiastic about the new science of criminalistics.

the system, Bertillon eventually devised eleven key physical measurements grouped into three general categories (the entire body; the head; the appendages). He also invented several standardized instruments to promote uniform recording procedures. Although pictures of offenders had been in use for some time, Bertillon standardized the types of photographs (full front; full profile). During the 1890s he incorporated fingerprints into his system because they represented one more piece of physical evidence.

By 1900 the Bertillon System had become the standard method for classifying criminal records in Europe and America. But Bertillon's contribution to criminalistics did not rest solely upon his famous system. He also had a number of important ideas for improving the collection and analysis of evidence. Among other things, Bertillon introduced the use of photography to preserve a crime scene; he developed a means for preserving footprints; and he advocated handwriting analysis as a crucial tool in investigations. These ideas were important steps in the development of police laboratories where the physical evidence of a crime could be subjected to scientific analysis.

While Bertillon concentrated on the problem of identifying criminals, Hans Gross devoted most of his time to the difficulties of gathering and interpreting evidence. Gross (1847-1915) was the son of an Austrian army administration officer. After completing his formal education, and earning a Doctor of Jurisprudence degree in 1870, Gross became an examining justice, a court official responsible for the detection of crime.

As a court prosecutor, Gross soon learned about the inadequacies of ordinary patrolmen and detectives as state witnesses in criminal trials. He discovered that their only resources in solving cases were individual shrewdness and practical experience, a combination of skills not every officer possessed. Furthermore, policemen had no systematic methods for dealing with physical evidence. In fact, they frequently overlooked important clues or failed to appreciate their significance. During the 1870s Gross searched for solutions to these problems, reading widely to familiarize himself with the latest scientific theories and methods of his era.

Gross published the results of his studies in 1883, in *Handbuch für Untersuchungsrichter als System der Kriminalistik (Manual for the Examining Magistrate: A System of Criminalistics)*. This seminal work was based on two assumptions: 1) the police should become familiar with the psychology of criminal behavior; and 2) the police should adopt any technical and scientific procedures which might be useful in analyzing a crime scene and its evidence. The second assumption became the basis of modern criminalistics. Every chapter dealt with a major issue in a systematic fashion. Gross wrote in considerable detail about the proper qualifications for police investigators, and he provided the first explanation of the appropriate techniques for analyzing a crime scene. Other chapters described the kinds of special equipment an investigator needed and discussed the role of experts in criminal cases. Gross also wrote about the importance of bloodstains and other physical evidence. His book was so thorough that it remains significant after nearly a century.

Having placed crime detection on a scientific basis, Gross next helped make criminalistics a respected subject for advanced study. Between 1898 and 1914 several European universities established professorships in scientific crime detection. Gross held several of these appointments before returning to his hometown to accept a professorship at the University of Graz in 1905. Later, in 1912, he opened one of the first Criminalistic Institutes, an idea which spread quickly to other universities in Lausanne, Rome, Bucharest, and Vienna. Gross and other pioneers in criminalistics trained dozens of students in this new field, and as these graduates took positions in law enforcement they spread the doctrine of scientific police work. Their expertise and availability made it possible for many European cities to establish police laboratories prior to 1914. Thanks to the efforts of men like Bertillon and Gross, European police were thoroughly committed to scientific approaches to their work by World War I.

## European Achievements: Fingerprinting

Bertillon based his famous system on the assumption that every individual's physical features are unique. Anthropological studies at the time supported this assumption, but unfortunately they were wrong. In 1904 federal prison officials at Leavenworth discovered two convicts who had precisely the same measurements. This discovery undermined the Bertillon System and created the need for a more accurate identification method. Although it had not yet been widely accepted, the solution to this problem had already been developed. Dactyloscopy, the technique of collecting, classifying, and identifying fingerprints, was destined to become yet another major contribution Europeans made to the emergence of police science.

Amateur scientists were once again in the forefront of criminalistic innovations. Dr. Henry Faulds and Sir William J. Herschel pioneered the study of fingerprints. Faulds was an English Presbyterian minister who worked as a missionary in Japan; Herschel spent his career as a British civil servant in India. Neither man had any training in law enforcement. They developed their interest in fingerprints through highly specialized circumstances related to their work, and neither knew of the other's research for many years.

Faulds (1843-1930) began collecting fingerprints as a hobby during the 1870s. In 1879 the Japanese police asked Faulds to try his luck at identifying a burglar from some fingerprints he had left. Shortly afterward, Faulds did so. He then exceeded that feat by developing a method for lifting latent prints and using the evidence he collected to identify yet another thief. Convinced that he now had developed a scientific means for crime detection, Faulds published an article about his research in the prestigious journal *Nature* in 1880. He thereby became the first person to recognize the use of fingerprints for identifying individuals in criminal cases.

Independently of Faulds and at the same time, William Herschel (1883-1917) arrived at similar conclusions from a different perspective. Herschel had a practical problem to solve in his work as a magistrate: he needed a way to prevent fraud in settling native claims against the British government. He accomplished this by using an Asian superstition that manual contact with a business contract created a taboo against its violation. Claimants were required to acknowledge payments by affixing their partial, inked prints to legal papers. In 1877 he proposed that the British record the prints of all Indian prisoners as a way to discourage recidivism. The prison officials rejected his idea, and Herschel retired in 1879 without pursuing the matter further.

Except for a bitter fight between Herschel and Faulds over which man had "discovered" fingerprints, nothing significant occurred in the use of this new idea until 1888. Then Sir Francis Galton, one of England's most renowned scientists, received an invitation to lecture about the Bertillon System at a leading scientific institute. In preparing for his speech, Galton investigated fingerprints as an alternative method of identification. What he found intrigued him. Galton obtained Herschel's collection of prints and used it to prove two critical ideas which the amateur scientists had only asserted. First, Galton determined that an individual's prints do not change over his lifetime. Second, he demonstrated that each individual's prints are unique. Galton then made his last important contribution by devising the first system for classifying prints. This system appeared in his classic book, *Fingerprints,* published in 1892. As a result of Galton's work, Scotland Yard in 1894 adopted a modified version of the Bertillon System which included prints.

After some further refinements, European police quickly accepted fingerprints as an important tool. Elsewhere, progress was much slower. Argentina, in 1896, actually became the first nation to adopt fingerprints as the official means for identifying criminals. This achievement was due to Juan Vucetich, an Austrian immigrant who developed his own classification system independently of other researchers. The American police lagged behind, although an important breakthrough occurred in 1904 at the St. Louis World's Fair, where Scotland Yard detective John Ferrier demonstrated fingerprinting to an interested group of police officials. The St. Louis police promptly established the first fingerprint bureau in the United States. But the prevailing philosophy of policing, which sacrificed professionalism to politics, hindered progress. Too few policemen had a commitment to improving their work by scientific means.

European advances in criminalistics had created a credible basis for connecting law enforcement to science by 1914. This was a major contribution to the development of police professionalism. European police officials rapidly adopted criminalistics because the traditions of centralized administration and responsible civil service gave them the authority and ability to do so. American police reformers would eventually capitalize on these achievements too. Once they acquired power, these reformers would increase the prestige of policing by incorporating scientific precision, impartiality, and decisiveness into crime detection. The American public would learn to respect lawmen who successfully used this European heritage. But improvement in the image and performance of the police awaited other developments within the United States.

## Society and Politics in American Cities

Urban America underwent extraordinary changes between 1920 and 1965, which affected the ways Americans lived, worked, and thought. While none of these developments involved the police directly, they reshaped the society which law enforcement served. After 1920 a new social and economic environment would encourage the police to adopt a different approach to their work.

The American economy shifted its emphasis during the 1920s. Prior to World War I businessmen had developed the nation's natural resources, transformed agriculture, built a national transportation system, and created the world's most productive iron and steel industry. After 1920, businessmen turned to the production of consumer goods. Factories which made consumer products needed large land areas to accommodate their assembly lines and sought space on the edges of cities. Workers followed the factories into suburbia. The central cities therefore lost thousands of jobs and residents.

Cities also lost many of their inhabitants because of suburbanization. By the mid 1960s nearly 70 percent of all Americans would be living in metropolitan areas. Within those areas, the most rapid growth occurred in the suburbs. The American dream of homeownership was fulfilled primarily by buying a house in a new subdivision outside the central city. By 1970 suburbanites outnumbered city residents.

As the upper classes moved to the suburbs, they left behind people who were increasingly unlike them. Dramatic changes in immigration, and new trends in population movements within America, produced a very different type of inner-city resident. After Congress severely restricted European immigration beginning in 1921, thousands of Spanish-speaking immigrants from Mexico, Puerto Rico, and Cuba streamed into the United States. Like the Europeans before them, most of these people settled in cities, in neighborhoods close to the downtowns.

Black Americans joined the cityward migration. Job opportunities attracted them to cities, beginning in World War I. Thousands, and then millions of blacks left rural areas in search of better wages, working conditions, and living standards. Northern factories hired large numbers of them, while others found employment in hotels, restaurants, nightclubs, and other booming service industries. By the mid-1960s black Americans had essentially relocated themselves. Nearly 75 percent of them lived in cities. Like the Spanish-speaking immigrants, blacks concentrated in the inner-city neighborhoods.

These new city residents shared four things in common: they were nonwhite, unskilled, poor, and powerless. Mexicans, Puerto Ricans, Cubans, and blacks would be subjected to enormous discrimination. Their ability to improve themselves would be restricted because whites would systematically exclude them from high paying jobs, good schools, and decent housing. Economic changes reinforced social discrimination. These newcomers had arrived in cities at a time of decreasing demand for unskilled labor. American industry now needed well-trained, highly skilled workers, and nonwhites (with some exceptions) did not have those qualifications. Poverty had driven these people to seek opportunities in the cities, but for many of them poverty would remain a way of life. And until the 1960s blacks and Spanish-speaking Americans would be almost powerless to help themselves. Whites dominated urban politics and paid little attention to the needs of the new inner-city residents.

Urban politics had to adjust to two basic developments after 1920. First, the organization of politics altered. Secondly, voters' expectations and attitudes changed. Both changes resulted from the ways urban society and economics evolved after World War I. Politicians did not become less important, nor did they necessarily become less powerful, but they did have to modify their behavior to deal with new situations and ideas.

Metropolitan fragmentation was one important trend which affected the organization of politics after 1920. Suburbanites increasingly incorporated as separate political units. In the long run, this fragmentation meant an enormous duplication of services and a decline in per capita tax revenues in the central cities. Politicians therefore found it nearly impossible to organize effective solutions to problems shared by all the communities within a metropolitan area.

The use of experts also affected politics. During the Progressive era many Americans became convinced that cities could improve their services by employing people specifically trained to perform certain tasks. After 1920, cities across the nation began hiring thousands of experts who complicated the lives of politicians in two ways. First, the use of experts deprived politicians of valuable patronage. Secondly, municipal departments run by experts were harder to control. Experts regarded politicians as ignorant meddlers who should be resisted whenever possible.

Changes in voter expectations and attitudes, which also affected politics, reflected the increasing importance of middle-class values which stressed efficiency, honesty, and economy as the basis of sound government. Until the 1920s urban politics had been notorious for being so totally opposite to these values. Corruption, inefficiency, and excessive costs certainly did not disappear from local government. But compared to the nineteenth century, these problems became less common. Political organizations and officeholders had to make serious efforts to implement the standards which the largest voting block in the cities demanded.

The predominance of middle-class values and the deconcentration of political power in a transformed metropolis contributed substantially to the emergence of a new model for law enforcement. Expertise, honesty, and efficiency were the basis for professionalism. These ideals had shaped the development of many professions prior to World War I, and the progressives had laid the groundwork for applying these standards to police work. After 1920 the concept of professionalism could be used as the framework for police reform because middle-class Americans understood its advantages and supported its application to law enforcement. Urban politicians no longer had the ability or the desire to block this development. Reformers would now acquire the independence to reshape police departments according to their own desires.

## Police Reform, 1920-39: Initial Developments

Police professionalism did not immediately become the dominant model in law enforcement. Professionalism would triumph only after nearly three decades of struggle. In these initial years, progress came in two forms: 1) efforts to redefine the police mission and 2) changes forced upon departments by the Great Depression.

The effort to redefine the police mission concentrated on a single idea: crime fighting. It did not matter that the police had a long and important historical role in community relations work or that they spent a great deal of their time with mundane affairs. What mattered was the public's *image* of the police. The average citizen who knew nothing about routine police work did know about crime. Crime concerned and frequently frightened him. In order to change their image the police realized they needed to emphasize the dramatic aspects of their work. They set out to do exactly that.

During the 1930s J. Edgar Hoover, as director of the Federal Bureau of Investigation, did a great deal to advance the crime-fighter image. A variety of gangs and individuals were making spectacular names as bank robbers and desparadoes. Hoover, in a stroke of genius, labeled these people "public enemies" and ordered his agents to hunt them down. Within a few years the FBI violently ended the careers of John Dillinger, Baby Face Nelson, Pretty Boy Floyd, and Ma Barker. The nationwide pursuit of these criminals, followed by their demise in an orgy of bloodletting, captivated the public. Hoover used this campaign as a means to make the FBI the most important law enforcement agency in America. But his efforts reinforced the growing image of all policemen as crime fighters. (Hoover and the FBI are treated in more detail in Chapter 11.)

The police also sought scientific support for their new image. Fingerprinting had been making slow progress since its initial appearance before World War I. The International Association of Chiefs of Police lobbied unsuccessfully for years to establish a national bureau which would collect and analyze prints. Progress had been somewhat better in the states. By 1921 five states had established identification bureaus. Then in 1924 Congress finally authorized such a bureau within the Justice Department. Following this victory, the IACP, with Hoover's help, increased its efforts to establish a nationwide system of fingerprint agencies. By 1931 almost half the states had done so. During the thirties Hoover began offering the FBI's services in identifying prints and in training local officers in the use of this kind of evidence. The United States had finally accepted fingerprints as the basis for criminal identification.

Science and technology bolstered the police crime-fighting image in other ways as well. The St. Valentine's Day Massacre prompted a group of Chicago businessmen to establish the nation's first crime detection laboratory at Northwestern University in 1929. Three years later the FBI founded its laboratory, setting an example which encouraged several state and local governments to follow suit. After ignoring criminalistics for so long, the American police were moving rapidly to match and exceed European progress in this area. Radios and automobiles introduced policemen to the wonders of technology. The first radio patrol car appeared in Detroit in 1929. During the thirties police departments across the country largely abolished foot patrols, put their men in cars, and coordinated their activities through radio communications.

Police officials rapidly became devoted to scientific and technological innovations because these developments had the greatest immediate potential to transform the policeman's image. Criminalistics helped overcome the notion that the average cop was a dumb brute who beat confessions out of prisoners. Scientific investigations required intelligence and skill, not brute force. Patrol cars and radios made the police more mobile and more able to respond rapidly to calls for help. Gone (supposedly) were the patrolmen who slept on their beats and who were never around when needed. Technology had made the police more effective and efficient. Reality did not always match the new image, but a public long accustomed to the old-fashioned, corrupt, incompetent cop was impressed by the change and delighted with the idea of a scientific crime fighter.

The Great Depression also made important contributions to the growth of reform. Financial problems overcame political opposition to a major reform objective: greater departmental centralization. During the 1930s the number of precinct stations in most cities declined significantly. Police chiefs, inspired by the example of European administrators, seized this opportunity to increase their power. They switched more men to patrol car duty and proliferated the use of specialized squads which operated from central headquarters. More patrolmen came under the direct orders of headquarters personnel who used the radio network to monitor their activities more closely. Membership in specialized squads also enhanced supervisory controls, since these men now answered directly to a superior officer rather than to a ward politician.

Hard times also made more qualified police recruits available. For the first time in history, police work became attractive to men from the middle class who had better educations than the average, old-style patrolman. The presence of these recruits enabled administrators to find men who could understand the importance of criminalistics and who would make good commanders. In addition, police chiefs now had the excuse they needed to raise intelligence and educational standards for applicants. Men who were less-well-trained now found it more difficult to obtain positions, or, if they were already on a department's roster, they found it harder to win promotions. The Depression therefore contributed to an upgrading in the overall quality of police personnel.

## Police Reform 1939-65: The New Professionals

By the end of the 1930s the police had made considerable progress toward establishing their claim to professional status. One last obstacle remained: the absence of an effective national leadership which could achieve autonomy from politics. The initial period of reform prepared the way for the emergence of men who would assume leadership roles after 1939. Most of these men rose through the ranks of local departments to become police chiefs. Some came from the FBI, where professionalism had received an early and enthusiastic boost from Hoover. All had one thing in common: they had chosen a career in law enforcement at a time of widespread experimentation in policing. They therefore experienced at firsthand the impact of the crime-fighting image, scientific detection, and technology on the public's attitude toward the police.

Orlando W. Wilson and William H. Parker became the two most prominent spokesmen for the new professionalism. Wilson learned police reform while a patrolman under August Vollmer at Berkeley in 1921. As police chief in Wichita, Kansas, beginning in 1928, Wilson transformed the police force. He sought more qualified, better educated recruits. At the same time, Wilson began a program to upgrade their training. His national reputation began to develop when he convinced the Kansas League of Municipalities to create a statewide police training school in 1931, and appoint him the school's director. Prominent reformers from around the country lectured to policemen-students about the latest innovations in their work.

Technology fascinated Wilson; he became a leading, if controversial, expert in its use. During his term as Wichita's police chief he attracted widespread attention by conducting the first systematic study of patrol cars. He decided that single-man squad cars were both feasible and necessary because they fulfilled the requirements of professionalism. He argued that single-man cars were efficient, effective, and economical —three key ideas in the professional model emerging in the 1930s. Brushing aside patrolmen's complaints about their personal safety when they had no partner to depend upon, Wilson claimed that the public received better service with single-man cars. This idea aroused considerable interest. The ensuing debate, which continued for the next four decades, placed Wilson at the center of an important controversy which enhanced his growing reputation.

By 1939 Wilson had achieved national prominence, but he had also irritated too many Wichita politicians for the last time. His political support gone, Wilson resigned as a police chief and accepted a professorship in police administration at the University of California at Berkeley. College training for policemen was a relatively new idea in the United States. The first complete police curriculum was offered at San Jose State College only in 1931. Congress helped popularize this notion by authorizing funds for vocational training in law enforcement in 1936. By the end of the decade several thousand officers were attending classes, but the outbreak of war halted this promising beginning. Wilson, though, was now in a position to become one of the pioneers in college programs for policemen. After World War II ended, he founded the first professional School of Criminology. As dean of this school, Wilson became an extremely influential reformer. The essence of his ideas summarized the basic ingredients of the new professionalism: 1) complete independence from politics; 2) a highly centralized command structure; 3) a college-educated rank and file; 4) the application of the most modern technology available to police work; and 5) absolute obedience and minimum discretion at the level of patrolmen. Wilson's students spread his doctrine across the nation. More than one hundred graduates of his school eventually achieved important positions in local law enforcement and implemented his ideas.

In 1960 Wilson carried the reform banner to Chicago, a city notorious for its boss system and its resistance to police professionalism. Typically, Wilson demanded complete freedom from political interference as a condition for accepting the offer to become chief of police. Ward heelers howled, but Mayor Richard Daley agreed. For the next seven years Daley consistently supported Wilson in any controversies which arose. Operating with the protection of Chicago's most powerful politician, Wilson proceeded to implement reform. He began by re-organizing the department's administrative structure. Precincts were consolidated into new units called districts. Wilson then insisted on a precise chain of command to control his men. Superior officers and their orders had to be obeyed, or individuals faced a variety of disciplinary actions. At police headquarters, Wilson reduced the staff and sent many officers back to the field. He restricted the number of people who reported directly to him by creating a small number of assistant-to-the-chief positions. Each assistant handled a particular administrative area, leaving Wilson free to deal with general policy and further reforms. Technological change became a hallmark of his administration. Wilson introduced the latest communications equipment. Experiments with this technology enabled him to distribute the department's personnel more efficiently. Eventually, the police could respond to a call for aid within five minutes. Wilson retired in 1967, generally praised by grateful Chicagoans who were convinced that he had professionalized their police.

William H. Parker's fame rested on his career as chief of police in Los Angeles. Although he was not a protegée of Vollmer, many of Parker's career experiences paralleled Wilson's. Parker began as a patrolman in Los Angeles in 1927. He demonstrated an early commitment to professionalism by earning a law degree and by becoming a member of the California bar in 1930. An adept politician, Parker used his legal training to advance his career. By 1934 he was the department's trial prosecutor and an assistant to the chief. After serving in the army during World War II, Parker gained invaluable administrative experience by participating in the reorganization of the police in several German cities from 1945 to 1947. Home again, he graduated from Northwestern University's Traffic Management School. Returning to the Los Angeles Police Department (L.A.P.D.), he became an inspector of the traffic division. Parker underscored his commitment to professionalism in 1949 when he became a deputy chief in charge of prosecuting dishonest cops.

Parker became police chief in 1950 when a scandal forced the mayor to find someone with credentials in the new professionalism. Unlike Wilson, Parker assumed office without securing immediate freedom from political interference. He had to fight to achieve department autonomy. An uproar over charges of police brutality gave him the opportunity he sought in 1951. Parker conducted an intensive investigation which resulted in the dismissal or punishment of over forty officers. Shortly afterward Parker turned over some evidence of vice-squad corruption to prosecutors before a scandal erupted. Both incidents demonstrated to the public that he could handle internal problems without interference. Thereafter Parker had all the political independence he needed. In fact, he became a formidable political figure who used his power to advance reform and to undermine criticism of his department.

Firmly in power, Parker launched a campaign to transform the L.A.P.D. His greatest success, so typical of the new professionalism, came in administrative reorganization. The command structure was simplified. Then Parker combined several headquarters divisions into a single Bureau of Administration which provided general services (planning, internal investigations, etc.) to more specialized bureaus. Parker was especially fond of planning, another mark of the new professionalism. He used planning as a major propaganda weapon in his campaign to increase public respect and admiration for the police. Planners had instructions to implement middle-class values as the basis for further reforms. They worked hard to increase police efficiency and to reduce costs. Every savings, every new indicator of efficiency, became the subject of press releases in Parker's continuous public relations campaign.

Efficiency came in several forms. Parker aggressively sought ways to get every possible policeman on the streets. He freed some 200 men for patrol duty by forcing the county sheriff to assume his responsibilities for guarding prisoners. After another battle, the California Highway Patrol took over traffic control duties on the freeways crisscrossing Los Angeles. That freed more men for other work. Parker also adopted one-man patrol cars, a move which allowed him to enhance police visibility by increasing the number of cars on the streets.

On a more mundane level, changes in booking procedures and traffic control also reduced costs and made more effective use of personnel.

Parker also made rigorous personnel selection and training a major characteristic of the L.A.P.D. Less than ten percent of the applicants who passed the required civil service exam actually were accepted as recruits. Higher standards of physical fitness, intelligence, and scholastic attainments weeded out many men. Others failed the psychiatric examinations which Parker now required as part of the screening process. Once accepted, recruits attended a thirteen-week academy where a rigorous physical program, rigid discipline, and intensive study in basic skills and criminal law caused many more to drop out. Those who survived soon learned that they had to maintain their high performance levels on the job. Parker thus molded an image of a tough, competent, polite, and effective officer by controlling recruitment. During the 1950s this image made the L.A.P.D. the model for reform across the nation. By the time of his death in 1966 Parker had become one of the most prominent reformers of his generation.

The 1950s marked a turning point in the history of professionalism. Following major scandals, reformers came to power across the nation. Politicians had real choices between the traditional and new models of policing because a number of professional police reformers were available for the first time. With an enraged middle class threatening their livelihoods, the politicians began opting for reform. Robert V. Murray became police chief of Washington, D.C., in 1951; Wyman W. Vernon assumed the helm in Oakland, California, in 1956; James Slavin arrived in Denver in 1962; and Edmund L. McNamara took over Boston's police in the early sixties. Many other cities also acquired chiefs dedicated to the new model of policing. By 1965 the gospel of professionalism had triumphed.

## SUGGESTED READINGS

The history of twentieth century law enforcement is just beginning to attract the attention of American scholars. Samuel Walker, *A Critical History of Police Reform: The Emergence of Professionalism* (Lexington: Lexington Books, 1977) and Robert M. Fogelson, *Big City Police* (Cambridge: Harvard University Press, 1977) approach police reform from somewhat different perspectives, but both are excellent studies for students to consult for further elaboration of the themes of professionalism. William J. Bopp assesses Wilson's career in *"O. W.": O. W. Wilson and the Search for a Police Profession* (Port Washington: Kennikat Press, 1977). Joseph G. Woods, "The Progressives and the Police: Urban Reform and the Professionalization of the Los Angeles Police" (unpublished Ph.D., University of California, Los Angeles, 1973) is the only full-length biography of a modern police department. Woods deals extensively with William Parker's career in his closing chapters. European scholars have done most of the work on the history of criminalistics and its pioneers. Henry T. F. Rhodes, *Alphonse Bertillon* (London: Harrap, 1956), Douglas G. Browne and Alan Brock, *Fingerprints: Fifty Years of Scientific Crime Detection* (London: G. G. Harrap, 1953), and George W. Wilton, *Fingerprints: History, Law and Romance* (London: W. Hodge and Company, 1938) are all useful works in English. Shorter introductions to criminalistics can be found in articles on Bertillon, Gross, and fingerprinting in two edited books: Hermann Mannheim, ed., *Pioneers in Criminology* (2nd ed.; Montclair, N.J.: Patterson Smith, 1972), and Philip J. Stead, *Pioneers in Policing* (Montclair, N.J.: Patterson Smith, 1977).

# 8

# Varieties of Criminal Behavior: The 20th Century

**A**lthough the crime-fighting image favored by advocates of police professionalism was useful in promoting change, it also posed some problems. Police reformers implied that professionalism would, among other things, reduce crime. But this claim rested on shaky foundations. Crime rates, as well as changes in specific criminal activities, respond to broad social trends, not just to police intervention. In order to understand the limitations upon police reform, therefore, it is important to consider what we presently know about crime in the twentieth century.

In general, the same sorts of professional thieves and street criminals who had harassed citizens for a hundred years or more continued their depredations. Economic prosperity, the unequal distribution of wealth, and social prejudices, as usual, offered criminals innumerable opportunities and incentives for their behavior. Techniques altered sometimes, but the objectives of these malefactors remained constant. Major social conflicts between minorities and the dominant society prompted several outbreaks of collective violence. Protests against economic and social injustice, and fierce resistance to such protests, formed the basis of these confrontations. The fact that all these activities, from petty theft to massive riot, were hardly new did not comfort its victims. A concern about crime therefore remained a major theme in modern America.

### Professional Crime

Thieves who steal for a living continued to plague American society throughout the twentieth century. As always, economic and social trends influenced both the specific nature of their crimes as well as their life-style. The increasing affluence of American society and the growth of a consumer economy spread material goods more widely than ever before. Professional thieves found in the diffusion of these goods a steady source of income. New business practices, changes in the age structure of society, and new social developments created additional possibilities for criminal activities. In order to take advantage of these possibilities, most professional criminals had to "hustle" for a living. They could not afford to specialize since they did not know when changing conditions would produce new opportunities or foreclose old gimmicks. Hence the average professional constantly engaged in a wide variety of crimes.

Confidence games are an excellent example of the ways professional thieves adjust to changing circumstances. The period from the mid-1890s to the 1920s was probably the heyday of large-scale con games. For approximately thirty years con men fleeced a host of victims in various big cons. These swindles were based primarily on fake stock market exchanges or fake bookmaking operations. Victims believed they were obtaining inside information about stock deals and race results and bet huge sums. In order to deal with these gullible, wealthy victims, con men created elaborate organizations in such cities as Los Angeles, Denver, Kansas City, Atlanta, and Miami. Huge scores, sometimes amounting to $100,000 from a single victim, meant these thieves could afford expensive life-styles and the best in police protection. Early in the 1920s, though, hard times began to appear. Several crusading district attorneys prosecuted many of these con men and publicized their techniques in order to educate the general public. The postal inspectors joined the attack and pursued big con operations relentlessly. By 1938 the inspectors had broken up the last of the major gangs, and an important era in underworld history ended.

Although vigorous law enforcement had undermined one of the most lucrative operations ever devised, con men did not disappear. Instead, they sought new opportunities. The changing age structure of the population during the late 1940s and 1950s provided several enticing possibilities. At that time, the number of old people and widows was increasing because of enhanced life expectancy. Con men victimized this population in at least two ways. First, many senior citizens on pensions were looking for ways to supplement their incomes. Secondly, many were lonely. Con men invented work-at-home and lonely-hearts schemes to bilk these people. The amounts con men earned through these swindles was not particularly large in each case, but the cumulative totals could provide a comfortable living. When these ploys attracted too much attention, especially from postal inspectors, confidence games apparently entered a period of decline in the 1960s. Recently, however, variations on very old games are reappearing, again victimizing older citizens. The drop game, which dates back to the early nineteenth century, seems to be enjoying a vogue in the late seventies. Confidence operators (who now are frequently women) pretend to find a valuable package and then persuade a pre-selected victim that he or she should share in this good fortune. Of course, the thieves ask for a cash advance as a gesture of good faith, and they quickly disappear once the money is in their hands. Victims typically lose $2,000 to $5,000 in these games, proving that inventive swindlers can always make a good living.

Armed robbery by professional criminals also showed some distinctive trends. The historical data available on this crime indicate that there have been two periods of especially intense activity: from the end of World War I to the mid-1930s; and from the late 1960s to the present. Different conditions account for each period. Armed robbery had not been very common in nineteenth century cities because money had not been especially well protected. Professional thieves had achieved technological skills superior to safes, and they therefore preferred burglary to robbery because it was less risky. But more effective safeguards gradually emerged by the twentieth century. Financial institutions purchased safes which were now so well designed that they were temporarily impregnable. Banks redesigned their interiors to make access to cash storage areas much more difficult. They also installed alarms connected to local precinct stations. But these institutions, and others such as savings and loan associations, payroll offices, and the financial mail, remained tempting targets because the economy still depended heavily on cash transactions. Criminals therefore faced the problems of striking swiftly and efficiently to forestall time-consuming resistance. Guns solved those problems. Firearms prompted obedience and discouraged heroics by the victims. Thus armed robbery, which had been a crime common in rural areas and small western towns in the late nineteenth century, came to the cities. Immediately after World War I armed robbery reached nearly epidemic proportions. Between 1920 and 1921, for example, thieves committed thirty-six mail robberies netting them over six million dollars.

This first wave of armed robberies ended when the risks involved became greater than the potential rewards. Federal postal inspectors were especially effective against gangs which robbed the mails. (Several of these criminals also committed robberies of local banks and payroll offices as well; hence federal intervention contributed to solving local crimes.) By 1933 the inspectors had eliminated the last major threat, the Roger Touhy gang in Chicago. Then legislation in 1933 placing banks under federal protection brought the FBI into the struggle. Although the major threat to banks had already ended, and the Depression sharply constricted the amount of cash available, the FBI made a reputation by pursuing robbery gangs which made mediocre livings off small-town banks. Professional armed robbers in general seemed to have temporarily switched to other activities because hard times drastically reduced the average score and because the FBI was developing a fearsome reputation by killing off a few notorious bandits.

Changes in the post-World War II business habits encouraged a resurgence in armed robberies. Many businessmen had ceased keeping large amounts of cash on hand. Instead they arranged to have armored car companies transfer their cash receipts to local banks. Although these vehicles were built to cope with potential assaults, they were not invulnerable. Furthermore, they offered a tempting target because they carried more cash than the average thief could hope to steal in any single commercial robbery. Thieves demonstrated that they could deal with this challenge as early as 1950, when a group of robbers plundered a Brinks armored car in Boston. Such robberies remained infrequent, though, because of the difficulties involved and because there were easier targets available. The growth in air travel offered an example of an easier score. Businessmen began using air freight to ship lightweight, extremely valuable merchandise such as jewelry. Thieves started raiding such shipments as soon as they could learn airport routines and identify employees who would help them for a price. By the late 1960s airport robberies became another problem with which lawmen had to cope. Finally, suburban growth after World War II caused difficulties for banks which tried to offer convenient services to their customers. Bankers responded to the threat of losing business from suburbanites by opening branches around a metropolitan area. These branches emphasized relaxed atmospheres and courteous service. Unlike the formidable home offices, therefore, these branches were not well designed for protecting their contents. Furthermore, they were located near major highways. Armed robbers found these branch banks very easy targets, and a rash of robberies began in the late 1960s, continuing to the present time. (The average modern bank robber is not a professional criminal, but the risks of capture have decreased enough since the 1930s to attract a few professionals back into this activity.)

The art of picking pockets seems to be one professional crime which has entered into irreversible decline. "Class cannons" have apparently decreased from about 5,000 or 6,000 at the end of World War II to less than 600 in the mid-1970s. The reasons for this decline are far from clear. Although fewer people now carry large amounts of cash, they do carry credit cards, and there is a thriving illegal market for "plastic money." Problems with recruitment may be crucial to explaining the decline. This crime requires considerable skill, an ability to blend into a crowd, and a talent for close, if surreptitious contact with victims. For some reason pickpockets do not appear to be attracting younger criminals who have those qualities. It may be that younger professionals prefer other forms of theft because they are more lucrative, or it may be that picking pockets is no longer a high-status occupation in their opinion. Shoplifting is one crime which has fallen into disrepute among professionals. The same decline in status may have occurred for pickpockets—a development which would explain a lack of interest among younger, ambitious thieves. Whatever the reason, it seems clear that pickpockets are disappearing after centuries of activity.

Aside from pickpockets, most professional thieves appear to have adapted quite well to changing opportunities. Burglars learned new skills in forging checks and money orders once they found the cash kept in safes had declined dramatically. And they turned to residential burglary as a more reliable source of salable commodities. Such adjustments typify the resourcefulness of these criminals. Hustling to make a living by whatever means comes to hand, they continue to amaze and frustrate their victims and the police.

## Street Crime

Street crime continued to be a major problem in American cities as well. Like professional crime, much of this behavior differed little from nineteenth century patterns. Gangs roamed slum neighborhoods and engaged in a variety of deviant behaviors. Their activities continued to disturb ghetto residents as well as outsiders. Many of the poor followed long established precedents in expressing their anger or frustration by sudden violence. They attacked family and friends, sometimes with devastating results. Murder, assault, petty larceny, and amateur burglary therefore remained staples of slum life throughout the twentieth century. But there were some important changes within the basic framework of nonprofessional crime. The most disturbing changes involved an increase in violent crime (especially robbery) and a shift in the drug use patterns in American society.

Both of these developments appear to be related to the complex ways social changes affect individuals and groups. Unskilled labor, for example, was essential to America's rapid industrialization in the late nineteenth century. But it is increasingly less necessary to our modern, technologically sophisticated economy. People who have no skills therefore have major difficulties trying to find steady, decently paying work. Suburbanization after 1920 further complicated economic problems for these people. Large numbers of clerical and other jobs became available in the factories and shopping centers being built in suburbia. But the number of jobs available in the old central cities decreased, and unskilled workers did not have the resources to seek employment beyond the city limits. Social discrimination excluded many inner-city residents from moving to the suburbs where they would have been closer to the burgeoning job market. Prejudice also inhibited the development of solutions (such as work training programs) to the problems of the unskilled. Political changes reduced the ability of local politicians to help with city jobs and other favors. And, as more voters moved to the suburbs, politicians paid less attention to the needs of inner-city residents. Teenagers and young adults, who bore the brunt of these changes, responded in various ways which aggravated the problems of their local communities.

Street crimes by black teenagers in the 1930s and early 1940s demonstrate the havoc youths with few prospects for achievement could wreak on their communities. During the 1920s black neighborhoods in several cities had developed tenuous but important ties to white society. Jazz music, soul food, and other aspects of Negro culture had suddenly become popular. Whites flocked to speakeasies and restaurants in search of diversions and new experiences. These customs provided the basis for an emerging small business community within the ghettos, and for a time there seemed to be a good chance that this incipient growth would develop into an important economic activity. But teenage criminals ended this possibility. Muggings became common as whites explored ghetto entertainment. With the rise in these robberies, white customers began to shy away from black restaurants and nightclubs. By the mid-1940s, the threat of robbery had undermined a promising economic development in the ghetto. The demise of these black-owned businesses cost the ghettos an opportunity to create a "home industry" which would have been a source of jobs, income, and pride for local residents.

A second peak in teenage street crimes has more recently threatened the social fabric of black lower-class communities. More than economic development is at stake because the whole social structure of the ghettos seems in trouble. With the decline in restraints on criminal behavior since the early 1960s, violent robberies have been on the increase. The vast majority of victims are blacks; hence the surge in these robberies has increased the fear, frustration, and distrust in neighborhoods where hope was already in short supply. Money is often not particularly important to the perpetrators. Instead, many teenagers commit these crimes to acquire prestige among their peers. These youths are more concerned about their social status as tough characters than they are about the effect of these robberies on their communities.

Drug abuse has apparently become another means to establish social status. In the nineteenth century opium, morphine, and heroin were so widely used that Americans paid little attention to addicts. This situation changed dramatically early in the twentieth century. Reformers and law enforcement officials combined to criminalize drug abuse. The basic legislation accomplishing this, known as the Harrison Act, passed Congress in 1914. Although the Harrison Act was designed primarily to regulate the drug industry, officials interpreted it and subsequent legislation in such a way that supplying drugs to an addict became a crime. This interpretation forced addicts to become part of the underworld and dramatically changed patterns of addiction. Middle-class addiction declined drastically. By the 1920s, though, addiction, was increasing in lower-class black, Italian, and Jewish neighborhoods. Drug use was also becoming increasingly common among musicians and other entertainers. These new patterns indicate, at least in part, that drugs had become a way to defy new standards for normal behavior. Defiance is an important theme in the slums. The poor have no control over the rules which increase their difficulties. Hence, flouting those rules can be one way to acquire status among similarly afflicted peers.

Heroin was the principal addictive drug for several decades. Since the 1920s heroin use seems to have fluctuated in accordance with fashions within the drug subculture. An "epidemic" of addiction occurred following World War II, and lasted until 1949. After a brief interlude, heroin use increased again in the 1950s. Finally, another "epidemic" erupted in the late 1960s, lasting until the early 1970s. In all these cases heroin experimentation seems to have been related to changing ideas about deviant life-styles. Lower-class adolescents who sought to create a "cool" life-style and self-declared social rebels such as the Greenwich Village "beats" in the 1950s were examples of this approach to heroin use. When addiction's unpleasant side effects would become too obvious, or new drugs promised more exciting experiences, heroin use would decline. Thus when amphetamines became widely available in the mid-1960s, many drug users made them the dominant fashion. By the 1970s, there were so many kinds of drugs competing with heroin that it seems to have declined considerably in importance. (Reduced supplies because of federal intervention may also have contributed to the shift to other drugs.)

Marijuana has had a somewhat different history from that of opium and heroin. It first appeared in the United States during the early twentieth century. Mexican laborers attracted by job opportunities in the Southwest brought this drug with them. They introduced it to lower-class blacks, and marijuana smoking began to spread into the lower South. New Orleans then became an important center for the further diffusion of the drug in the 1920s and 1930s. The city's jazz musicians, black and white, adopted marijuana smoking as part of their life-style. When these musicians moved North, they brought this habit with them to places like Chicago. By the late 1940s marijuana had become popular among jazz music fans across the country. For approximately the next twenty years this drug was regarded as a necessary part of the avant-garde world of entertainment. (In the 1970s the avant-garde would prefer cocaine, another drug whose exorbitant price gave it great snob appeal.)

By the late 1950s marijuana was also beginning to spread into the middle and upper classes. A growing interest in jazz and the "beat generation" made these early contacts with the drug possible. The great explosion in "pot" smoking did not occur, however, until the late 1960s. Young people everywhere adopted marijuana as part of their protest against the Vietnam War and the hypocrisy they saw in their parents' generation. Pot smoking not only increased; it also became a major characteristic of youth culture generally. As a result, the demand for marijuana has steadily increased through the 1970s.

Heroin, marijuana, and the barbituate and amphetamine drugs (which became available in the 1960s) have had different effects on street crime. The possession of these substances is in itself a crime in most states. Marijuana, though, may not be addictive and is relatively inexpensive. And it rarely induces antisocial behavior. Pot smokers do not therefore engage in other forms of crime because they use marijuana. On the other hand, the addictive drugs such as heroin have contributed to the increase in crime. It is impossible to determine precisely how much of that increase is due to addicts who steal to support their habits. They seem to prefer burglaries because addicts usually want to avoid confronting victims. Burglary, however, involves property which takes time to convert to cash. When desperate for a fix, addicts are likely to commit robbery, an offense in which the addict's lack of self-control often leads to violence.

Robbery, burglary, and drug addiction are only part of the street crime problem. Aggravated assault and murder have also increased significantly, especially among blacks. The amount of street crime has helped undermine neighborhood stability in the inner cities. It has also thoroughly frightened suburbanites who are no longer as immune to this threat as they once believed. With the causes of this behavior so deeply rooted in youth and ghetto culture, as well as in a continuing high birth rate among minorities, it is likely to remain a significant problem for some time to come.

## Collective Violence

Although relatively infrequent, collective violence is one of the most spectacular and disturbing forms of criminal behavior. The long history of such violence in this country begins in the late eighteenth century. Since that time Americans have witnessed or participated in scores of riots, vigilance movements, and lynchings. These incidents have been caused by groups who are attempting either to preserve or to change existing social, economic, or political arrangements. In the twentieth century most collective violence has erupted over three problems: unionization, racial conflict, and political protest.

Labor history is filled with violent episodes. The fundamental cause of much of this violence has been the issue of union recognition. Workers sought to create organizations to defend their interests. Employers vigorously opposed those organizations. Strikes over union recognition therefore have traditionally had the greatest potential for violence. The casualties in such confrontations reached appalling proportions. In 1905, for example, a teamsters' strike in Chicago resulted in 14 deaths and 233 other casualties. During the most violent period of labor strife, from 1911 to 1916, dozens of people died in battles between strikers and an assortment of police, strikebreakers, and company guards. Violence declined following World War I when employers launched a successful national campaign to undermine unions. With their organizations in disarray or dissolution, workers were temporarily left to fend for themselves. Franklin Roosevelt's support for unions after 1933 reversed that trend. But employers resisted unionization bitterly, thereby provoking the last major episode of union-related violence. This resistance peaked in 1937, when Chicago policemen killed 10 pickets and wounded some 90 others in a police riot.

New laws and institutions which appeared in the 1930s undermined this sort of violence by removing its principal cause: union recognition. The National Labor Relations Act (1935) made recognition of unions a fundamental fact of American life. A National Labor Relations Board, created by this law and given expanded powers shortly afterward, had the authority to settle labor disputes. With the power of the federal government behind them, unions quickly claimed a prominent place in the economy. Violence decreased dramatically as a result, although it has not disappeared completely. This was one example of how political and institutional changes can make social conflict manageable.

Racial violence also has a long history in this country. In the twentieth century, though, there has been an important change in the basic reason for the outbreak of rioting. For most of our history, race riots erupted because of competition between whites and blacks for jobs and housing. Frequent assaults usually occurred along the borders between neighborhoods. The attacks provoked spiralling violence which only required a culminating incident to spark a riot. Chicago's 1919 riot followed this pattern. Large numbers of Negroes had settled in the city during World War I. As their numbers increased, they sought more housing in areas adjacent to the ghetto. White residents, angry at blacks who were finding jobs in nearby factories, and alarmed by the ghetto growth, violently resisted this expansion. Adolescents of both races fought frequently, escalating tensions. Finally, in July 1919, a black youth at a beach accidentally drifted into a white bathing area. He drowned after several whites started stoning him. The whites then decided to continue the violence by storming into nearby black neighborhoods. Mobs of primarily white youths beat, stabbed, and stoned any blacks they could catch. Enraged blacks fought back. After a week of rioting, 38 people lay dead and over 500 were injured. Community riots of this sort occurred elsewhere in the early twentieth century.

The last important community riot broke out in Detroit in 1943. But then the reason for rioting began to change. A new pattern emerged. The new form of riot usually began with a confrontation between blacks and the police over a relatively trivial matter. While unimportant by itself, the incident served to focus the frustrations and intense anger of ghetto residents over continuing discrimination and agonizing poverty. Their rage exploded into violence which was directed at targets *within* the black community. Usually this meant the rioters attacked the symbols of white oppression, such as stores and public buildings owned by whites. In addition, these riots involved massive looting. Looters stole both to strike at whites who owned the property and to satisfy their own urge for material possessions. Deaths occurred in these riots when the police intervened to halt the violence and looting. A riot in Harlem in 1943 was the first example of this new pattern. It remained a unique event until the 1960s. Then lower-class blacks who had not benefited from the Civil Rights Revolution vented their considerable rage in a series of riots from 1964 to 1968. Scores of people were killed, hundreds injured, and property losses amounted to millions of dollars.

For reasons which are still unclear, the epidemic of ghetto riots ended abruptly after 1968. It may be that the Black Power movement, with its violent rhetoric and emphasis on community pride, helped channel the frustrations of ghetto residents into more constructive behavior. Strident language may have satisfied the urge to protest at the same time that self-help programs gave blacks a needed sense of purpose and accomplishment. In addition, the police had become much more sensitive about handling confrontations with blacks. They combined this newfound sensitivity with a prompt but controlled show of force when necessary. With a more sophisticated approach to police-ghetto confrontations, the chances for a major riot probably declined. Finally, civil rights leaders also had become more aware of lower-class blacks' needs. They sought and obtained a variety of government programs hopefully designed to deal with many aspects of ghetto residents' problems. All these developments do not completely explain the sudden end of the rioting, but they appear to have made significant contributions.

Political violence is yet one more basis for rioting in America. This type of riot is relatively rare, but it has occurred in at least three different periods in our history. It first erupted in a small number of incidents immediately after American independence. Then it resurfaced during the 1830s and 1840s. Finally, political violence broke out once more in the late 1960s. In this last episode, violence was coupled with a rejection of basic social and political assumptions. Participants rejected the validity of American institutions and the nonviolent settlement of differences. White and black radicals, who belonged to such organizations as the Students for a Democratic Society and the Black Panthers, advocated rebellion. Although they were a small minority, these radicals managed to attract considerable attention. By manipulating the news media and adopting confrontation tactics they caused an extraordinary amount of violence. At the 1968 Democratic National Convention in Chicago, for example, radicals provoked a police riot. None of their other efforts matched the success of that incident. Ambushes and shoot-outs with the police into the early 1970s perpetuated the radicals' reputation for violence but these episodes never won them the following the radicals hoped for. Police suppression and desertions from their ranks reduced these frustrated revolutionaries to futility.

**Trends in Crime**

Until recently, the general trend in crime had been rather encouraging. For over a hundred years, from the 1850s to the 1950s, the rate for serious crimes had gradually declined. This was true not only in America, but in western Europe as well. Whether in England, France, Germany, or Scandinavia, the story was the same. As these nations became more industrialized and more prosperous, the amount of crime decreased significantly. True, there were some temporary reverses. A crime wave swept the United States following the Civil War. Germany, France, and America experienced an upsurge in crime after World War I. Despite these episodes, however, the dominant trend in the crime rate was clearly downward. By the 1930s crime had reached historic lows.

In the United States this trend was probably due to several things. First, and in many respects most importantly, the birth rate had been declining since World War I. The Great Depression reinforced this tendency toward smaller families through economic necessity. Fewer youths in the crime-prone years (14-24) were wandering the streets as a result. Secondly, congressional restrictions on immigration, passed in the 1920s, stemmed the flow of Europeans into the country. Simul-

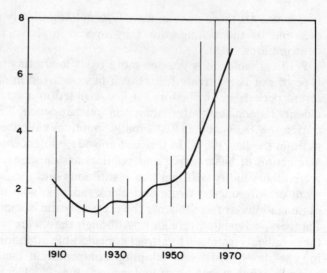

The common trend in known crimes of theft and violence in western societies, 1910-1970. *Courtesy Sage Publications.*

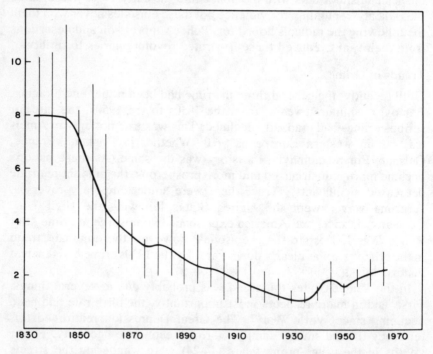

The common trend in convictions for crimes of theft and violence in western societies, 1835-1965. *Courtesy Sage Publications.*

taneously, economic hard times after World War I and during the Depression discouraged southern blacks from moving into northern cities. In both cases, there were fewer newcomers to urban life whose adjustment problems would have contributed to the crime rate. Finally, the Depression and World War II may have enhanced feelings of community solidarity. People shared common experiences of hardship and patriotism in the effort to overcome economic difficulties and to win the war. Criminal violence might have decreased because of this solidarity.

Then, quite dramatically, this historical trend ended. After 1960 crime in western Europe and America rose sharply. England experienced enormous increases in the rates for burglary, robbery, and assault. Other nations had similar sudden reversals. In the United States, where the crime rate had always been higher than in other nations, this surge in criminal activity amounted to an epidemic. Between 1964 and 1974 rates for murder and aggravated assault doubled; robberies more than doubled. Burglary, rape, auto theft, and drug abuse also increased significantly. Criminals became more violent, using vicious, unnecessary force more frequently perhaps than any time since the nineteenth century. These increases leveled off after 1974, but the rates remained extremely high by contemporary standards.

We do not yet fully understand the reasons for this outbreak of crime. There is some agreement, however, about the major contributing causes. An extraordinary shift in the birth rate after World War II, in both Europe and America, laid the basis for the explosion in crime. The members of this postwar baby boom reached adolescence between 1959 and 1963. Already numbering in the millions, this group continued to expand rapidly. In the fifteen years from 1960 to 1975 the adolescent population of the United States, for example, increased 63 percent. This vast population would have had a significant impact on crime rates no matter what else was happening in society. Indeed, a rise in youth crimes accounted for much of the increases in Europe as well as the United States.

Three developments probably aggravated the surge in crime in the United States: the emergence of a youth subculture; the massive influx of blacks into large cities; and the Vietnam War. An adolescent subculture relatively free of adult supervision developed through a combination of prosperity, changes in social values, and new teenage experiences. Americans enjoyed an unparalleled prosperity in the 1960s. They used much of their affluence to shower their children with material goods. Adolescence became for many a period of considerable comfort and few responsibilities. Teenagers did not need to work to help the family or to acquire spending money. Institutions such as schools were hard pressed to control these youths because of their sheer numbers.

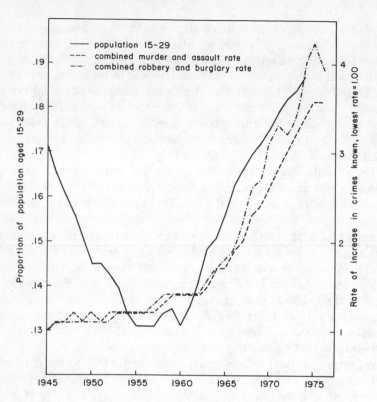

Youth population and crime in the United States, 1945-1976. *Courtesy Sage Publications.*

There were too few adults available (or concerned enough) to cope with the problems of teaching these teenagers responsible behavior. As a result, adolescents increasingly turned to their peers for guidance, respect, and status. But the effect of using their peers to help them define acceptable behavior could be quite devastating. Affluence was not universal. Not all teenagers had the ability to participate equally in the materialism of their subculture. Caught between their normal desire to emulate other teenagers' life-styles and their inability to pay, many adolescents turned to casual crime as a solution.

Negro Americans resumed their urban migration after 1940. By 1970 nearly 75 percent of all blacks lived in cities. They sought better living conditions and economic opportunities; they found massive discrimination and squalor. Prejudice, and changes in the black community, made race a major consideration in any explanation of the increase in crime after 1960. Birth rates for Negroes have been considerably higher than for whites. As a result, the black population as a whole is relatively young. The ratio of adolescents to adults is therefore higher for blacks than it is for whites. On this basis alone, there would be more crime among blacks than among whites. But the extent of black crime is increased by a prejudice which has historically deprived Negroes of the chance to obtain decent work. They have the highest unemployment rate of any minority group, and the rate among teenagers typically reaches 50 percent. Those who are employed frequently find themselves in low paying jobs where advancement is blocked by discrimination and a lack of skills. Black teenagers who want to participate in the adolescent subculture thus have severe problems. Crime is an all too obvious solution for some youths in these circumstances.

Ironically, the success of the civil rights movement may have contributed to the rise in crime among blacks. That reform crusade won major benefits for middle-class blacks, but not for the poor. Laws

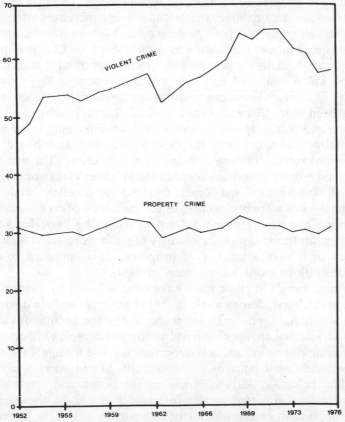

Percentage of arrestees for violence and property crime who were black, 1952-1976. *Courtesy Sage Publications.*

against various forms of discrimination, combined with more liberal attitudes about race, enabled middle-class Negroes to participate more fully in American society. They responded in part by seeking better neighborhoods for their families. With their departure from the ghettos, the cohesiveness of black slum communities began to crumble. Middle-class blacks no longer exercised as much control over the values and behavior of individuals in the ghettos. Cultural restraints on violent reactions to continuing discrimination and the frustrations of poverty lost their effectiveness. The result was a dramatic increase in violent crime. Since black criminals usually victimize fellow blacks, the amount of violence within the ghettos rose significantly. Robbery and assault became especially common and remained major problems for poor blacks into the 1970s.

The Vietnam War's impact on crime is extremely difficult to assess because there were so many other social changes and problems which occurred at the same time. Historically, crime increases after any war. But precisely why is difficult to determine. Vietnam veterans may have had more problems readjusting to society because Congress provided inadequate benefits for several years to pay for training and other programs which had been given to previous veterans. The pronounced tendency to draft lower-class youths, and especially blacks, may also have been more disruptive than normal. These youths had the most problems and the fewest resources for reestablishing themselves. It is possible, therefore, that the lack of help and draft-board policies convinced some returning veterans to turn to crime. The war also encouraged some collective violence among upper-class youths who regarded it as immoral and illegal. By 1967 some college students protesting the war were beginning to reject the notion of civil disobedience, a protest philosophy which did not question the basic legitimacy of social institutions. Instead, a minority of students rejected fundamental values such as the sanctity of property. This approach to antiwar demonstrations led to more violent protests.

In sum, trends in crime rates have been affected by changes in two basic areas. First, demographic shifts in birth rates and age distributions have accounted for a significant proportion of the fluctuations in crime. Secondly, social changes have had subtle and complex effects on those fluctuations. New values, new opportunities, and foreign wars have disrupted traditional patterns of community life in ways which affect criminal behavior. Urban growth in the South and Southwest, for example, has attracted people from older cities. As these residents seek opportunities elsewhere, their departure seems to lessen social tensions and crime rates in their former neighborhoods.

Crime remains a major problem although there have been definite fluctuations in its general trend. Some of these fluctuations are apparently related to developments in western society as a whole. Juvenile crime, for example, has increased in Europe as well as in the United States due to higher birth rates following World War II. But juvenile crime in America seems more common and more violent.

Unfortunately, changes in law enforcement do not seem to alter general trends in crime. From a historical perspective, the police cannot cope with the broad currents of criminal activity. The decline in crime from the 1930s to the 1950s, for example, began before police professionalism transformed local law enforcement. Contrariwise, the immense effort to deal with the recent surge in crime seems to have had no effect that we can prove. This does not mean that new policing ideas have no value. Specific techniques, such as plainclothes details in high crime areas, can affect specific offenses. But the overall trend remains discouraging. The causes of crime continue to be entangled in the changing fortunes and misfortunes of society.

## SUGGESTED READINGS

Two important collections of essays which examine trends in crime in both Europe and America are: Ted Robert Gurr, et. al., *The Politics of Crime and Conflict: A Comparative History of Four Cities* (Beverly Hills: Sage Publications, 1977) and Hugh Davis Graham and Ted Robert Gurr, eds., *Violence in America: Historical and Comparative Perspectives* (rev. ed.; Beverly Hills: Sage Publications, 1979). The President's Commission on Law Enforcement and Administration of Justice, *Task Force Report: Crime and Its Impact—An Assessment* (Washington, D.C.: Government Printing Office, 1967) also examines general trends, but for a short time period. Useful general studies of America's contemporary crime problem include James Q. Wilson, *Thinking About Crime* (New York: Basic Books, Inc., 1975), Robert S. Weppner, ed., *Street Ethnography: Selected Studies of Crime and Drug Use in Natural Settings* (Beverly Hills: Sage Publications, 1977), and Charles E. Silberman, *Criminal Violence, Criminal Justice* (New York: Random House, 1978). Various books deal with the world of the professional thief. Among the more interesting of these are Edwin H. Sutherland, *The Professional Thief* (Chicago: University of Chicago Press, 1937), Bill Chambliss, ed., *Box Man: A Professional Thief's Journey* (New York: Harper & Row, 1972), Peter Letkemann, *Crime as Work* (Englewood Cliffs, N.J.: Prentice-Hall, Inc., 1973), and Thomas Plate, *Crime Pays!* (New York: Simon and Schuster, 1975). Street crime is usually examined in the context of gang activities or juvenile delinquency in general. Marvin E. Wolfgang, et. al., *Delinquency in a Birth Cohort* (Chicago: University of Chicago Press, 1972) is one of the most influential of these studies, as is Lewis Yablonsky, *The Violent Gang* (Baltimore: The Macmillan Company, 1966).

The classic study of gangs is Frederic M. Thrasher, *The Gang: A Study of 1,313 Gangs in Chicago* (Chicago: University of Chicago Press, 1927). John E. Conklin, *Robbery and the Criminal Justice System* (Philadelphia: Lippincott, 1972) studies general trends in this important crime during the 1960s. James Willwerth, *Jones; Portrait of a Mugger* (Greenwich, Conn.: Fawcett Publications, 1974) is a rare and fascinating study of one of the most feared types of criminals. There are many studies of collective violence. Several articles in the works by Gurr and Graham, cited above, deal with various aspects of this phenomenon. In addition, the following books are useful special studies: *Report of the National Advisory Commission on Civil Disorders* (New York: Bantam Books, 1968); National Commission on the Causes and Prevention of Violence, *Rights in Conflict* (New York: Bantam Books, 1968); William M. Tuttle, Jr., *Race Riot: Chicago in the Red Summer of 1919* (New York: Atheneum, 1970); and Robert M. Fogelson, *Violence as Protest: A Study of Riots and Ghettos* (Garden City, N.Y.: Doubleday & Company, Inc., 1971).

# 9

# Organized Crime in the 20th Century

**P**ublic perceptions of organized crime have had an important impact on the development of law enforcement. Americans are both fascinated by and fearful of a presumed national crime conspiracy which corrupts government, undermines policing, and murders rivals. Police reformers and other lawmen have used this combined fascination and fear to promote their own goals. In the process, our knowledge of organized crime has more often been obscured than clarified. Although serious historical research has only begun recently, its findings have already significantly altered our understanding of organized crime's development.

Despite its reputedly spectacular nature, illegal enterprise is based upon three characteristics which first emerged in the nineteenth century. The first of these is the concept of multiple partnerships. Any illegal business has certain needs which vary according to the type of activity. If, for example, an underworld figure wants to open a gambling casino, he will need a place to house the casino, employees to run it, a manager to supervise operations, and police or political protection. He will probably not have all the skills and knowledge required to do all these things himself. Hence, he will seek partners. Each partner will have a special talent to contribute to the project's success. One man will be an experienced manager; another will provide influence with local authorities, etc. This partnership arrangement is not based upon the idea that one man is "the boss." Instead, the partners are equals. Each man, furthermore, is free to pursue other business deals as he sees fit. In sum, the structure of illegal enterprise is decentralized and composed of multiple, frequently complex partnerships.

Secondly, illegal enterprise provides services to the public. Some services, such as gambling and prostitution, have been furnished on an organized basis for over a hundred years. More recently, new demands have opened other opportunities for the underworld. Liquor during Prohibition was the most famous example; narcotics, since the 1930s, is another. The demand for services varies over time and affects the development of illegal enterprises. Changes in the population sometimes account for these variations. During the early twentieth century, for instance, the United States had an excess of men. That large, single-male population made prostitution extremely profitable and encouraged greater organization to meet demand. Once the population imbalance disappeared, after the 1920s, there were relatively fewer customers and prostitution became less centralized. (Other developments such as new standards of morality and new technology also affected the business of prostitution.) The essential point here is that illegal enterprise does not always expand. It does seek new opportunities, though, and is therefore heavily dependent upon changing public tastes and standards for its success.

Finally, various ethnic groups in America's cities have contributed significantly to the growth of illegal enterprise. The Irish were important in gambling as early as the 1860s. In more recent times, the Italians have received most of the public's attention because of our fixation with the Mafia. Italians, however, were not the only group engaged in underworld activities. In fact, they are probably a minority within illegal enterprise. Blacks, Chinese, Cubans, Mexican-Americans, and, perhaps most important of all, Eastern European Jews, have made major contributions to "organized crime." These ethnic groups have been involved in this kind of activity for one important reason. Americans who want illegal services have typically relied upon minority groups to provide them. Most members of these groups live ordinary, useful lives, but a small number of them have used crime as a means to social and economic success. Illegal enterprise is not, therefore, dominated by any single ethnic group. Rather, it is a mosaic which reflects the diversity of American society generally.

The history of "organized crime" since 1920 illustrates the important role these three characteristics played in its development. Building upon the extraordinary opportunities of the 1920s, a generation of skillful, ruthless men used their experience and wealth to create extensive, criminal networks after 1933. They did not, however, dominate every aspect of illegal enterprise after Prohibition. Ex-bootleggers could not possibly have monopolized all the opportunities which emerged following Repeal. Other men, who had no backgrounds in bootlegging, forged their own empires from the various demands for illegal services which appeared during and after the 1930s.

## Prohibition, 1920-33

Americans adopted Prohibition as a patriotic gesture during World War I. Ironically, the war ended before Prohibition began. But the fighting in Europe had provided a convenient rallying point for a reform which some people had sought for decades. Ever since the 1830s, a small but influential number of reformers had persistently agitated against alcohol. These people, generally long-established, white, Anglo-Saxon Protestants, found the behavior of other immigrants (especially their drinking habits) appalling. For these reformers, prohibition became one way to control these ethnic groups. It was also a means of asserting their superiority over the decadence of the more recent arrivals. This crusade did not become a major issue in national life until after 1900. Better organization, increasing immigration, and the need for sober factory workers were some of the reasons for the slowly increasing effectiveness of prohibition until the war broke out. By 1917 several states and hundreds of local communities had voted themselves dry. America's declaration of war against Germany aroused intense patriotism which found expression in, among other things, a commitment to banning all liquor. Before anyone except the Prohibitionists understood the implications, the states had ratified the Eighteenth Amendment to the Constitution.

The National Prohibition Act of 1919, better known as the Volstead Act, created the framework for enforcing the new amendment. Congress refused to provide for an adequate federal police under this act. Instead, enforcement responsibilities were divided among the commissioner of internal revenue and state, county, and local police. This meant that the politicians who controlled local law enforcement would have a major role in Prohibition. Since those politicians responded to public opinion, enforcement depended upon the degree of support for Prohibition from one community to the next. In general, rural and small town Americans supported Prohibition more than urban residents did.

City dwellers violated the Volstead Act primarily because their attitudes toward liquor had changed considerably since the nineteenth century. Immigrants, who concentrated in cities, had always regarded drinking as an important leisure activity. But now the middle classes agreed. Liquor had become an important way to ease the tensions of middle-class life. It was also to be enjoyed for its own sake as well. Young adults and emancipated women in the Roaring Twenties regarded drinking as a major diversion. Middle-class inhibitions against public drinking did not disappear entirely, but they relaxed sufficiently to open a new, very large market to bootleggers.

Bootleggers faced three problems as businessmen. First, they needed to acquire their product. There were various solutions to this difficulty, beginning with the relatively simple answer of theft. Millions of gallons of liquor were stored under lock and key at bonded warehouses across the country. During the early twenties much of this liquor disappeared. Another solution to the acquisition problem involved importing booze from Canada and the West Indies. This approach required bootleggers to establish connections with criminals in other cities, especially Detroit, Cleveland, and the eastern ports from Boston to Miami. Finally, manufacturing beer and alcohol, either in breweries or "alky cooking" plants located in ethnic neighborhoods, offered yet another possibility. Joe Saltis, for instance, owned several breweries in Wausau, Wisconsin, which produced beer for his Chicago customers. The Genna brothers, on the other hand, distributed equipment for stills among their Italian neighbors on Chicago's Near West Side and collected the product for distribution.

Each approach to the acquisition problem required different skills, but from the standpoint of future developments those bootleggers who created supply networks based on intercity contacts would become the most important entrepreneurs. Johnny Torrio, for example, was extremely active and successful in this area. During the early 1920s Torrio created the organization which Capone and others would inherit in 1925. Both Torrio and Capone had friends and acquaintances in the liquor-smuggling business. These contacts proved useful in channeling booze into Chicago. Later, in 1932, Torrio brought together the seven largest East Coast smuggling groups in a syndicate which dominated the supply of imported liquor in the Northeast. His partners in this venture were some of America's most famous Jewish, Italian, and Irish criminals: Lucky Luciano, Meyer Lansky, Bugsy Siegal, Yasha Zatzenberg (all from New York City); Nig Rosen (Philadelphia); Longy Zwillman (Newark); Charles Solomon (Boston); and Daniel Walsh (Rhode Island). This group supplied liquor to bootleggers in midwestern cities, thereby creating relationships which would be useful after 1933.

Storing and distributing alcohol was a second problem for bootleggers. Wholesale bootleggers had to acquire warehouses and fleets of trucks. This equipment was highly vulnerable to various business risks. Hijackers plagued truck convoys, forcing bootleggers to hire armed guards to discourage them. Violence was inevitable in these circumstances. Most of the deaths associated with bootlegging in the early twenties involved hijacking incidents. Warehouses offered temptations to thieves, and carried the additional risk that local officials might seize and destroy the contents. Political influence therefore became a necessary part of every wholesale bootlegger's operations. Capone and Torrio cultivated close ties with Chicago's Republican political machine, headed by William H. Thompson. During Thompson's terms as mayor (1919-23; 1923-27) the Capone organization had little to fear from the police. Similar political ties existed in New York, Boston, Philadelphia, Cleveland, and other cities.

The last business problem for bootleggers involved retail sales. Some bootleggers established their own outlets; others tried to build a clientele among independent speakeasy owners. In either case, competition between wholesalers could become intense. No single person or syndicate could control an entire city. Rivals constantly sought new territories, or they intruded on their competitors' turf. They used various tactics to expand their markets. Price cutting was a standard ploy in developing new outlets or in encouraging retailers to switch from one supplier to another. Police raids could also be useful. Speakeasy owners afraid of losing their business because of the embarrassment these raids caused their customers often agreed to buy from a wholesaler who threatened to use this tactic. Violence also emerged as a marketing tool. Rivals sent strong-arm men to disrupt their competitors' businesses and engaged in battles with one another in the streets. Conflicts over territory became the primary reason for murder after 1925. In Chicago over 400 gangsters died in these struggles before Prohibition ended. That was not typical, however; other cities had far fewer deaths associated with bootlegging.

Although Chicago's death toll was unusual, the organization of the Capone bootlegging syndicate in this city provides a good case study of this illegal enterprise. In its prime, the Capone group consisted of four senior partners: Al and his brother Ralph, Frank Nitti, and Jack Guzik. Each senior partner established partnerships with other people to deal with a particular business. Ralph Capone, for example, was connected with Louis Lipschultz in the distribution of liquor to speakeasies. Ralph also represented the senior partners in the Smoke House, a highly successful gambling den run by Pete Penovich and Frankie Pope. The other senior partners invested in additional gambling houses, dog tracks, whorehouses, and in various phases of bootlegging. In each case, their partners received equal shares of the profits and simultaneously engaged in criminal enterprises independent of the Capone syndicate. Penovich and Pope, for instance, ran gambling operations of their own at a local racetrack. Far from being a tightly knit organization ruled by Al Capone, this syndicate was a sprawling, decentralized organization which had an extraordinary array of interests. Its structure permitted it to adjust to changes and new opportunities. When Capone went to prison for income tax evasion in 1931, the other senior partners continued business as usual.

Bootleggers who built large organizations by 1933 had learned valuable lessons which would serve them well. Their willingness to use violence obscured the fact that they had perfected some management techniques appropriate to operating intra- and intercity businesses. Furthermore, they had acquired valuable knowledge of, and in many cases personal acquaintance with, similarly talented men around the nation. Most were still fairly young—in their thirties or early forties. The bulk of their careers lay before them. Finally, they had large fortunes which they could invest in new ventures. Repeal therefore made little impression on these entrepreneurs; they simply looked for fresh opportunities.

### Illegal Enterprise During the Depression and World War II

The Depression had little effect on illegal enterprise. Bootlegging provided a tidy income for criminal entrepreneurs during the first four years of the national catastrophe. Following Repeal in 1933, gambling reasserted its dominant role in illegal services as many important criminals devoted increasing attention to its enormous potential. A few entrepreneurs dabbled in narcotics, but this product had only a minor role in their overall plans. Its potential lay in the future. Probably the most famous development in the thirties, though, had nothing to do with providing illegal services to the public. According to a myth popularized in the 1960s by law enforcement officials and journalists, this was the era when a national crime syndicate run by the Mafia emerged.

Faithful to its public image, the Mafia supposedly created this national syndicate in a bloodbath. This event, known either as the Castellammarese War or the Night of Sicilian Vespers, involved a clash between two generations of Italian gangsters. Men like Salvatore Maranzano and Giuseppe Masseria led the "Mustache Petes," older mafiosi, who had arrived in America prior to 1920 and who had recreated the Sicilian Mafia in the Italian slums. Prominent gangsters like Lucky Luciano, Frank Costello, and Vito Genovese represented a new Mafia generation. They resented the Mustache Petes who refused to expand beyond the Italian ghettos, grab wealth and power in the wider society, and establish the dominance of the Mafia nationally. The conflict erupted into warfare when Masseria was murdered in early 1931 and Maranzano declared himself boss of bosses. Luciano and his followers struck in September 1931. Maranzano and sixty Mustache Petes died in an orgy of killing which stretched across the nation. With the opposition eliminated, Luciano established a national crime council which has coordinated illegal enterprise throughout the United States ever since.

There are several things wrong with this colorful legend. For example, the Sicilian Mafia was not transplanted to America. Italian immigrants brought Mafia cultural attitudes with them, but not the organization. Those attitudes emphasized self-reliance, suspicion of outsiders, and distrust of government officials. All of these values were products of Sicily's unique historical development. But in America the social system which nurtured these attitudes was missing; immigrants had to adjust to new conditions and new cultural values. Furthermore, only a few mafiosi actually came to the United States, and then only during the 1920s when Mussolini was trying to eradicate them. There was too little time for these few men to dominate Italian underworld activities, to say nothing of crime generally. In sum, no Mafia organization, as the term is popularly understood, existed in 1931.

Another problem with the Castellammarese War is even more basic. Sixty or more murders of prominent Italian gangsters in the period of two nights (September 10 and 11) in cities across the country should have attracted at least mild interest among policemen and journalists. They chose to ignore the purge, however, for a very good reason. It never occurred. At most, four men including Maranzano died violently on the traditional date for the massacre. None of these murders involved Italian gangsters outside of New York.

Lucky Luciano and others did murder Masseria and Maranzano. They were second generation Italian gangsters who did resent what power the Mustache Petes had. But their takeover of New York's Italian gangs did not create the basis for a national Mafia crime council. Instead, they killed their local Mustache Petes to permit the development of a new type of criminal organization which combined Italian and American ideas. This process has been called the Americanization of the mobs. It occurred in different cities at different times. In some places Americanization happened well after 1931, and not every Mustache Pete died in the process. Many simply accepted the new approach to organization without much protest.

The new organization borrowed some terms and concepts from the Sicilian Mafia. But the basic rationale and structure were purely American. Luciano and his compatriots divided New York into five geographical districts, called *borgate*. Within each *borgata* there was a hierarchy which consisted of a boss, one or more *capodecinas*, and soldiers. The *capodecina* was a middle management person who coordinated the activities of ten men. Soldiers were actually small entrepreneurs who engaged in illegal enterprises within a *borgata*. A *consigliere* (counselor) completed the hierarchy. He adjudicated disputes between soldiers and the leadership. The whole system made a national crime council impossible. Individual bosses were free to pursue their own interests. Thus decentralization, not a rigid hierarchy, characterized relations between *borgate*. Luciano was not the crime czar of New York. In effect, the *borgate* system mirrored the multiple partnership concept with the important difference that bosses did not have to divide their profits among their peers. These arrangements gave Italian criminals the ability to expand beyond their own neighborhoods, but that did not mean they became the dominant ethnic group in the underworld. Instead, they now had the ability to make deals with Jewish, Irish, Polish, and black criminal entrepreneurs. Bosses and soldiers struck partnerships across ethnic lines. Luciano and Meyer Lansky invested in national projects together. In local neighborhoods, men like Joe Valachi found Jewish partners in ventures such as policy games.

While Italian gangsters occupied themselves with the *borgate*, other ethnic criminals pursued their own affairs. Black entrepreneurs were becoming important underworld figures because of the enormous northward shift of the Negro population following World War I. Forced into the ghettos of New York, Detroit, Chicago, and other cities, these people sought diversions from their misery and new ways to make money. Two illegal enterprises attracted the attention of a few blacks: prostitution and numbers. Negro involvement in prostitution dated back to the nineteenth century, but now they increased their contribution significantly. An abundance of black females made prostitution a ghetto growth industry. Since whites owned the ghetto's brothels, black entrepreneurs found most of their opportunities on the streets. Many women, unable to find work, became independent streetwalkers. Their earnings depended upon individual initiative and luck. Pimps provided the only organization among streetwalkers. They collected "strings" of girls and staked out territories to which they claimed exclusive rights. With physical force as their only means of maintaining control over their territories, disputes between pimps often ended violently. Pimping was sufficiently lucrative to make these entrepreneurs a prominent group in the underworld after 1920.

Numbers first appeared during the 1920s. West Indian blacks apparently introduced the game in New York, and it soon spread elsewhere. Originally, numbers was confined to the black ghettos, but by the thirties it had begun to attract whites as well. The game's huge profits caught the attention of entrepreneurs quite early. Large numbers syndicates appeared in several cities, and they became important ghetto businesses. A good-sized operation employed 300 or more people, and there were several syndicates in a single city. Literally thousands of blacks might depend upon this game for their livelihoods.

Numbers bankers played crucial leadership roles at a time when blacks had many problems and few solutions. The bankers became important politicians whose influence opened many doors for their constituents. Furthermore, these bankers frequently acted as community philanthropists, sponsoring improvements and other ghetto activities. Crime was thus becoming an important means of social and economic mobility for blacks.

Other forms of gambling attracted entrepreneurs in the 1930s. Horse racing had fallen on hard times during the Progressive era. Most state legislatures outlawed it. The sport began to revive during the twenties using pari-mutuel betting (bookmaking remained illegal). When the Depression started affecting tax revenues, state lawmakers supported reopening even more tracks as one way to fill the public coffers. By the mid-thirties racing had once again become a major form of entertainment. Since bookmakers needed accurate race results fast, some criminal entrepreneurs began supplying this need. Moe Annenberg was the most successful individual in this regard. He was a newspaper man who had acquired several dailies and racing sheets during the 1920s. In the early 1930s Annenberg established a monopoly on the wire service business and used this control to build a gambling empire. He had many partners who bought his service for local bookies. When Meyer Lansky opened a casino north of Miami about 1933, he made Annenberg a partner. Lansky was only one of many men who found it impossible to operate bookmaking without Annenberg. Federal tax problems drove Annenberg out of business in 1939, but his former associates formed Continental Wire Service in 1940 and carried on without him. Former bootleggers in a few cases also began investing in racetracks, especially in Florida and Cuba. This was not yet a major development, but it laid the groundwork for more ambitious schemes in later years.

A few important criminals also explored the profitability of narcotics. Louis "Lepke" Buchalter, one of the more savage gangsters at the time, was the most notorious example. Buchalter spent the twenties working as a hired killer and enforcer. Late in the decade he became involved in racketeering in New York's fur trade. Branching into other activities in typical entrepreneurial fashion, Buchalter joined a narcotics-smuggling syndicate about 1935. His partners included Yasha Katzenberg, an ex-bootlegger and associate of such luminaries as Meyer Lansky and Johnny Torrio. Katzenberg and his partners apparently invited Buchalter to join them because he had some useful connections among smugglers. This dope ring was thus a typical multiple partnership in which each participant contributed a special skill. Buchalter remained with this syndicate until federal narcotics agents broke it up in 1939.

Gambling, narcotics, and prostitution do not exhaust the entrepreneurial opportunities of the thirties and early forties. Racketeering in labor unions, the movie industry, and many small businesses also occupied the attentions of many criminals. Loansharking began to develop into a small but potentially interesting industry. And the war offered numerous temporary opportunities for profit in black-market activities. Ex-bootleggers did not dominate any of these enterprises, but they figured prominently in several of them. Jewish gangsters continued to play more significant roles than other ethnic criminals, but blacks and Italians were becoming more noticeable. In general, criminal businessmen learned how to apply the principles of multiple partnerships to the expanding opportunities of post-Prohibition America.

**The Modern Era**

Criminal entrepreneurs after 1945 had, as usual, a variety of lucrative investment possibilities. The three most important underworld growth industries were regional gambling centers, loansharking, and narcotics. Ex-bootleggers played crucial roles in the creation of gambling centers because it was an idea which made full use of their special talents. The other two businesses, however, attracted a newer generation of criminals drawn in some cases from different ethnic groups. Ex-bootleggers apparently had fewer investments in loansharking and narcotics. The older generation which had established itself during the 1920s simply could not dominate the dynamic, complex world of illegal enterprise.

Regional gambling centers developed where local economies depended heavily upon tourism. New Orleans was an example. Tourism was the city's second largest industry. Furthermore, New Orleans offered forms of entertainment designed for adult, rather than family, tastes. Fine restaurants, jazz concerts, and Bourbon Street strip shows drew thousands of tourists eager to spend their money. Gambling was simply another diversion which these people enjoyed. The presence of so many tourists throughout the year ensured large profits to gamblers. They responded by opening major casinos in New Orleans, Hot Springs (Arkansas), Miami, Covington and Newport (Kentucky), and Las Vegas.

Criminal entrepreneurs living in tourist centers could not run these casinos without help. They might not have sufficiently sophisticated personnel available, and they might not know where to find them. Money was even more of a problem. In general, regional gambling centers developed in cities not noted for having extremely wealthy bootleggers during Prohibition. Entrepreneurs in these cities might have a good deal of money, but not enough to finance regional casino operations. Hence outside investors from other cities were essential. These outsiders turned out to be those ex-bootleggers who had invested in gambling in the East and Midwest during and after Prohibition. By the 1940s these men had extensive knowledge about the skills needed to run large gambling operations, they knew many men with those skills, and they knew entrepreneurs in several cities who were also involved in gambling.

Las Vegas became the most famous example of a regional gambling center. Nevada's legislature had legalized gambling in 1931 in an effort to attract tourists. The new law did not immediately benefit Las Vegas, though. Prior to 1945 construction on Hoover Dam and the development of military installations caused more population growth than gambling did. Bugsy Siegal's plans changed that. Late in the war Siegal became the West Coast representative for Trans-America Wire Service. He used this position to force Las Vegas gamblers to make him a partner in their operations. In 1945 Siegal became convinced that Las Vegas had a great future as a gambling center. Since the city had few facilities or attractions for tourists, Siegal conceived the idea of a self-contained entertainment center. He wanted to build a casino-hotel complex which would include a restaurant and nightclub. This was an expensive idea, so Siegal organized a syndicate with several of his ex-bootlegger friends to raise the money. Meyer Lansky was his most prominent co-investor. After a year of work, Las Vegas' first major casino, The Flamingo, opened in December 1946.

After some initial problems, the Flamingo began to show a profit. Siegal's dream came true, but he did not live to enjoy it. He was murdered in June 1947, presumably because of disputes with his partners over his management of this venture. Las Vegas, however, prospered. The Flamingo's profits attracted the attention of many criminals. Moe Dalitz, one of Cleveland's most important illegal entrepreneurs, organized a syndicate which built the Desert Inn, and later, the Stardust Inn. Phil Kastel, a New Orleans underworld figure associated with Frank Costello in New York, found several partners to help him build the Tropicana. Other ex-bootleggers from Boston, Philadelphia, Chicago, and Minneapolis made huge investments. By the early 1950s they had erected many of the important casinos which have made Las Vegas synonymous with gambling.

Loansharking first assumed its modern form in the 1930s. This enterprise developed in response to the needs of three groups who were poor credit risks for legitimate lenders. Small businessmen who had cash problems were one important source of customers for loansharks. Bettors and bookmakers who could not cover their gambling losses formed a second group. Finally, thieves who needed money while they were between jobs borrowed from loansharks. Violence played a key role in this business. Loansharks had to have some means for ensuring repayment, but their business had no legal standing. They turned to violence, then, as a technique which encouraged prompt payments.

Like bootlegging, this was a business which offered opportunities to young men raised in lower-class ethnic neighborhoods. Loansharks, however, were born too late to participate in bootlegging. Instead, many of them spent their early careers engaged in violent street crimes, an ideal preparation for loansharking. By the late 1940s these criminals were reaching an age where continued involvement in street crimes was less attractive to them. They began looking for other ways to make a living. Gambling syndicates which could use their talents in enforcement roles opened new vistas for them. The pioneers in the juice racket all had ties to such syndicates.

The most important developments in loansharking occurred in Chicago. Sam De Stefano was perhaps the most prominent loanshark in the 1950s. He was a product of the city's slums and a member of the notorious Forty-Two Gang. Prior to World War II De Stefano's violent career earned him three prison terms. After his release in the late forties, De Stefano became a West Side gambler's partner and began building his loanshark business. His political connections with Chicago's First Ward Democrats, and his friendship with important underworld figures like Tony Accardo, contributed to his success. De Stefano was typical of the independent entrepreneurs who flourished in the fifties. During the early sixties, however, relatively powerful syndicates emerged which coordinated loansharking more closely. They assigned territories and established a clearing house which checked to see whether customers were borrowing from several loansharks. Thereafter, this business became one of the more important branches of complex, multi-service syndicates.

Drug use is one of the most perplexing problems in modern America. After a long period of low demand, or even relative decline, the demand for narcotics increased after World War II. This demand reached near epidemic proportions in the sixties and early seventies according to many observers. While fluctuations in drug abuse are difficult to explain adequately, the post-1945 increase may be due to developments in the general society. The immense growth of black ghettos since the forties, and the social problems which resulted from that growth, probably account for the fact that heroin use is heavily concentrated among blacks. Marijuana, on the other hand, became practically a symbol of white middle-class youths' rebellion in the sixties. The demand for "pot" skyrocketed and then stabilized as marijuana smoking acquired respectability among young adults. In more recent times cocaine use has become a status symbol among the avant-garde elite.

Italian criminal syndicates dominated drug smuggling and distribution until the early 1960s. Immediately following World War II, Italian drug manufacturers became the most important source of narcotics flowing into America. These firms dealt with local smugglers who had contacts with East Coast mafiosi such as Geatano Lucchese, a New York City *capo*. After federal protests forced the Italian government to shut down this trade, Turkey became the principal United States supplier.

The dramatic increase in the demand for heroin and marijuana in the sixties undermined Italian domination of the drug trade. As the decade progressed, drug smuggling and distribution became a chaotic, decentralized business reminiscent of the wide-open days of early Prohibition. New ethnic groups, including blacks, Anglo-Americans, Cubans, and Mexican-Americans became involved in all aspects of the business. Southeast Asian, Mexican, and South American supply routes developed and allowed these new entrepreneurs to circumvent the Italians. Changes in smuggling techniques encouraged further decentralization. Small airplanes which could easily evade radar detection quickly became a major method for smuggling. "Mother ships" —freighters loaded with tons of marijuana—followed regular schedules along the East Coast, stopping at prearranged points to unload their cargoes. These techniques allowed dozens of small syndicates, sometimes designed to handle only one deal, to proliferate. A few large, well-organized syndicates began to appear in the mid-seventies, but narcotics remains an especially disjointed enterprise.

Illegal enterprise is thus a complex activity which constantly evolves in response to peculiarly American opportunities. Europe has virtually nothing to compare with our criminal syndicates. The Sicilian Mafia may have some similarities, but it is apparently undergoing change as Sicilian culture adjusts to modernization. Elsewhere in Europe syndicate crime is a minor problem. The basic reason for this is quite simple. European criminals do not act as middlemen dispensing illegal services or goods. The mobs which do exist are parasitical, i.e., they engage in extortion or similar activities. Furthermore, these mobs are excessively violent, a fact which brings rapid legal retribution. Since these syndicates provide no services, they have been unable to develop any influence in European criminal justice systems.

American syndicates, of course, continue to have considerable influence with our police, courts, and politicians. Criminal entrepreneurs developed this influence by exploiting differences in cultural values at various times in our history. Local law enforcement agencies, which also reflect those same conflicts, found it difficult to cope with illegal entrepreneurs. Police agencies have adopted rather extraordinary strategies to deal with this problem. The Mafia myth is an interesting recent example of such strategies. During the 1960s, for the first time in the long history of illegal enterprise, the police managed to convince a very large number of citizens that the Mafia was a genuine threat to society. This myth helped create a political consensus supporting new laws to deal with organized crime. But the myth also obscured the actual organization and development of syndicates. It was an inaccurate reading of history. Hopefully, a more accurate reading will suggest more effective solutions.

## SUGGESTED READINGS

Most of the immense literature on organized crime has been written by journalists more interested in entertaining their readers than in helping them understand this complex phenomenon. As a result, we do not yet have enough good historical studies dealing with most aspects of illegal enterprise. John Kobler, *Capone: The Life and World of Al Capone* (Greenwich, Conn.: Fawcett Publications, 1972) and Hank Messick, *Lansky* (New York: G. P. Putnam's Sons, 1971) are two good biographies of major entrepreneurs. Mark H. Haller has pioneered in the serious historical study of organized crime in several excellent articles: "Organized Crime in Urban Society: Chicago in the Twentieth Century," *Journal of Social History,* V (Winter 1971-72): 210-34; "Bootleggers and Gambling, 1920-1950," in the Commission on the Review of National Policy Toward Gambling, *Gambling in America* (Washington, D.C.: Government Printing Office, 1976), Appendix I, pp. 102-43; and, with John V. Alviti, "Loansharking in American Cities: Historical Analysis of a Marginal Enterprise," *American Journal of Legal History,* XXI (1977): 125-56. Ivan Light, "The Ethnic Vice Industry, 1880-1944," *American Sociological Review,* XLII (June 1977): 464-79 is another important study which is all the more valuable because it does not concentrate on Italian-Americans. Humbert S. Nelli, *The Business of Crime: Italians and Syndicate Crime in the United States* (New York: Oxford University Press, 1976) is the best study of its subject and an extremely important book. Other important contributions to an understanding of Italian-American involvement in organized crime are: Joseph L. Albini, *The American Mafia: Genesis of a Legend* (New York: Appleton-Century-Crofts, 1971), Francis A. J. Ianni and Elizabeth Reuss-Ianni, *A Family Business: Kinship and Social Control in Organized Crime* (New York,: Russell Sage Foundation, 1972), and Annelise G. Anderson, *The Business of Organized Crime: A Cosa Nostra Family* (Stanford: Hoover Institution Press, 1979).

# 10

# The State Police

**T**rends in crime after 1900 contributed to major new developments in the history of law enforcement. In the nineteenth century, with rare exceptions, policing had been a local activity. The states had delegated their order-maintenance duties to local communities while the federal government had played a relatively minor role in law enforcement. In sum, republican theory closely resembled actual practice. But some criminal activities which began to affect more than one locality strained that close connection between theory and reality. Eventually the states, and especially the federal government, expanded their policing roles significantly. By the 1970s their intervention had created far more centralization in law enforcement than republican theory allowed. Centralization raised serious problems about civil liberties, privacy, and abuses of police power. The next two chapters examine the ways concerns about particular criminal activities helped justify a vast expansion in the policing responsibilities of the state and national governments.

Changes wrought by urbanization and industrialization eventually forced state politicians to reconsider their responsibilities. Communities became more interdependent and interconnected. Factories located in large cities depended upon raw materials from mining areas. City merchants developed large rural markets for their goods. And rural Americans relied on their city cousins to produce the tools and amenities which would lend aid and comfort to their lives. Railroads, and later highways, encouraged the flow of ideas and goods. As these arrange-

155

ments became more complex, they also became more vulnerable to disruptions. Disorders in one part of a state could cause hardships in another area. Furthermore, the improvements in transportation opened new opportunities in rural areas to urban criminals. New problems with criminal behavior and threats to public safety therefore undermined the assumption that local communities could always cope with these problems.

The history of state policing can be divided into three broad stages. First, in the initial two decades of the twentieth century, state governments sought to cope with the negative consequences of rapid urbanization and industrialization. Secondly, they dealt with the immense problems of traffic regulation which occurred with the introduction of automobiles. This effort began in the 1920s and culminated in the 1930s. Finally, in more recent years, state governments have begun to coordinate all the law enforcement efforts within their jurisdictions.

### Nineteenth Century Experiments

Prior to the twentieth century, only two states—Texas and Massachusetts—created state police agencies. Circumstances peculiar to each state were responsible for these early experiments. In Texas, an isolated and dangerous environment forced early settlers to raise a quasi-military force to protect themselves. Once in operation the Texas Rangers added new responsibilities to their work as time progressed. Massachusetts' experiment had completely different origins. The legislature created a new police agency in response to cultural conflicts over liquor. Such different origins also had different results. In Texas the Rangers became famous, in Massachusetts, the state police became notorious. The fate of each agency was closely intertwined in its principal functions and in the attitudes which the public adopted toward them.

The Texas Rangers emerged from the necessities of frontier life. Indians harassed American settlers in the Mexican province of Texas almost from the onset. Mexican officials could offer little assistance. Widespread Indian raids severely strained the government's slender military resources. It could not guarantee continuous protection to any settlement within its immense northern provinces. Thus, when the Americans proposed to deal with the problem themselves, the Mexican government expressed no objections. Beginning in 1823, these settlers raised unofficial militia companies to repel raids and to launch counterattacks. These activities earned the Rangers widespread support because they performed duties which benefited all segments of the community. In 1836, when Texas declared its independence from Mexico, the Rangers had become a fixture in the area's frontier life.

Community defense remained the Rangers' principal responsibility until the 1850s, when they acquired new duties. The Republic of Texas' legislature granted the force permanent status about 1840 and ordered it to patrol the Mexican border. In addition, the Rangers continued to fight Indians. These defense activities culminated in the Mexican War in 1846. While serving with the United States Army, the Rangers earned reputations for bloodthirsty savagery. Returning to Texas, they found the state undergoing some changes which affected their future role. Economic developments were particularly important. Texas had become a cotton producer and its trade with the rest of the United States was expanding. An emerging prosperity brought new problems, however. Highway robberies increased; runaway slaves became a major nuisance; and Mexican immigrants seeking work were entering the state illegally. These problems forced the Rangers to engage in more general policework, beginning in the 1850s.

Civil War and Reconstruction interrupted the Rangers' activities. In 1865 a Republican legislature actually abolished the force and substituted its own, highly unpopular, state police. When the Democrats returned to power in 1874, they restored the Rangers to their former roles. Operating from semipermanent camps with a small number of full-time officers, the Rangers once again fought Indians and provided law enforcement services to isolated communities. Their reputation for bloodthirsty behavior also continued. Many prisoners died while "escaping," others were lynched or tortured. Negroes and Mexicans suffered the most, as Rangers shot and beat them with impunity. The Rangers in this period bore little resemblance to an organized police. Personalized "justice" against minorities, though, made them highly popular with white Americans.

Their behavior did not improve in the twentieth century. But the state changed considerably. Texas cities began to grow rapidly, businessmen promoted railroad construction; and the discovery of oil created a boom-town atmosphere. Economic growth attracted thousands of new settlers. In sum, the frontier came to an end as the state's economic and social structure became more complex. And with this growth the need for a more disciplined, less lawless police increased. The Rangers could not adjust. After 1915 their reputation plummeted as previously acceptable behavior seemed increasingly out of place. The legislature finally acted to control the Rangers in 1935. It created a Department of Public Safety which had jurisdiction over their activities. The department drastically curtailed their once excessive behavior, and an era in frontier law enforcement came to an end.

Massachusetts' experiment with a state police was born in controversy in 1865 and suffered from continuous hostility until its demise ten years later. A clash of cultural values lay at the heart of the controversy. Native-born Americans loathed the Irish Catholic fondness for hard liquor. Their loathing was based in part on ethnic and religious intolerance. But it also derived from their belief that drunkenness was sinful and criminal. Needless to say, the Irish held contrary opinions which they expressed vigorously. Since Boston's politicians had to respect their constituents' views, they did not strictly enforce laws against drunkenness. In order to overcome this lax attitude, a coalition of rural residents, prohibitionists, and others successfully fought to create a state police. The new organization had the authority to deal with general crime problems, but they were supposed to pay particular attention to enforce vice laws.

The new force enjoyed its greatest successes in 1866 and 1867. State constables made several thousand arrests in Boston for violations of the liquor laws. Elsewhere in the state the new officers had little trouble with vice, and concentrated on more serious crimes instead. They gradually created a reputation for effective detective work in robbery and murder cases. Rural residents appreciated this sort of police work. But the controversy over liquor enforcement obscured those achievements. Constables encountered considerable hostility in Boston. More importantly, their best efforts seemed to have no effect on the crime problem. As opposition to their activities continued, a movement to abolish the force gathered steam. Their opponents succeeded in reducing the number of state police in the early 1870s; they also forced through the legislature a series of laws which relaxed liquor statutes. Finally, in 1875, the legislature abolished the force, replacing it with a small number of state detectives who worked in rural areas.

Neither of these two early organizations had much influence on subsequent developments. The Rangers did inspire some short-lived imitators in Arizona and New Mexico early in the twentieth century. Small police forces appeared in both states to deal with criminals. But political opposition and abuses of their power led to their rapid demise. When an influential model for state policing did emerge, it developed in response to different sorts of problems than those which had inspired these early experiments.

## A New Model for State Policing: Pennsylvania

Early in the twentieth century rural crime and disorder in the industrial states of the Midwest and Northeast began to reach serious proportions. Railroad construction in these areas had spurred economic development and reduced rural isolation. Factories and mines had opened, promoting even greater prosperity. But prosperity also brought problems. Thieves discovered that small towns now had well-stuffed bank vaults. Burglaries became a major rural crime, beginning late in the old century and continuing into the new. Desperately poor workers, especially in the mining areas, organized unions and struck for better wages and working conditions. Murders, sabotage, and riots became common as employers fought to crush these strikes. Local sheriffs and constables were incapable of dealing with serious crime and industrial disorder. As elected officials, they too often lacked the will or ability to cope with these new circumstances.

Western Pennsylvania was especially troubled by the consequences of industrial growth. A major mining region, the area became notorious for violence. State officials contributed to the violence by abdicating their peace-keeping responsibilities. In 1865 the legislature in effect turned authority for maintaining the peace over to private corporations. A law creating the Iron and Coal Police gave employers the right to hire men to protect their interests. With no scruples about violence, the Iron and Coal Police broke up union meetings and strikes by beating and shooting workers. The miners retaliated whenever possible. During the 1890s labor problems became even more complex. Employers hired thousands of Italians, Slavs, and other Eastern Europeans. Conflicts among these ethnic groups, and with Americans, became common. Different attitudes toward religion, leisure, national celebrations, and other matters proved fruitful sources of trouble. Also in the 1890s, the United Mine Workers emerged as a major union. Its organizing activities and efforts to improve the miners' lives provided plenty of opportunities for more confrontations with the Iron and Coal Police.

Growing concern over ethnic conflict and labor violence finally stirred state officials into action. The anthracite coal strike of 1902 was the turning point. President Theodore Roosevelt appointed a commission to investigate the causes of this strike. In its report, this commission blamed the state for much of the trouble in the coal fields, pointing out that the absence of effective law enforcement encouraged violence. Pennsylvania's new governor, Samuel Pennypacker, began a campaign to remedy this situation. He suggested, and the legislature finally approved, the creation of a state police. The new organization began operations in 1905.

Governor Pennypacker disregarded every American precedent in his search for an appropriate model for his new state police. Flouting tradition, he looked to the military for his example. The American army had been fighting Filipino guerrillas since 1898. When the savage fighting led to high casualties, atrocities, and declining morale, the army switched strategies. It created the Philippine Constabulary in 1901. Composed of Filipino recruits led by soldiers of fortune, the Constabulary hunted guerrillas in the jungle while the regular army occupied the settled areas. This strategy succeeded, although the

Constabulary suffered high casualties and developed a fearsome reputation. Pennypacker admired both the Constabulary's effectiveness
and its reputation. He set out to create a version of the Philippine Constabulary in Pennsylvania.

Pennypacker chose John C. Groome, a National Guard officer, to
command the state police. Groome created an organization which
conformed precisely to the governor's ideas. First he went to Ireland
to study the Royal Irish Constabulary (the model for the Philippine
Constabulary). Returning home, Groome selected 228 men from a huge
list of applicants to staff his police. All his officers had National Guard
or regular army experience. Ninety percent of the other men had
served one to three tours in the army. Some had been officers in the
Philippine Constabulary. As events would demonstrate, Groome looked
for other qualities besides military experience. He sought men who
displayed physical stamina, devotion to duty, reckless bravery, and
contempt for foreigners. After a rigorous period of training, Groome
assigned the men to four troop commands concentrated in the western
mining areas of the state.

The state police did impose order on the mining districts. And they
did so without playing favorites. Violence could no longer be used as
often or as casually as it had been. When striking miners, for example,
launched a sniping attack on strikebreakers, the troopers arrested
them and confiscated their weapons. Management, on the other hand,
discovered that their Iron and Coal Police could no longer break heads
with impunity. Nor could they rely on the troopers to disrupt peaceful picketing. For the first time in Pennsylvania's long history of industrial strife, the state government was using its power to maintain
the peace.

But the state police used their power in other ways and for other
purposes as well. Groome's admonition to his men that "One State
Policeman should be able to handle one hundred foreigners" set the
tone for this aspect of their work. Motivated largely by prejudice, the
state police set out to teach immigrants urban-industrial discipline.
They did so first by establishing their physical supremacy over ethnic
Americans, and secondly by attacking "inappropriate" conduct.
From the outset, troopers conducted systematic sweeps through immigrant areas. They invaded homes, confiscated weapons, and subdued
protests without any particular attention to legal niceties. Riot sticks
and fists quelled dissent. Troopers appeared at immigrant cultural
events where they intimidated the participants into abandoning traditional behavior, especially heavy drinking. Picnics, christenings,
weddings, and other social events became more decorous. The immigrants learned "appropriate" behavior which conformed to the American ideals of their watchful state police.

Pennsylvania's police imposed order and discipline on the mining districts by World War I. The troopers could then devote their attention to more routine matters. Success encourages imitation, though, and several states copied Pennsylvania's model. Between 1908 and 1923 fourteen states established similar organizations. Most of these were in northern industrial states. In nearly every case these states sought to eliminate the same sorts of disorders which had plagued Pennsylvania. There was, however, one significant variation from the basic model. State policing in the West was generally less impartial and more violent than in the East. Nevada, for example, established its state police in 1908 after a major labor dispute. Local copper companies hired the new officers as watchmen for their mines. State policing in Nevada therefore began with a clear probusiness bias. Colorado and Oregon created their state police in 1918. Both were paramilitary organizations which also sided with local industrialists. Colorado's police became so controversial for their antilabor behavior that the legislature disbanded them in 1923.

The decline of the labor union movement and European immigration after 1917 undermined the need for a Pennsylvania-style state police. In the staunchly probusiness atmosphere of the 1920s, unions lost thousands of members. They became too weak, and the public was too hostile, for them to seriously challenge their employers. World War I and congressional immigration restriction laws discouraged European migration to the United States. Cut off from new recruits who could revitalize their ethnic cultures, immigrants already in the United States slowly acculturated. The state police no longer had to deal with social and industrial discipline. Other public agencies, such as schools, assumed those chores in rural areas. Freed from those responsibilities, the police now turned to new problems.

**Traffic Regulation**

Automobiles transformed American life. They altered economic development, affected social attitudes and behavior, and revolutionized urban growth. For the first two decades of the century there was little evidence that this invention would have such profound effects. Beginning in the 1920s, however, those effects became increasingly obvious. So did the problems which autos caused. Those problems had an important impact on the development of the state police. For the first time in their brief history troopers came into frequent contact with the middle class. Like miners and immigrants before them, the middle class needed to modify some aspects of their behavior. But previous tactics, especially brute force, were not applicable to this new group of offenders. The state police needed a new approach to their work to cope with middle-class drivers.

Traffic regulation became a major problem when the number of automobiles increased enormously. Cars were initially toys for the wealthy
and a few zealous inventors. They were hard to make and expensive
to buy. In 1900 there was perhaps one auto for every ten thousand
people. Then Henry Ford revolutionized his industry in 1914 by mass
producing a cheap, durable car, the Model T. Other manufacturers
copied his methods and the number of autos mushroomed. By 1930
the ratio of cars to people was 1:5.3. Practically every family owned
one. During the 1920s these people began exploring the countryside
on weekends and on vacations.

Highway construction encouraged driving and complicated traffic
control. Prior to the twenties America had few paved roads outside
of its cities. Congress began to remedy this situation in 1916 with
passage of the Federal Aid Road Act. This law provided limited federal
funding for highway construction. State legislatures responded by
taxing gasoline to raise matching funds. Then in 1921 Congress increased the federal contribution to construction. It also established
building priorities by creating the first interstate highway system.
Although this original system took many years to complete, the number
of miles of paved roads increased 100 percent by the end of the twenties.

Motorcycle squad duty. *Courtesy of St. Louis Police Library.*

Travel outside cities now became easier and more attractive. But once beyond the supervision of urban policemen, drivers found little to restrain them. Speeding, reckless driving, accidents, and injuries increased significantly by the close of the decade.

Criminals also took advantage of these developments. They had been plundering small-town banks and post offices for decades, but the auto made their work easier. Now they did not have to confine their activities to towns near railroads. Cars and highways gave them a new flexibility to explore previously untapped areas. Furthermore, the road system and the auto's mobility insulated them from arrest. Trains traveled fixed routes on regular schedules, two characteristics which thieves had to take into account in their planning. By using cars, though, criminals could strike at anytime and use a variety of escape routes. They were therefore even more difficult to cope with than before.

State governments responded to these developments in two ways. First, some states authorized police agencies which had broad powers to deal with criminal as well as traffic problems. But others chose to establish more limited organizations which dealt only with traffic. This second solution became the dominant trend. During the twenties eight legislatures created state police departments, while six limited themselves to highway patrols. In the 1930s, though, only eight more state police agencies were set up while eighteen highway patrols were established. And several of the more grandiose-sounding state police organizations were actually restricted to traffic matters by law.

Once in operation, these police had to establish new methods for controlling ordinary drivers as well as criminals. They disciplined middle-class citizens by combining service with mild restraints. Michigan's state police, for example, began offering traffic safety education in rural areas in 1925. A few years later Texas troopers gave free vehicle inspections. None of the controls which legislatures and the police imposed were especially drastic. Michigan apparently was the first state to study where accidents occurred and to assign troopers to those areas, beginning in 1936. This idea reduced accidents and gave officers a ready response to irate speeders whom they stopped. Licensing tests and speed limits were also mild controls. Few people flunked the exams and the police were too undermanned to catch every speeder. These regulations and services did not seriously impede the middle class' enjoyment of its new mobility.

The state police had to improve their communications and information systems in order to control criminals. Progress occurred slowly in both areas. By 1934, for example, twenty-four states had bureaus of criminal identification. These bureaus played an important role in promoting the use of fingerprints in police work. Technology helped solve the problems posed by the new mobility and flexibility of criminals. Telephone systems and two-way radios were sufficiently developed by the early 1930s to permit new police tactics. In 1933 Michigan introduced the roadblock technique. State troopers could seal off an area where a major crime occurred within ten minutes. The troopers captured twenty-two thieves during the first year of operating with roadblocks, and other states quickly adopted the idea.

Whatever their official title—highway patrol or state police—the new agencies which emerged between 1923 and 1940 made an important contribution to bringing automobile use under control. Accidents and fatalities declined. Criminals found their work had become more risky. State troopers generally enjoyed excellent reputations. Their work was rarely tinged with political overtones and they stressed courteous relations with the public. Until the 1940s, at least, the state police were America's elite lawmen.

### Conclusion: The Modern Era

State policing entered a period of consolidation after World War II. The various departments began to break their close ties with the military by no longer recruiting officers so exclusively from the armed services. Public interest in these police forces declined as their novelty wore off. And the state legislatures contented themselves with minor bureaucratic adjustments in the structure and authority of the various departments. For a time it seemed that the states had fulfilled their order-maintenance responsibilities and that no new initiatives would occur.

For reasons which are not entirely clear, state governments began to reassess their policing responsibilities in the late 1950s. This renewed activity concentrated in two areas: police performance and general law enforcement. Legislatures sought to improve police performance in various ways. Beginning with California and New York in 1959, several states adopted uniform training and recruitment standards for their police agencies. Some states sought to increase local protection within rural communities. They offered to locate some troopers in small towns instead of in regional headquarters. State governments also eagerly sought computer ties to the National Crime Information Center which began operations in 1967. By tying into this system, the state police enhanced their ability to trace suspects' records.

Organized crime has had the most direct impact on state efforts to expand their general law enforcement responsibilities. Concern over this problem also began in the late 1950s, following the famous Mafia meeting in Appalachia in 1957. When organized crime emerged as a major theme of law enforcement during the 1960s, several states created crime commissions to coordinate efforts to deal with this problem. This trend culminated in the late sixties with the New England State Police Compact. Each state agreed to participate in a regional alliance to concentrate resources against organized crime activities. This is perhaps one area where state government could make a significant contribution to dealing with one of the nation's most difficult crime problems. Organized crime derives much of its immunity from the fact that it is rooted in a local community's social, economic, and political life. Local lawmen therefore have considerable difficulty coping with these particular criminals. State policemen, however, are somewhat less susceptible to those difficulties because they are not part of the local community. They may be relatively more effective against illegal entrepreneurs than their local counterparts.

Federal efforts to combat crime also contributed to the enhanced state role in law enforcement. The Omnibus Crime Control and Safe Streets Act of 1968 increased state responsibilities and authority significantly. Congress assigned the task of coordinating criminal justice planning to the states. State planning agencies obtained considerable control over the distribution of federal funds to local communities. They also received their own monies for research, training, education, and technical programs. For the first time in their history the states had become an integral part of a national effort to deal with crime and to improve policing.

State policemen remain more concerned with traffic than with organized crime. The continuing central role of automobiles in American life has made this necessary. Safeguarding the nation's transportation network therefore consumes most of their time. Developments since the 1950s have affected state government more than the state police. Previously spectators to most aspects of law enforcement, the states now provide a fuller range of policing services to their citizens. Specialized activities such as narcotics squads, organized crime commissions, and scientific laboratories have become increasingly common. The proliferation of these services indicates that the states are assuming a more active role in law enforcement. Although this is one of the more interesting trends in modern policing, we as yet have no general assessment of its impact. Further study may reveal that this change is of comparable importance to the shift which occurred in the 1920s, when traffic replaced disorder as the primary concern of the states.

## SUGGESTED READINGS

There is an extraordinary absence of historical works on the state police. And what is available is often biased or out of date. Katherine Mayo, *Justice to All: The Story of the Pennsylvania State Police* (New York: G. P. Putnam's Sons, 1917) suffers from both problems although it is still a classic study. Bruce Smith, *The State Police: Organization and Administration* (repr.; Montclair, N.J.: Patterson Smith, 1969) attempted the first survey of this subject, but his work is now very dated. The same can be said of two other studies: Bruce Smith, *Rural Crime Control* (New York: Institute of Public Administration, Columbia University, 1933), and August Vollmer and Alfred E. Parker, *Crime and the State Police* (Berkeley: University of California Press, 1935). Both books are, however, valuable for what they reveal about their topics in the 1930s. Frank R. Prassel, *The Western Peace Officer: A Legacy of Law and Order* (Norman: University of Oklahoma Press, 1972) contains useful information on state policing in the West. Walter P. Webb, *The Texas Rangers: A Century of Frontier Defense* (Austin: University of Texas Press, 1935) is similar in tone to Mayo's work on the Pennsylvania police. John P. Kenney, *The California Police* (Springfield: Thomas, 1964) is a too brief overview of a unique but important system of state law enforcement.

# 11

# Federal Law Enforcement: The 20th Century

Prior to 1900 the federal government had played only a limited role in law enforcement. It had concentrated on protecting the mail and the national currency, and on safeguarding its revenues. This minimal policing effort reflected the relative unimportance of the central government in American society generally. Congressional activities and attitudes reinforced this limited approach to law enforcement. Postal inspectors and Secret Service agents might perform necessary work, but congressmen thought they might also be a potential threat to civil liberties. Congress, therefore, kept agency budgets low and regarded requests for more men with great suspicion. Any expansion of federal law enforcement thus had to await fundamental changes in the responsibilities of the national government and in the attitudes of elected federal officeholders.

Basic changes in both areas began early in this century. Starting in the Progressive Era, Congress passed a large number of laws which vastly expanded the federal government's importance. Congress based this legislation on federal authority in three crucial areas: foreign trade, interstate commerce, and national security. As a result, law enforcement responsibilities multiplied. In addition, various Presidents, cabinet officers, and department heads vigorously expanded policing activities. They regarded more effective federal law enforcement as necessary and in the public interest. Gradually, Congress became convinced too, at least until the early 1970s. New laws and new attitudes therefore became the basis for the tremendous expansion in federal policing during the twentieth century.

167

This expansion did not occur all at once. Public concerns dictated what sort of laws Congress passed. Those concerns varied over time and did not always apply to police problems. Vigorous executive leadership depended upon the interests and personalities of Presidents and their subordinates. Not every President, cabinet officer, or department administrator cared equally about expanding federal law enforcement. Given these general considerations, the increase in federal policing proceeded sporadically. The three most important periods of expansion coincided with crises in domestic reform and foreign wars.

### The First Era of Expansion, 1908-24

Public attitudes and national necessities combined in the first quarter of the century to expand federal policing. During the Progressive Reform period Americans became convinced that the central government had to help solve many of the nation's problems. This belief caused voters to elect politicians who advocated increased federal power. Theodore Roosevelt and Woodrow Wilson were typical representatives of this new attitude. Both men encouraged laws and administrative decisions which, in some cases, created new federal policing responsibilities. World War I ended reform, but it did not halt the growth of federal authority. Congress decided it had to enact laws to safeguard national security. Then, in the aftermath of the war, a misguided hysteria over internal security swept the nation. Both during and after the war the public supported vigorous federal law enforcement against aliens, dissenters, and other presumed enemies. In response, federal police agencies established a mixed record of commendable effectiveness and deplorable violations of civil rights.

Attorney General Charles J. Bonaparte began the process of expansion. Frustrated because the Department of Justice lacked investigative officers, Bonaparte asked Congress for authority to hire some in 1908. He needed these agents to investigate charges of corruption and business violations of the law—two favorite Progressive concerns. When he was turned down, Bonaparte decided to act on his own. On July 1, 1908, he created the Bureau of Investigation within the Justice Department. Roosevelt ordered the Secret Service to transfer eight agents to the new bureau. By administrative fiat Bonaparte had established the agency which would develop into the Federal Bureau of Investigation.

The bureau's first important opportunity to expand occurred in 1910. Reformers had by then become convinced that organized rings of procurers shipped unwilling women across state lines and forced them into a life of prostitution. Congress responded to this concern by passing the White Slave Traffic Act (Mann Act). This law prohibited the interstate transportation of women for immoral purposes. Charged with responsibility for enforcing the Mann Act, the bureau responded with an immediate expansion in manpower. It grew from a few dozen agents to nearly three hundred. Until the 1930s the bureau conducted numerous investigations into the illicit sexual behavior of ordinary Americans. These investigations had little impact on the business of prostitution, but they helped justify the bureau's existence.

Reformers' concerns over personal, private conduct did not stop with prostitution. Drug abuse also alarmed them. In the nineteenth century, drug addiction had been fairly common but it had not been a matter of public concern. Although a few criminals were addicts, there was no relationship between crime and narcotics. Opium, morphine, and heroin were readily available in various forms at local drugstores at cheap prices. No one had to steal to support a habit.

This situation changed radically early in the twentieth century. Doctors became much more cautious in prescribing narcotics because of their growing knowledge about addiction. The medical profession began to campaign for more intelligent use of drugs and greater controls over them. At the same time, an international reform movement developed to restrict the world trade in opium. Humanitarians in Europe and America held conferences and passed resolutions demanding an end to this traffic. In 1909 Congress passed the Opium Exclusion Act as the first concrete result of this reform agitation. Then in 1914 the medical profession, large drug companies, and the reformers supported passage of the Harrison Act. A landmark law, the Harrison Act was designed to regulate drug importing, manufacturing, and dispensing. Persons engaged in any of these activities had to register with the Collector of Internal Revenue, pay special taxes, and keep detailed records. The law was not, however concerned with the individual addict.

Congress made the Bureau of Internal Revenue within the Treasury Department responsible for enforcing the Harrison Act. Given this mandate, the bureau's director established the Narcotics Section in the Miscellaneous Division. The federal role in drug enforcement problems expanded gradually from these obscure beginnings. First, the Treasury Department made a crucial decision which immediately changed the position of drug addicts in American society. In 1919 the department decided that a doctor could not legally prescribe for an addict. By a single stroke, addicts were deprived of legitimate drug supplies. Predictably, the demand for illegal supplies promptly rose. Criminals began smuggling narcotics into the country to meet this demand. In response, Congress passed the Narcotic Drug Import and Export Act in 1922. This law established penalties for illegally importing, distributing, selling, or possessing drugs. Once a mere Section, Narcotics became a full-fledged Division in the Bureau of Internal

Revenue in 1920. Its manpower also increased as the battle against illegal drugs expanded.

Although important, the efforts to regulate personal -behavior had less impact on federal law enforcement than World War I and its aftermath. Laws affecting prostitution and narcotics produced relatively limited policing efforts. The war, however, caused a considerable growth in law enforcement activities. Congress did not create any new agencies, but it did expand the responsibilities of existing ones. Simultaneously, a government-sponsored campaign to marshal support for the war effort produced a massive hatred of foreigners and paranoic suspicion of dissent. Americans displayed a willingness to subordinate basic liberties to national security. While there were some spies and saboteurs at work during the war, the reaction to them was excessive. Even when peace returned, and there was absolutely no threat to national security, massive violations of civil rights continued.

Two laws provided the authority for this increase in federal policing activities. First, Congress passed the Espionage Act in 1917. This law imposed heavy fines and prison sentences for anyone who aided the enemy, obstructed recruitment, or mailed seditious literature. Secondly, Congress severely restricted freedom of speech and press in the Sedition Act of 1918. It was now a crime to "utter, print, write, or publish any disloyal, profane, scurrilous or abusive language" about government or its leaders. Superficially, the provisions of both laws made sense in a time of national emergency. Problems arose, however, in the ways these acts were interpreted and applied.

Post office inspectors, Secret Servicemen, and Bureau of Investigation agents all worked to enforce these laws. The inspectors reviewed postal employee records in a hunt for disloyal personnel. Seditious literature also attracted their attention. The definition of sedition was so broad that this task occupied a great deal of their time. Several newspapers were suppressed and their editors were imprisoned for making statements critical of the war effort. Both Secret Servicemen and bureau agents worked in counterespionage and antisabotage efforts with considerable success. In addition, the bureau investigated enemy aliens and enforced the draft laws. "Slacker raids" in 1918 rounded up thousands of draft age men who did not have proper identification. Those arrested were treated roughly and held in violation of their civil rights. Further investigations revealed that practically none of these men had violated the draft laws. All but a few had to be released. The hasty investigations, sudden mass arrests, and disregard for basic legal procedures which occurred in the "Slacker raids" typified the carelessness of federal policing during the war. Hundreds of loyal Americans who disagreed with various official policies suffered as a result.

Even greater abuses occurred with the war's end. A development known as the Red Scare caused near hysteria across the nation. Various events combined to produce this episode, which erupted in the winter and spring of 1919-20. The Russian Revolution and widespread political disorder in Europe following the war's end created the impression that bolshevism was spreading throughout the world. At home, anarchists launched a letter bomb attack on many prominent citizens. Most of the bombs never reached their destinations. A few did, but none of the intended victims was hurt. The explosions, however, convinced Americans that radicalism threatened the nation's social and political foundations. Numerous strikes in major industries added to the turmoil. Labor unrest led many people to believe that Communists had seized control of the working class. While untrue, demagogues made the most of the accusation. Frightened by these events, the public demanded protection, and the federal government responded.

Attorney General A. Mitchell Palmer established a General Intelligence Division in the Department of Justice and appointed J. Edgar Hoover its director. This new division collected information on radicals throughout the United States. Within two years, Hoover had prepared dossiers on 450,000 people, 60,000 of whom he designated as important radicals. That amazingly high figure indicated a major threat, if accurate. But it was not. Hoover obtained that inflated estimate by believing everything his poorly trained, overeager agents reported. They infiltrated thousands of meetings of groups suspected of radicalism. Even mildly liberal organizations were suspect. The agents habitually overestimated the membership of these "radical" groups and over-reacted to speeches and casual comments. When the agents sought information on individuals, they collected gossip, malicious rumors, and any other data which fit their preconceived notions. None of this information was checked for accuracy. But Hoover proceeded to use this "intelligence" as the basis for action. Federal agents made mass arrests of presumed radicals across the country. The Palmer Raids, as they were called, did not solve any serious crimes. Instead, innocent citizens found themselves in jail charged with the most nebulous offenses. Civil rights and venerable legal procedures simply did not exist for the new federal agents. Except for about 400 persons who were shipped to Russia at the Justice Department's insistence, all those arrested were eventually released. Not, however, before they had been smeared by Palmer's unfounded accusations. Eventually, Palmer's excessive behavior provoked a reaction, and the Red Scare ended in the spring of 1920.

Public reactions to these abuses ended the first era of federal law enforcement expansion. The various agencies, especially the FBI, had grown too rapidly in response to reform and wartime demands.

Agents lacked adequate training and often had backgrounds which ill-equipped them to respect civil rights. Several FBI agents, for example, had been private detectives who had unsavory reputations. Politicians regularly interfered in bureau affairs. To solve the bureau's multiple problems, the attorney general appointed J. Edgar Hoover director in 1924. Even with this appointment, a new era in federal policing had to await the emergence of yet another series of national emergencies which would justify further expansion.

## The Federal Bureau of Investigation, 1932-54

Red Scare excesses, and the inept enforcement of Prohibition, temporarily undermined public support for more federal policing. Important politicians also discouraged expansion. Presidents Coolidge and Hoover regarded crime control as primarily a local responsibility. They therefore resisted suggestions that the federal government should assume a more active role in law enforcement. While Prohibition agents attracted the public's wrath for their corruption and inefficiency, most federal officers avoided controversy. They concentrated on necessary but less spectacular tasks. Postal inspectors, for example, worked successfully to eliminate a resurgence of major mail robberies. J. Edgar Hoover spent the late 1920s cleansing his bureau of political hacks. He rebuilt the bureau by carefully selecting highly qualified new agents, by imposing rigorous discipline, and by stimulating high morale among his men.

Eventually, Hoover's appointment as director and his reforms would have important consequences. His early participation in the Red Scare established one of his most enduring and dangerous traits: his tendency to see Communists behind every social change. This paranoia caused enormous problems after World War II. But Hoover was also deeply committed to police professionalism. During the 1930s, he became a major spokesman for police reform by making the bureau a model of professionalism. He recruited college graduates, created the first federal crime laboratory (1932), and founded the National Police Academy (1935). These achievements did a great deal to enhance the prestige of efforts to improve the quality of police personnel and to encourage the spread of scientific crime detection.

Hoover's considerable importance as a police reformer depended upon the FBI's reputation as the nation's leading law enforcement agency. That reputation did not exist in the 1920s. Shortly after the Great Depression began in 1929, however, favorable conditions for the expansion of federal policing reemerged. Hoover, through a combination of luck and bureaucratic political skill, became the principal beneficiary of this changed situation.

The Depression threw millions of people out of work. Some of the unemployed turned to crime for a living, and property thefts therefore increased. In addition, important underworld figures like Al Capone, Dutch Schultz, and Louis Buchalter expanded their interest in racketeering, gambling, and other activities. The violence associated with these maneuvers often made spectacular headlines. And finally, a number of gangs which specialized in bank robbery and kidnapping emerged in the early 1930s. Initially, this apparent surge in crime did not provoke a demand for federal intervention. But that situation soon changed.

Three events caused an expansion of federal law enforcement: the Lindbergh kidnapping in 1932; the Kansas City Massacre in 1933; and the election of Franklin D. Roosevelt, also in 1932. Criminals abducted wealthy businessmen or members of their families with increasing frequency in the 1920s and early 1930s. These kidnappings prompted upper-class citizens to seek federal penalties for this crime as one way of discouraging criminals. Supporters of a federal law, however, encountered considerable resistance from states'-right advocates and other groups when they asked Congress for legislation. Then Bruno Hauptmann kidnapped Charles Lindbergh's son in early 1932. Lindbergh was not simply another wealthy American. As the first man to fly the Atlantic alone, he was a national hero. Everything he did, everything that happened to him, interested the public. Lindbergh's anguish over his son's abduction, and the subsequent discovery of the infant's body, provoked a national outcry. Overwhelmed by demands for action, Congress passed the Lindbergh Law in 1932. This legislation created a special unit within the FBI to handle kidnapping cases. Within four years Hauptmann had been captured and executed and the FBI was beginning to attract national publicity for its pursuit of other kidnappers.

An ambush and murder of five men, including an FBI agent, became the second episode justifying an increased federal police effort. On June 17, 1933, Pretty Boy Floyd and two companions made an abortive, bloody attempt to rescue a friend being returned to federal prison. Their friend died with four officers in a hail of machine gun fire. Promptly dubbed the Kansas City Massacre by the press, the killings shocked the law enforcement community and Hoover in particular. He launched a nationwide manhunt for the killers, even though he had very slender legal powers in the case. FBI agents cooperating with local police managed to capture one participant, who was subsequently executed. Floyd died in a gun battle with federal agents in 1934. The remaining gangster died in a dispute with underworld competitors. Hoover had initially ordered his agents into this manhunt because of his outrage over the killings. But the public's response to his actions encouraged him to look for other cases which would enhance the FBI's prestige. When John Dillinger attracted notoriety in 1933, Hoover sought a pretext to intervene. Dillinger's escape from an Indiana jail, in which he drove a stolen car into Illinois, gave Hoover his opportunity. After a spectacular pursuit agents finally killed Dillinger in Chicago in the summer of 1934. Ignorant of the FBI's clumsy handling of the case (agents bungled two capture attempts through haste and a refusal to cooperate with local police), an adoring public showered Hoover with praise. These cases, and several others, played a crucial role in fostering the FBI's image as the nation's leading law enforcement agency.

Hoover had a powerful supporter in his campaign to expand the FBI. Franklin Roosevelt had had an interest in better law enforcement since the 1920s. As President, Roosevelt sought increased federal policing authority. The favorable attention the FBI was receiving, and his own popularity, helped Roosevelt overcome congressional opposition to his ideas. In 1934 Congress passed a series of laws which vastly expanded the area of federal responsibilities. It now became a federal offense to rob a national bank; to flee across state lines to avoid prosecution; to engage in interstate racketeering; to transport stolen property across state lines, and to resist a federal officer. Congress assigned enforcement of these laws to the FBI. Hoover now had the public support and legal authority to pursue a policy of vigorous bureau expansion.

FBI Director J. Edgar Hoover. *Courtesy of Religious News Service.*

Roosevelt further increased Hoover's power by executive acts. In 1936 the President, concerned about Fascists and Communists in the United States, turned to Hoover for help. Roosevelt asked him to gather information on German, Italian, and Russian embassy activities. The FBI watched embassy personnel and reported who these people talked to in their travels around the country. This work was conducted with considerable secrecy because the FBI had no legislative authority to justify it. In the late 1930s the FBI's responsibilities increased enormously when Roosevelt gave the bureau authority over all domestic espionage, counterespionage, and sabotage matters. Hoover revived the notorious General Intelligence Division in 1940 and began collecting files on anyone who might be a threat to national security. All these responsibilities required more personnel. Hoover had 772 agents and other employees working under him in 1934, at the beginning of the bureau's expansion. By 1941 he had 4,370. The FBI had become one of the federal government's fastest growing agencies. Hoover's ambition and Roosevelt's favoritism combined with genuine national needs to produce an extremely powerful federal police force for the first time in American history.

There were great benefits and great dangers in Roosevelt's law enforcement policies. Hoover's success made him the nation's most famous and influential police officer. The public could now compare their local police's behavior with the FBI's professionalism. Unfavorable comparisons pressured local officials to do something about deficiencies. Thus hundreds (and eventually thousands) of officers attended the National Police Academy where they received intensive training in the latest techniques and ideas about policing. Academy graduates spread the gospel of professionalism and often became important police officials who advanced reform. The FBI also made important contributions to national security. Even before America entered World War II, the FBI broke up several German espionage rings. Sabotage was not even a minor threat during the war, thanks to the bureau's efforts. Indeed, the FBI's record in the war is one of its finest achievements.

Once hostilities ended, however, the less desirable effects of Roosevelt's policies emerged. Conflicts between the United States and Russia, and the successful Chinese Communist revolution in 1948, produced another round of public hysteria. The nation launched a witch-hunt for domestic scapegoats which lasted until the early 1950s. Politicians engaged in a great deal of demagoguery, using public fears to advance their own careers. Hoover fed the hysteria by announcing that many public officials had committed treason. This statement directly contradicted his assurances during the war that there were no Communists in government. Prodded by demands to do something, President

Truman created a federal loyalty program in 1947 and gave the FBI responsibility for investigating the backgrounds of all federal employees. Hoover thus obtained enormous power over the careers of thousands of public servants. He used this power to attack anyone who seemed "soft" on communism. During the notoriously irresponsible hearings conducted by Senator Joseph McCarthy, Hoover provided the senator with files on suspected subversives. Those files contained unverified gossip and other unreliable information which Hoover treated as absolute truth. As a result, many able public servants had their careers ruined.

The hysteria finally ended in 1954 with Senator McCarthy's public disgrace, but Hoover was more powerful than ever. His extreme conservatism had earned him important allies among southern congressmen. They admired his staunch anticommunism and his ideas on civil rights. Hoover regarded violations of black Americans' civil rights as a purely local problem even though the FBI had a federal mandate to investigate these offenses. Furthermore, he thought the civil rights movement, which was becoming a major reform crusade in the 1950s, was a Communist plot. As a result, Hoover refused to conduct even preliminary investigations of civil rights violations. Grateful southern congressmen supported his budget requests and defended him against all criticism. Until his death in 1972 Hoover was practically an independent institution. Not even Presidents could control him.

**Federal Policing Since 1954**

When the excessive concern over internal security declined in the early 1950s, the political justification for increasing federal police power temporarily ended. Further growth awaited new developments. Then, in the 1960s, aggressive politicians and new social crises once again produced a period of vigorous expansion. Concern over three problems brought about this growth. First, some officials became convinced that the federal government should join the fight against organized crime. Secondly, alarm over street crime provoked public demands for more effective law enforcement. Lastly, the civil rights crusade and protests against the Vietnam War created a number of law enforcement problems.

Prior to the 1960s federal officials had not been particularly concerned about organized crime. J. Edgar Hoover refused to believe national crime syndicates existed. Then Robert F. Kennedy developed an interest in the problem of organized crime. While serving as counsel to a Senate committee investigating labor-union racketeering in the late 1950s, Kennedy learned a great deal about underworld influence in legitimate economic affairs. At the same time, local lawmen had become interested in federal help against criminal syndicates in their communities. Political considerations, however, blocked co-operation between federal and local police officials. Hoover would not use the FBI to investigate criminal syndicates, and there was no one in Washington who could overcome his opposition. When Robert Kennedy became attorney general in 1961, he sought ways to resolve this dilemma. Joe Valachi's testimony before a Senate committee in 1963 gave Kennedy the political leverage he needed. Valachi claimed personal knowledge of a national crime conspiracy he called the Cosa Nostra. His evidence was extremely vague and contradictory, but other witnesses from various law enforcement agencies supported him. Valachi's testimony caused a national sensation. He contributed to the growing myth of an all-powerful national council run by Italians who dominated organized crime. That myth became an important justification for expanding federal law enforcement activities.

A rise in street crime also justified an expanded federal policing effort. Since offenses like burglary and mugging do not ordinarily come within federal jurisdiction, a public consensus that these offenses were a national problem had to emerge before federal agencies could intervene. Drug abuse became the key to developing that consensus. Popular opinion held that narcotics use caused street crime. Whether true or not, this idea focused attention on drugs as the root cause of crime. It followed that more effective narcotics controls would reduce crime. And the narcotics trade was one area where federal agencies could in fact help local police. They had jurisdiction over international and interstate commerce, and they had potentially greater resources than local lawmen. Concern over narcotics and crime therefore created the basis for public approval of a greater federal effort in these areas.

The civil rights crusade and the antiwar movement stirred enormous controversy and rubbed some very raw nerves in American society. Bombings and murders became all too common in the South and white terrorists struggled vainly to defeat the demand for racial equality. Major riots erupted in northern ghettos as enraged blacks reacted to economic exploitation, social repression, and police brutality. By the mid-sixties the growing protest against the Vietnam War further increased tensions. Violent demonstrations on college campuses and in cities across the country challenged fundamental social ideas and commitments. While politicians pondered the ideological issues, the police struggled to preserve public order. New congressional laws regarding civil rights and national security in wartime became the basis for federal intervention in the upheavals convulsing the country.

When Robert Kennedy moved to the Senate in 1964, he left the opportunity to expand federal policing to others. Lyndon Johnson began the process by creating the President's Commission on Law Enforcement and Administration of Justice in 1965. Its numerous suggestions prompted some immediate responses. The FBI, for example, established the National Crime Information Center in 1967. This computerized record bank collected information on a variety of offenses and a huge number of offenders. A network of terminals across the country tied local authorities to the central computer. A commission recommendation for coordinated attacks on organized crime contributed to the creation of the Strike Force concept. Each force would have personnel from several federal agencies who pooled their knowledge and skill to investigate and prosecute underworld figures. The first Strike Force began operations in 1966. Although important, these were only the initial steps in the expansion program.

New laws spurred the growth of federal policing. Congress passed the Omnibus Crime Control and Safe Streets Act in 1968. This law dealt with a large number of problems. In one of its most important provisions, the act created the Law Enforcement Assistance Administration (LEAA). This agency would make federal funds available to local police for educational programs and experiments in training and department organization. LEAA also would fund research on new ideas for crime prevention. The Omnibus Crime Control Act also authorized court-ordered wiretapping and electronic surveillance. Although intended as a weapon against organized crime, this provision could also be used against other targets as well. It therefore opened up some dangerous possibilities for suppressing civil liberties. Unsatisfied with this act, advocates of even greater federal power to deal with organized crime persuaded Congress to enact a second important law. In 1970 Congress passed the Organized Crime Control Act. This legislation created a witness immunity and protection program, extended federal jurisdiction over illegal gambling, and prohibited the investment of income from racketeering in legitimate interstate businesses. In sum, both laws established a more direct and wide-ranging federal role in the battle against crime.

President Richard Nixon used these laws and his executive authority to launch an extremely vigorous campaign against crime. This effort produced some solid achievements, but it also caused enormous abuses of police power. The attitudes and methods of the men in charge of specific activities were partly responsible for this mixed record. But Nixon, and Attorney General John Mitchell, bear the greater responsibility because they were not especially concerned about the means their subordinates used to obtain results. Nixon's campaigns against organized crime, drug smuggling, and civil dissent illustrate the strengths and weaknesses of his approach to law enforcement.

Nixon ordered a vigorous expansion of the Strike Force program to combat organized crime. Within two years (1970-71) the number of these groups increased from five to nineteen. By the end of 1971 there was a Strike Force in almost every major city which had important crime syndicates. Attorney General Mitchell helped them considerably by authorizing wiretaps, beginning in early 1969. Using leads developed from taps and other sources, Strike Forces quickly made some sensational revelations. In 1969 the New Jersey Strike Force secured indictments against Hugh Addonizio, mayor of Newark, and some seventy other public officials and criminal entrepreneurs. These men had created a lucrative contract kickback scheme involving extortion, criminal conspiracy, and tax evasion. When Addonizio and several others were convicted, the Strike Force idea gained considerable prestige. Over the next eight years these groups compiled an impressive record, obtaining convictions against several thousand underworld figures.

Widespread concern over drug abuse during the 1960s encouraged a major effort against smugglers and distributors. Federal law enforcement had been inadequate in this area for several decades. Congress created the Federal Bureau of Narcotics (FBN) in 1930 and President Hoover had appointed Harry J. Anslinger its director. Anslinger spent over thirty years trying to halt the flow of narcotics (primarily heroin) into the country. But his agency never had more than 200 agents, and he lacked the power or prestige to build the FBN into a major policing agency. Anslinger retired before public concern spurred a significant effort to combat drug problems. Beginning in 1968, a succession of various agencies struggled with drug smuggling and distribution. Congress finally reorganized all of them into the Drug Enforcement Administration (DEA) in 1973. The DEA quickly grew into a major federal police agency. By 1975, it had 3,000 employees and 500 special agents on loan from the Customs Service.

In the midst of these bureaucratic changes, federal officials adopted new strategies for combating drug dealers. Anslinger's old Federal Bureau of Narcotics had dealt primarily with Italian crime syndicates. His agents had concentrated on arresting individuals who were not always major figures in the drug traffic. Under the leadership of John M. Ingersoll, the Federal Bureau of Narcotics and Dangerous Drugs devised a more comprehensive approach. The FBNDD conducted a systematic investigation of worldwide drug trafficking. Agents identified 58 interrelated syndicates, composed of about 1,000 individuals, which presumably controlled nearly 80 percent of the cocaine, marijuana, heroin, and other drugs being distributed illegally throughout the United States. Having identified entire syndicates, the FBNDD planned and executed nationwide raids designed to eliminate them. The first such raid, in June 1970, resulted in 178 arrests in 9 cities across the country. Similar raids then became standard policy.

International diplomacy has also been used to combat drug smuggling. The first notable success in this regard occurred in 1971, when

Turkey agreed to discourage opium poppy cultivation in exchange for United States compensation to its farmers. In 1975 the Mexican government, with American help, began an aerial herbicidal spraying program which destroyed almost 85 percent of the poppy fields in Mexico. The Drug Enforcement Administration has sought to increase the effectiveness of police agencies in countries which grow or process cocaine and marijuana. DEA agents have trained special drug investigation units in Peru, Bolivia, and Colombia. In addition, Colombia for a time permitted United States aerial surveillance of pot ships loading in its ports. This arrangement made possible the seizure of forty of these vessels during 1977 and 1978. All of these efforts demonstrate a relatively more effective approach to dealing with this problem since 1968.

Civil dissent led to the most recent assault on basic liberties by federal police. J. Edgar Hoover regarded the tremendous social upheavals of the 1960s as Communist inspired, but he did not receive support for his views until Nixon became President. By that time both the black civil rights movement and the student protest against the Vietnam War had spawned some radical organizations. The Black Panthers and the Students for a Democratic Society (SDS) had captured national attention with their violent rhetoric and frequent clashes with local authorities. Hoover convinced Attorney General Mitchell that both groups represented a threat to national security—an accusation which Hoover never proved. Given a free hand, Hoover directed a massive campaign of disruption against the Panthers, SDS, and other groups. FBI agents infiltrated student meetings, recruited informants who provoked violence, wiretapped phones, and intercepted mail. CIA agents and officers from Army Intelligence also engaged in a wide range of similar activities. All this had the enthusiastic support of the Nixon administration. In fact, Nixon's appointees soon demonstrated a near obsession for using similar tactics against their political opponents as well.

The burglary of an FBI office in suburban Philadelphia in 1971 began a reversal of this attack on civil liberties. Documents which revealed the extent of the bureau's illegal activities were stolen and distributed to the public. For the first time in fifty years the FBI became the object of widespread criticism. Its defenders were placed in the awkward position of trying to justify inexcusable conduct. Various congressmen called for investigations and the bureau's prestige plummeted. Shortly thereafter, revelations about the CIA's domestic surveillance and the Watergate burglary scandal contributed to a growing movement to curtail the powers and behavior of federal law enforcement agencies. Congress strengthened the Freedom of Information Act of 1966 and passed the Privacy Act of 1974 in an effort to correct many of the problems which had surfaced during Nixon's first term.

Following Nixon's resignation in 1974, the mid-seventies became a period of adjustment and reevaluation for several federal policing agencies. The FBI was in serious disarray, especially after Hoover's death in May 1972. His successors had enormous difficulties overcoming both the worst aspects of Hoover's legacy within the bureau and the continuing public suspicion of the bureau's behavior. With some 20,000 employees the bureau continues to be the largest federal law enforcement agency, but its prestige and ability to dominate the profession of policing have been seriously undermined. President Jimmy Carter redefined the mission of the Strike Forces in 1978 by ordering them to concentrate on investigations of underworld control of legitimate businesses and labor unions. This shift away from prosecuting individuals will require some adjustments in the Strike Forces' tactics. Drug enforcement has perhaps been the most frustrating problem for federal agents. Rapid growth caused bureaucratic disorder in the DEA which was not adequately resolved until after 1975. In addition, political decisions and diplomatic failures have added to the drug problem. Nixon's associates often sought quick solutions which did not always deal with reality. When Turkey agreed to halt poppy cultivation, heroin supplies declined in East Coast cities. But heroin was also used in the West and Southwest, where Mexican and Asian supplies continued uninterrupted. Those suppliers quickly established contacts with black criminals on the East Coast, and the supply of heroin increased once more. White underworld drug suppliers, now in danger of losing income, encouraged the resumption of poppy cultivation in Turkey after 1974. Our agreement with Mexico to attack poppy growers through aerial spraying did not therefore represent another step in a sustained campaign. Heroin use, moreover, continued to spread (although it is doubtful that heroin *addiction* increased significantly).

Federal law enforcement changed substantially in the twentieth century. The increase in the number and size of various policing agencies reflected the national government's expanding role in American society. Rapid growth was not, however, the most significant development. A shift in the goals of federal policing was far more important. Prior to the 1960s federal officers generally dealt with narrowly defined problems. They did not seek to combat crime as a general phenomenon. Instead, agencies like the FBI acquired jurisdiction over particular offenses as those crimes assumed national importance. The offenders in these cases shared a common characteristic: their alleged or actual crimes denied them of social and political power. Americans have no sympathy for kidnappers, bank robbers, counterfeiters, and assorted other criminals. Federal officers could deal with these offenders as individual cases which had no broader complications. The Red Scare and McCarthyism did have disturbing implications, but the victims of federal excesses found little public concern for their plight. Furthermore, no one seriously questioned the role of federal law enforcement agencies in these episodes. Thus there was no real challenge to their authority or tactics. In sum, federal officers created a solid reputation for effective law enforcement in large part because of the tasks they were assigned.

The emphasis, and therefore the tasks, of federal law enforcement changed in the 1960s. Prodded by public fears, and perhaps emboldened by past successes, federal officials committed the national government to a broader attack on crime. They also launched an assault on illegal entrepreneurs and, most recently, on white-collar crime. Different strategies were supposed to deal with each aspect of these new responsibilities. The Omnibus Crime Control Act of 1968 created a bureaucratic structure for coordinating a national campaign against crime. Congress allocated enormous sums to improve policing. Between 1968 and 1975, LEAA alone spent nearly five billion dollars on various programs. At the same time Strike Forces and new drug agencies dealt with various aspects of organized crime.

More than a decade of effort has produced mixed results. Although there are many reasons for this record, three problems seem especially critical. First, politicians expected, indeed demanded, quick results. This pressure led to sloppy work. Secondly, federal officers lacked concrete knowledge about the scope and nature of the problems they now confronted. Strike Force personnel, for example, assumed the validity of the Mafia myth. Hundreds of presumed mafiosi therefore landed in jail without seriously undermining illegal enterprise. Ignorance about heroin addiction, how common it is, how it spreads, still leaves in doubt the efficiency of current drug policies. Finally, federal agents were now dealing with offenders who did have social, economic, and political power. Their power rested on the public demand for illegal goods and services. Federal successes, such as the apprehension of an entire drug syndicate, simply created room for other entrepreneurs to fulfill public demands. On the other hand, the influence which these entrepreneurs have in their local communities complicates efforts to build cases against them. And white-collar criminals, as the recent furor over the FBI's Abscam probe revealed, have considerable power to protect themselves from the consequences of their acts.

In sum, the expanded federal role in law enforcement has not proved to be a panacea. The crime problem may have been even worse without federal aid, but we have no way to prove that assertion. Further study and better strategies may resolve some of the problems facing contemporary federal policing. But at this point it is still too early to tell.

## SUGGESTED READINGS

The FBI has received most of the attention of authors who write on twentieth century federal policing. Don Whitehead, *The FBI Story* (New York: Random House, 1956) is the standard probureau work. Fred J. Cook, *The FBI Nobody Knows* (New York: Macmillan Company, 1964) is a solid, highly critical study. Sanford J. Unger, *FBI* (Boston: Little, Brown & Company, 1976) is the most exhaustive, and balanced, study now available. Other federal law enforcement agencies have not attracted much attention. Clark R. Mollenhoff, *Strike Force: Organized Crime and the Government* (Englewood Cliffs, N.J.: Prentice-Hall, Inc., 1972) is disappointingly shallow. Hank Messick, *Of Grass and Snow: The Secret Criminal Elite* (Englewood Cliffs, N.J.: Prentice-Hall, Inc., 1979) contains useful information on the history of drug enforcement since 1968. David F. Musto, *The American Disease: Origins of Narcotic Control* (New Haven: Yale University Press, 1973) is the best study of the period prior to 1940. Students should also consult the President's Commission on Law Enforcement and Administration of Justice, *The Challenge of Crime in a Free Society* (Washington, D.C.: Government Printing Office, 1967) and the commission's special reports.

A policewoman exemplifying the modern community service model of policing. *Courtesy Tony Castelvecchi.*

# 12

## Modern Policing

The sixties began in hope and ended in frustration. Civil rights activists mounted a successful national campaign to remove the legal barriers to full equality for black Americans. Presidents Kennedy and Johnson sponsored ambitious social programs to help the poor and eliminate urban blight. Dedicated reformers supported by enthusiastic followers and endowed with political power seemed on the verge of resolving many important problems. War and civil disorder abruptly altered the prevailing optimism. Ghetto rioters and student protesters focused on different grievances, but they shared a belief that the nation's social, economic, and political systems were malfunctioning. The rising crime rate contributed to the growing malaise. Criminal violence alarmed Americans who were already distraught over disorder and the war. These problems spilled over into the 1970s. Protests against the war did not end until 1974, when President Nixon finally negotiated an American withdrawal from Vietnam. Crime rates peaked that same year, but then stabilized at very high levels. The nation is still absorbing the turbulent legacy of the sixties.

Modern policing was an early casualty of all this upheaval. Their critical role in preserving the peace thrust the police into the center of every conflict regardless of its origins or outcome. No matter what they did, the police angered someone. This problem was especially acute in race relations. Aggressive patrol tactics in urban ghettos had become standard procedure in many cities. To the police these tactics were necessary to control potentially dangerous situations. Ghetto residents regarded them as harassment based on race prejudice (and they were frequently right). The civil rights crusade increased the tensions between these opposing views. As blacks gained political power, they demanded an end to these traditional techniques. Policemen interpreted these demands as attempts to subvert law enforcement. These conflicting views escalated misunderstanding on both sides and helped spark riots in the mid-1960s.

Police confrontations with college students further tarnished their image. During the 1960s college students supported basic social and political challenges to established values and ideals. The counterculture movement, with its emphasis on sex, drugs, and free speech, flouted many cherished notions about appropriate behavior. Student outrage at the Vietnam War complicated matters even further. Thousands of young people took to the streets to protest American intervention in Vietnam. From their perspective the war epitomized the corrupt nature of American society. The police understood none of this. Confronted with the excesses of student behavior, policemen mixed rage with contempt for students who seemed unable to appreciate their privileged positions. Mutual misunderstanding, in the context of the police role in preserving order, led almost inevitably to confrontations and violence.

The rapid increase in crime was perhaps the last, humiliating blow to the police. Crime-fighting was, after all, their specialty. Or at least that was what the public believed. And yet there was no denying the dramatic rise in all types of crime. The increase outstripped attempts to explain it as the consequence of better reporting techniques, changing attitudes, or economic developments. Already anguishing over riots and civil disorder, the public had little patience with such explanations. By the late 1960s crime had become a major political issue and the police were being subjected to searching criticism.

In response to these problems, reform reemerged as a major theme in policing. The professional model of law enforcement no longer seemed appropriate. Critics analyzed its faults and probed its consequences—an ironic turn of events since professionalism was still relatively new in the early 1960s. But the achievements of professionalism, and the highly volatile political environment of the era, complicated this reform movement in unexpected ways. New interest groups proposed contradictory solutions to the problems of professionalism. Academics, bureaucrats, and police patrolmen contended for dominance over the future of policing. The successes and failures of each group helped to shape modern policing into its current form.

## Rediscovering the Police: The Liberal Response

With a few exceptions such as Franklin Roosevelt, liberals had ignored the police since the end of the Progressive movement. Blacks had little political power prior to the 1950s; their complaints fell on deaf ears. The Depression and World War II also diverted attention from police problems. As a result, a small, dedicated group of police administrators had assumed control of reform. They developed and implemented the professional model. Strict, uniform law enforcement was one of the chief characteristics of that model, and bureaucratic pressures to execute that policy encouraged the aggressive patrol tactics which caused so much tension between the police and minorities. When the civil rights movement exposed these practices and labeled them unnecessary harassment, liberals renewed their interest in the police. Their dismay over what they discovered produced an alternative model for policing called community service.

University professors, social reformers, and journalists discovered that actual police behavior bore little resemblance to commonly held assumptions. First, they found that most police work does not involve crime. Policemen spend most of their time on very routine matters. Directing traffic, rendering various services, issuing tickets, and filling out forms were only a few of these mundane chores. Secondly, researchers uncovered the fact that policemen have a great deal of discretion in handling incidents. Indeed, arrests were not inevitable in every encounter. Furthermore, discretion extended to difficult decisions about if, when, and how to use force. Other studies probed the social backgrounds, attitudes, and work environments of policemen. Policing, they discovered, attracts recruits from the lower, or lower-middle class who have conservative social and political views. They conform easily to the requirements of police bureaucracy. But policemen also regard themselves as a misunderstood, much maligned group. Consequently, they are distrustful of outsiders and place great stress on loyalty to their fellow officers.

None of these revelations was particularly startling. Anyone who bothered could have discovered the same things years before. But this information was new to the liberals, and they found in these studies reasons why policemen mistreated minorities, abused students and protesters, and failed to cope with crime. Police officers were too often bigoted, intolerant of different viewpoints, and insensitive to change. They were also too accustomed to using force, especially on those who challenged their authority. Furthermore, the police failed to appreciate the social and economic causes of crime. Criminals, from the liberal point of view, were victims of their environment, not malevolent beings. The liberal indictment of the police contained a great deal of truth. And it became the basis for their solution to police reform.

According to the liberal diagnosis, the police needed to reorient their work toward a community service model. The implications of this idea were never completely clarified, but the model essentially required a revolution in police bureaucracy, attitudes, and behavior. Policemen should, above all else, stress services, not crime fighting as their principal activity. They should establish close relationships with neighborhood residents. People should be encouraged to suggest changes in police practices. They should also be organized into neighborhood crime prevention groups. Personal contacts between officers and residents should be based on mutual respect and cooperation.

The community service model also envisioned transformed officers. Ideally, they would come from the same background and speak the same language as the people they served. This implied that officers would have to be recruited from minority groups. But they would also have a college education which would teach them self-control and knowledge about the world. In order to make maximum use of these new officers, the police bureaucracy would have to be decentralized. Police chiefs would relinquish some control over policies and tactics to allow greater initiative. Local commanders would establish community centers where neighborhood residents could work with their police. Community service was, in sum, designed to return the control of the police to the neighborhoods. In that regard, it was an idealized version of nineteenth century policing.

Ironically, an idea primarily intended to make policing responsive to minorities worked best in small, homogenous middle-class communities. Victor Cizanckas, of Menlo Park, California, was the first to apply this model rigorously. Cizanckas became police chief in 1968, and immediately introduced his reform program. He abandoned military titles and uniforms, recruited college graduates with social science degrees, and decentralized decision making. Cizanckas downplayed police technology and the use of force. Officers were encouraged to enlist citizens in neighborhood crime control programs. And Cizanckas gave his men substantial responsibilities in deciding policies. His efforts were rewarded by an increase in department morale, an improved public image, and a decrease in local crime.

Although many small departments adopted Cizanckas' methods, large ones did not. Cincinnati's four year experiment (1971-75), the Community Sector Policing Project, illustrates some of the problems this approach encounters in large departments. The police chief chose a district which had a high percentage of blacks and a high crime rate for this experiment. Teams of officers were assigned to sections within this district. Each team had responsibility for providing nearly all the police services within their sectors. In contrast to Cizanckas' experience, the results were extremely disappointing. Serious crimes did not decline, and the police's image did not improve among area residents. Bureaucratic inflexibility caused this failure. Police administrators did not change the way they evaluated individual performance. An officer had to be sure he wrote enough tickets and made enough arrests to satisfy quotas. He could not waste time talking to local residents about their problems. Several bureaucrats also undermined the experiment by reassuming powers they had delegated to local team leaders. Without control over duty assignments, rosters, and other administrative details, team leaders lacked the flexibility to adapt to local conditions. In retrospect, this experiment seems more a publicity ploy than a serious attempt at reform.

Bureaucratic inertia was not the only problem impeding the spread of the community service model. The police were generally hostile to this idea because it contradicted their own conception of their work. And thanks to the success of professional reform prior to 1965, they had the ability to resist obnoxious innovations. O. W. Wilson, William Parker, and other reformers had removed the police from urban politics. Police chiefs could choose to experiment with reform, but if they did not want to no one could force change upon them. Most chose to ignore the substance of the community service model. But if the liberals' solution to reform had little impact, their critique of policing was valuable. They informed the general public about the realities of police work. And their support for college training encouraged thousands of officers to continue their educations. These are achievements whose consequences are difficult to measure. Hopefully, a better-informed public and a better-educated police can provide support for other reform efforts.

## Bureaucrats as Reformers

Although police administrators were generally indifferent to liberal reform proposals, that did not mean they opposed change. On the contrary, several police chiefs became dedicated reformers. They differed from liberal critics, however, as to the nature of the problems facing the police. And they had their own solutions.

By the 1960s a new generation of police administrators was assuming power in many cities. Trained in the original ideology preached by the pioneer professionals, these men accepted most of the basic goals of their mentors. Freedom from political interference of any kind remained the basis of their faith. These new professionals were prepared to make major changes in the structure of their departments in order to preserve that independence. In effect, they used that legacy to block new attempts to interfere in their fiefdoms.

The second generation of police professionals felt that their basic problems could be reduced to a single point: professionalism had not progressed far enough. Standards had to be raised; outmoded equipment had to be replaced; tactics had to be refined. And corruption had to be eliminated. In addition, these administrators realized they needed to mollify a restless public. Otherwise their precious political independence could be jeopardized. Thus discipline had to be tightened to respond to minority grievances. Community relations needed improvement, especially by recruiting blacks and hispanics. And officers had to cultivate a more friendly public image. In sum, bureaucratic reform stressed sound professional management and good public relations.

Bureaucratic reform could produce important changes. The most important example was Los Angeles. At his death in 1966 William Parker left a department which many regarded as the most professional police organization in the country. But it was also a department which overtly defended conservative white interests with uniform, even stringent law enforcement. Its relations with minority groups were tenuous at best, and its officers had a general reputation for arrogance. When Edward Davis became chief in 1969, he introduced a three-stage reform over the next six years. Essentially, he believed bureaucratic decentralization would encourage greater initiative among patrolmen and better community relations.

Davis began his reform campaign in 1969 by introducing the Basic Car Plan. He assigned the officers from each patrol car to a permanent territory. These men met monthly with area residents to discuss problems. Since this idea required patrolmen to alter their behavior somewhat, Davis redefined performance standards. Officers would be judged by the relative lawfulness of their areas. The Basic Car Plan seemed to improve police morale and community relations. Davis therefore adopted the second stage of reform, the Team 28 Experiment, in 1972. He created a team of patrol, traffic, and investigative officers, assigned them a territory, and delegated some authority to implement policies within their area. This was the first step in bureaucratic decentralization. Because the team combined police specialties and had a permanent territory, it was a miniature precinct. The last step in reform began in 1974. Davis decentralized the entire bureaucracy and introduced the Neighborhood Action Team Policing program. Central headquarters retained some functions, such as recruitment and training. But Davis combined all the police districts into four bureaus, each commanded by a deputy chief who had considerable authority. Team policing became standard within each bureau.

After some initial problems, Davis' reforms seemed to produce results. The crime rate declined for the city as a whole, and it dropped

30 percent in Watts, the city's black ghetto area. On the other hand, the new policies were not uniformly successful because not every patrolman and administrator adjusted easily to the changes. Citizen complaints continued, and indicated that there were still problems with arrogance, lack of sympathy, and other matters. Overall, though, the department's reputation had improved. Davis managed to preserve the LAPD's prominence as an effective, innovative organization.

Comprehensive reform remained a rarity. Most administrators resisted challenges to traditional ideas and practices, as their reaction to the Kansas City Preventive Patrol Experiment (1972-73) illustrates. Chief Clarence Kelley had earned a reputation as an important reformer by the time the Police Foundation sought his help with this experiment. With Kelley's cooperation, the foundation tested the effectiveness of traditional patrol techniques. The results were rather startling. Within the test area, three different approaches to patrol had no effect on the crime rate, or on the delivery of police services, or on citizen fear of crime. Furthermore, the study concluded that 60 percent of all patrol time is wasted effort. Officers could make more effective use of that time by doing other things.

Kelley responded to these findings by shifting officers from routine patrol to community-related policing. The reaction elsewhere was not so positive. Administrators across the country attacked the experiment's conclusions. There were indeed problems with the survey, but the critics overreacted. More was at stake here than just another irritating reform idea. Preventive patrol is regarded as *the* essential police activity. It enables the police to provide continuous community surveillance; it enhances police visibility—the public can see that officers are doing their jobs; and it deters crime. Or so the police argue. The Kansas City Experiment struck at the basic assumptions supporting the most typical policing idea. Bitter denunciations erupted so quickly because this study struck such sensitive nerves. In the debate which followed, the opponents managed to obscure the implications of the experiment by attacking its methodology.

The reaction to the Kansas City experiment defined the limits of bureaucratic reform. Police administrators have occasionally been willing to change the organization of their departments. They have even been willing to delegate authority and encourage initiative among their subordinates. But they refuse to reconsider the basic assumptions and tactics of police work. Their standard solutions to problems are better management, more men, and new equipment. Although these solutions have not significantly reduced crime or improved community relations, administrators cling to them: Reform from within police departments thus remains rooted in traditional assumptions.

### Militancy and Orthodoxy: Police Unions

Bureaucratic resistance to change is only one source of opposition to police reform. Another is the rank and file. They have recently acquired the political power to influence not just reform but policing generally. Although they have been hostile to change, their opposition does not necessarily imply an irreversible resistance. Rather, their opposition seems to derive from the combined effects of a separate police tradition and the environment in which unionism first developed during the 1960s.

The effect policing has had on patrolmen had been habitually ignored. Reformers insisted that political meddling was the central issue in law enforcement. This assumption shaped the way we have viewed police behavior. Serious deficiencies, such as corruption and brutality, therefore originated in political decisions to appoint incompetent, venal, violent men to the police. According to this analysis, police behavior would improve if departments could be freed from political interference. This assumption has influenced police reform since the nineteenth century. Patrolmen have been regarded as dependent objects which responsible officials could manipulate in the public's best, nonpartisan, interests.

Recent research has begun to undermine this conception of patrolmen. We are discovering that corruption and brutality can be acquired traits learned by participating in the subculture of policing. But the more important point is the existence of a subculture which shapes individual behavior in conformity to group traditions and expectations. This subculture did not emerge in the twentieth century when social scientists first discovered it. Rather, it originated in the experiences of nineteenth century policemen and has had a continuous existence ever since.

Until the 1960s, the assumptions of police reform seemed to work quite well. Professional administrators did acquire political independence in many cities. They did improve the efficiency, effectiveness, and behavior of their officers. But the professional police reformer, assumed that he would always be able to control his men. When events beyond his control politicized the rank and file, the administrator faced a situation for which he had no ready solution. Police militancy emerged as an independent new force. It drew its cohesion from the reactions of the patrolmen's subculture to practical problems and rapid social change.

Patrolmen had usually been underpaid, overworked, and misunderstood. But they had never had any sense of shared frustrations beyond the confines of their own departments. That changed in the 1960s. Events which pinpointed common concerns on a national basis for the first time provided the foundation for their militancy. The Berkeley

Free Speech Riots in 1964 began this process. Public reaction focused on the violence of students and policemen, but patrolmen everywhere were more concerned by the inability of the Berkeley police to obtain community support in enforcing the law. That underscored the isolation which the police subculture taught officers to expect. In 1966, Mayor John Lindsay's attempt to impose a Civilian Review Board on the New York Police produced a second crisis. Policemen across the nation regarded this as an effort to politicize law enforcement. If successful, Lindsay would appoint black activists, liberals, and radical college students to the board. These were people hostile to the police; they would oppose uniform law enforcement, substituting "community standards" as their policies. At least this was what New York's Patrolmen's Benevolent Association (PBA) claimed. The PBA launched a political campaign to defeat Lindsay, and won in a popular referendum.

The patrolmen learned several lessons from these and other incidents: Berkeley taught them that the general public no longer gave them automatic support. Public condemnation of the Chicago police riot during the Democrat's national convention in 1968 emphasized this point. Secondly, patrolmen discovered that their administrative superiors could not be relied upon to protect them from outside meddling. Lindsay had not encountered any resistance from department bureaucrats with his proposal. Finally, and most importantly, they had learned that they could protect themselves by organizing. Various sorts of police unions sprouted across the country and clashed successfully with their titular superiors in the late 1960s and after.

Rank and file militancy coincided with the emergence of reform. This proved unfortunate, especially in large police departments which already had other problems with implementing change. Patrolmen tended to assume that liberal reform was merely an effort by outsiders to undermine the integrity of law enforcement and the independence of police departments. They opposed bureaucratic reform for different reasons. Administrators initially refused to treat unionism seriously. Instead they tried to discipline union members into submission. Patrolmen responded by rallying around their union leaders and adopting a traditional labor-management dichotomy in their attitudes. This latter development was perhaps inevitable to some extent. But it was also unfortunate because patrolmen had accepted the basic assumptions of the professional police model. In the midst of change, the patrolmen had become the principal defenders of professionalism. A less antagonistic approach to police unionism might have at least enlisted rank and file support for changes in the name of improved professionalism.

With so many interest groups offering or resisting suggestions for change, police reform became muddled. Bureaucrats followed the paths of least resistance and poured millions of dollars into new technology. Police unions concentrated on improving working conditions and better pay, two areas where they had considerable success. Liberal reformers had to content themselves with a few show-case experiments in community service policing and an enormous increase in the number of policemen attending college. Eventually, we may also look back to the more radical developments, such as the Kansas City Preventive Patrol Experiment, as milestones on the way to a reconceptualization of the role of policing in modern society. We may be on the verge of discovering a more sophisticated approach to law enforcement which combines the virtues of the community service and professional models. But at the present time it is impossible to say how important this last reform movement will be in the long history of policing.

## SUGGESTED READINGS

There are several excellent studies of police behavior, beginning with William A. Westley, *Violence and the Police: A Sociological Study of Law, Custom, and Morality* (Cambridge: The MIT Press, 1970). Jerome H. Skolnick, *Justice Without Trial: Law Enforcement in Democratic Society* (New York: John Wiley & Sons, 1966), Jonathan Rubenstein, *City Police* (New York: Random House, Inc., 1973) and James Q. Wilson, *Varieties of Police Behavior: The Management of Law and Order in Eight Communities* (Cambridge: Harvard University Press, 1968) are also important works. There is no comprehensive study of modern police reform but Gerald E. Caiden, *Police Revitalization* (Lexington: Lexington Books, 1977) is a good compendium for introducing the complexity of the movement. Herman Goldstein, *Policing a Free Society* (Cambridge: Ballinger Publishing Co., 1977) is the best summary of reform ideas and flaws. In the absence of historical works on the rise of police unions, William J. Bopp's *The Police Rebellion: A Quest for Blue Power* (Springfield: Charles C. Thomas, 1971) is the best introduction available.

# A Retrospective View of Policing

**T**here has always been a fundamental tension in American policing between what the public expects and the police do. And there has always been some way to mediate this tension. Reform is therefore the prevailing theme in the history of our law enforcement agencies. The dominant theme in this reform is the effort to make the reality of police work conform to our ideal conception of it. Policing, like other institutions, faces a hazard characteristic of American society. We are constantly trying to remake what it is into what it should be.

Our political ideology makes possible this continuous search for the ideal. Republicanism dictates a decentralized political system in which ultimate power resides with the average citizen. Those who are interested can therefore accumulate power by organizing like-minded individuals and attempt change. At the same time, republicanism espouses the idea that ordinary people know what is best. Entrenched interests cannot therefore deny the legitimacy of suggestions for change because ultimate wisdom does not reside with them. Nor can those interests block change. They may deflect it, or temporarily frustrate it, but they cannot stifle it. Historically, then, change is relatively common because it is an integral part of the political system.

The particular direction change takes depends upon historical circumstances. In the nineteenth century, white Anglo-Saxon Protestant Americans dominated the political system long enough to design and implement the preventive police idea. They were the first "public" interested in new ways to enforce laws. Rapid social and economic changes had caused considerable disorder, and a new police seemed to be a logical solution to that problem. Their mandate to the preventive police was complex, however. Certain people and acts were deemed more dangerous than others. Basically, the original mandate presumed a strict enforcement of laws which dealt with street disorders and predatory crime. The streets were to be made safe and property secure. Other forms of criminal behavior, such as business fraud, were not designated as part of this mandate.

Such a vague mandate invited abuse. The new police promptly set about defining their own concept of their work. An absence of any meaningful, centralized administrative controls encouraged this development. Officers were recruited from the neighborhoods they would patrol and they were not trained in the law. Ignoring the idea of strict law enforcement (except where it suited their purposes), the early patrolmen created a system based on personalized enforcement. They dealt with the problems which bothered their neighbors. And because of the heterogeneous nature of urban society, where conflict was so common, these officers learned the value of force quite early. By sharing their experiences with fellow officers, these early patrolmen created the original police subculture which would become a powerful instrument for socializing new recruits to the realities of their work. In effect, these officers evolved the first community service model of policing.

But the first reformers had not intended such a model. The police therefore needed some means to mediate the gap between reformers' intentions and policing realities. For most of our history urban politicians performed that vital service. The police did not, of course, bend these politicians to their will. Rather, patrolmen became members of ward organizations. Politicians did, however, protect the community service approach to policing from irate critics. That model, after all, suited their own purposes.

The first model for policing had some inherent problems which rapidly discredited it among critical observers. Corruption, violence, and favoritism were rife within the departments. To some extent these problems derived from the nature of nineteenth century community service policing. Personalized law enforcement gave individual officers enormous discretion in dealing with illegal but widely accepted behavior such as prostitution and gambling. Violence was a characteristic form of behavior in lower-class ethnic neighborhoods; using physical force was therefore a commonly accepted practice. And in ethnic ghettos favoritism was an important tool in establishing effective relations. Bringing drunks home, or escorting unruly children back to their mothers, earned officers gratitude from the people they policed. Politicians obscured these aspects of community policing with their own policies. They cared little about an applicant's personal qualities as long as he was a good organization man. Financial arrangements with important vice figures encouraged officers to feel there was nothing wrong with their own accommodations with these people. Regardless of their origins, all of this behavior stirred controversy and demands for change. Reformers based their proposals on the obvious excesses, overlooking the other, more subtle characteristics of community policing.

By the late nineteenth century reformers had accepted as an article of faith that political meddling lay at the heart of all police problems. There was sufficient evidence to lend credence to this belief, and the drive to eliminate politics from law enforcement became the central concern of reform for several decades. Although this campaign took time, it succeeded. Changes in urban society between 1890 and 1940 undermined many old political machines. With their power gone they were easy targets for a new generation of reformers.

This new generation borrowed its ideas from the past. Strict law enforcement would at last have its day under the guise of police professionalism. Dedicated administrators replaced venal politicians as the new bosses in policing. They made important improvements in the recruitment, training, and management of their officers. And the changes which had undermined the old political machines made it possible to implement the professional model rather easily. Efficient, uniform law enforcement suited the needs and attitudes of a predominantly middle-class suburban society.

But again there was an underlying reality which belied the claims of the new reformers. Localized law enforcement allowed enormous room for variations. The professional model never conquered every department, and older style policing has not disappeared. Furthermore, the new reformers concentrated on structure, not substance. They tinkered with the command hierarchy, introduced better technology, uprooted officers from the neighborhoods, and gave them better educations. But these men still had to patrol the streets. They still encountered situations not covered by regulations. And they continued to relate their experiences to the traditions of their subculture. Police professionalism had not closed the gap between reality and ideals.

If police professionalism did not fulfill its promises, it did serve to shield officers from a public scrutiny of their work. Americans have always been impressed by statistics, and police administrators made numbers a fetish. Press releases, annual reports, and special studies reduced practically everything policemen did to some sort of statistic. This gave the comfortable illusion of productivity and efficiency and relieved the curious of any need to probe beneath the numbers. Administrators took great pride in these statistics. Data analysis seemed to be a powerful tool for reducing behavior to controllable routine.

The social upheavals and skyrocketing crime rates of the 1960s and 1970s severely undermined the claims of the professional model. For the first time in the history of law enforcement we are confronted with an embarrassing problem. Prior to the 1940s Americans could blame "crime waves" and the lack of social order on political interference in policing. But since World War II, we have assumed that the professional model could deal with crime and disorder. The central cause of previous failures, after all, had been removed. Now that assumption is no longer tenable because modern reform has had no clear effect on crime either. The question becomes: what exactly can the police do about crime?

One of the curiosities of the search for answers to that question is that no one seems to be asking street cops their views on the subject. Police administrators have their solutions: more men, more money, more equipment. Liberal reformers have a different answer—a return to community policing. Politicians also have joined the search for solutions. They offer the services of state and federal government in a coordinated effort to bring powerful resources to bear on crime problems. Some of these proposals are indeed useful, but they also clash with the republican traditions of local control over law enforcement. It may be that federal and state aid is essential in combating crime. But we must guard against the dangers of centralization which the history of federal policing, in particular, reveals. Academics have also joined the search for solutions. We are currently spending enormous sums on an extraordinary array of "scientific" experiments designed to reduce crime. These studies are conducted by talented, highly trained experts in the social sciences and business management. So far, their results are contradictory and usually only mildly encouraging.

All of these responses conform to a historical pattern. We have never consulted the other experts on crime, street cops. There are some eminently understandable reasons for this, given the general reputation we attribute to policemen. But a good part of this failure to ask their opinion is simply prejudice. Academics, politicians, and bureaucrats arrogate to themselves knowledge about crime and law enforcement which they often do not have. The reality of policing is suppressed. Perhaps it is time to reverse that tendency and to tap a reservoir of information about crime which has been available for over a hundred years. We may not find all the answers we need, but we won't know that until we ask.

# Index